M·A·K·E IT
C·O·U·N·T·R·Y

EDITORIAL

Editor, Family Circle Books — Carol A. Guasti
Assistant Editor — Kim E. Gayton
Project Editor — Leslie Gilbert Elman
Book Design — Bessen, Tully & Lee
Cover Photo — William Stites
Typesetting — Vickie Almquist, Alison Chandler, Caroline Cole, Maureen Harrington
Editorial Assistants — Celeste Bantz, Kristen J. Keller

MARKETING

Director, Family Circle Books & Licensing — Margaret Chan-Yip
Promotion/Fulfillment Manager — Pauline MacLean Treitler
Fulfillment/Planning Coordinator — Carrie Meyerhoff
Administrative Assistant — Lynne Bertram

Published by The Family Circle, Inc.
110 Fifth Avenue, New York, NY 10011

Manufactured in the United States of America

10 9 8 7 6 5 4 3 2 1

Library of Congress Cataloging in Publication Data
Main entry under title:

Family circle make it country.
Includes index.
1.Country decorating.   2.Country crafts and cooking.
I.Family Circle, Inc.   II.Title: Make It Country.
ISBN 0-933585-13-6

Other Books by Family Circle

THE BEST OF FAMILY CIRCLE COOKBOOK
1986 FAMILY CIRCLE COOKBOOK
1987 FAMILY CIRCLE COOKBOOK
1988 FAMILY CIRCLE COOKBOOK
1989 FAMILY CIRCLE COOKBOOK

FAMILY CIRCLE BUSY COOK'S BOOK

FAMILY CIRCLE GOOD HEALTH COOKBOOK

THE FAMILY CIRCLE CHRISTMAS TREASURY
1987 FAMILY CIRCLE CHRISTMAS TREASURY
1988 FAMILY CIRCLE CHRISTMAS TREASURY
1989 FAMILY CIRCLE CHRISTMAS TREASURY

FAMILY CIRCLE FAVORITE NEEDLECRAFTS

HINTS, TIPS & SMART ADVICE

To order **FamilyCircle** books, write to Family Circle Books,
110 Fifth Avenue, New York, NY 10011.

To order **FamilyCircle** magazine, write to Family Circle Subscriptions,
110 Fifth Avenue, New York, NY 10011.

T·A·B·L·E & O·F
C·O·N·T·E·N·T·S

INTRODUCTION 1

Chapter I: COUNTRY LOOKS 2
The Heart of the Home 6
Rooms to Live In 14
The Bathing Room 36
Lasting Impressions 40

Chapter II: COUNTRY STORAGE 44
Everything In Its Place 46
Faux Antiques 54
Basket Bonanza 62
Country Collections 64

Chapter III: COUNTRY TOUCHES 66
Quilts and Afghans 70
Patchwork Pillows 84
Around the Home 88

Chapter IV: COUNTRY SCENTS 110
Pleasing Potpourris 112
Yesterday's Blossoms 120
Beautiful Arrangements 128
Forever Flowers 134

Chapter V: COUNTRY GARDENS 142
    The Good Earth 146
    Window Gardens 160
    Herb Gardens 168

Chapter VI: COUNTRY COOKING 174
    Hot and Hearty Supper 178
    Homemade Soups 184
    Family Reunion Picnic 188
    Grandma's Baked Goodies 196
    Breads and Spreads 202
    Pick of the Crop 210
    Side Dishes and Sauces 226

    CRAFTS BASICS AND ABBREVIATIONS 230

    MATERIALS SHOPPING GUIDE 242

    INDEX 243

    CREDITS 249

W·E·L·C·O·M·E
T·O C·O·U·N·T·R·Y

Think "country" and you think of warm pine floors and braided rugs . . . of plump patchwork pillows . . . wicker baskets . . . and all the comforts that make everyone feel as though they've "come home."

In this book, you'll find illustrated examples of different country styles. The roots of country decorating are diverse, and range from the pristine serenity of the Shakers to the eclectic abundance of Victoriana, from rustic Southwestern decor to intricate New England scrimshaw. Country decorating is as individual as it is ingenious—it makes the most of what you have, and is thrifty with both money and resources. We show you ways to express your personal style by blending the period and regional elements you love best against any backdrop, authentic farmhouse to city townhouse.

Because country isn't just a "look", we've included ideas and projects that incorporate country into many aspects of your life. There are beautiful crafts to make, such as Americana samplers and colorful quilts. You'll also discover fragrant potpourris to mix and lovely flowers and herbs to grow in your backyard or on your windowsill. And since the heart of the country home is the kitchen, this book wouldn't be complete without a chapter on country cooking. You'll find the type of recipes that are handed down for generations: nothing fancy; just hearty and delicious food!

In short, country is a celebration of the home. It is comfortable and familiar, informal and intimate. Country is a collection of things you love best; styles that make you feel comfortable, a way of life that is as familiar and reassuring as an old friend.

COUNTRY
L·O·O·K·S

Home is where one starts from.
—T.S. Eliot

Today's country style is both traditional and contemporary. It combines elements of period styles—Colonial, Federal, Victorian—with the way we like to live today: relaxed and comfortable.

This chapter, filled with ideas and "dream" photographs, will whet your appetite for country style. Because color can transform a room more quickly, easily and inexpensively than any other decorating device, we'll point out how the color scheme in each room works: dark walls don't have to be gloomy, and pale neutrals needn't seem stark. For instance, the beautifully simple bedroom in the photo at left uses a fresh white bedspread and white walls, pine furniture and a hardwood floor as a backdrop that can be accented to reflect the changing seasons: pastels for warm weather, red tartans for cold winter days. Other country touches in this room include a cross stitch sampler, a hearth rug, a basket to hold kindling and fresh flowers on the mantle.

Redecorating often can be a costly proposition. But the essence of country is evolution, not revolution—that's what makes country decorating so wonderful. Whether you're painting or papering, adding a piece of furniture or a simple accessory, take it one step at a time. Simply put, the look of country comes from the heart: it's a collection of things you love best, colors and patterns that say "welcome home."

*What makes this a country kitchen?
The hanging pot rack and Shaker
plate rack . . . a ready-to-work feeling
with utensils in the open, and close at
hand . . . butcherblock countertops . . .
baskets everywhere!*

T·H·E H·E·A·R·T
O·F T·H·E H·O·M·E

Spring is Here

♦ Welcome spring with a cozy breakfast nook bedecked in checks of moss green and coral. The patchwork tablecloth, ruffled pillows and tie-on chair backs add to the inviting country atmosphere. Directions for the Springtime Table Setting begin on page 8.

♦ The toy lamb, copper cookware hanging near the fireplace, baskets suspended from an exposed ceiling beam and the "Americana" painting above the mantel all lend an authentic air to this farmhouse kitchen.

♦ What makes it country? The patchwork table setting . . . pots full of cheerful pink geraniums scattered about the room . . . the sunny, informal look.

A Taste of French Country

♦ Ceramic tiles are the unifying element in this modern kitchen with French country overtones. The walls and countertops are covered in white tiles with multi-hued speckles and edged with blue tiles.

♦ A *trompe l'oeil* (fool-the-eye) border over the window adds a whimsical note.

♦ The island, with a handy second sink, doubles as a work station and snack bar. The wooden cabinets conceal storage bins, and appliances not in use.

♦ What makes it country? Warm hardwood floors . . . bricks that recall an old baker's oven . . . an unadorned bay window.

SPRINGTIME TABLE SETTING

General Directions:

1. Cutting Squares: The cutting sizes given include a ¼-inch seam allowance. Draw each pattern on brown paper or manila cardboard and cut it out. Or draw the squares directly on the wrong side of the fabric. Be sure the corners are squared and the measurements are accurate.

2. Stitching: Pin two squares right sides together and raw edges even. Stitch exactly ¼ inch from the raw edges. Unfold the joined squares and press the seam to one side. When joining rows together, pin them so the vertical seams match.

RACK 'EM UP

Add a bold stroke of personal style to your kitchen with an inventive pot rack. Search flea markets, yard sales, junk shops and hardware stores for an unusual item that can do double duty as storage for your kitchen utensils.

Be sure the rack is securely fastened to the ceiling joists or wall studs — not just to plaster or drywall — and that the hooks are strong enough to handle the weight of pots and pans.

Here are a few stand-ins for the standard pot rack:

·

- ◆ *wrought iron gate*
- ◆ *wooden sled*
- ◆ *antique metal chandelier*
- ◆ *large, thick picture frame with hooks added and hung from the ceiling*
- ◆ *PVC pipe or copper tubing to create your own rack*
- ◆ *old grates*
- ◆ *2- to 3-inch-thick decorative curtain rod*
- ◆ *shutters hung from the ceiling with hooks*
- ◆ *old wooden ladder*
- ◆ *pegboard*
- ◆ *Shaker-style peg rack*

Use meat hooks, postal bag hooks, antique coat hooks, or mix and match decorative hooks to hang pots, pans and utensils.

SPRINGTIME TABLECLOTH AND NAPKINS
(72 x 84-inch tablecloth; 21-inch square napkins)

Materials: 44- to 45-inch-wide medium weight cotton or cotton-blend fabric: 1½ yards each of coral (C), white (W), and coral plaid (CP), 1 yard each of green check (GC) and green plaid (GP); 22-inch square of coral or white fabric for each napkin; matching threads; 4¼ yards of muslin for tablecloth back.

Directions (¼-inch seams allowed):

1. Cut out 6½-inch fabric square patches in the following amounts: 42 from the coral (C), 42 from the coral plaid (CP), 22 from the green check (GC), 20 from the green plaid (GP), 42 from the white (W).

2. Stitch together the patches in the following order: **Row 1:** C, GC, CP, W, C, GP, CP, W, C, GC, CP, W, C, GP. **Row 2:** W, C, GC, CP, W, C, GP, CP, W, C, GC, CP, W, C. **Row 3:** CP, W, C, GC, CP, W, C, GP, CP, W, C, GC, CP, W. **Row 4:** GP, CP, W, C, GC, CP, W, C, GP, CP, W, C, GC, CP. **Row 5:** C, GP, CP, W, C, GC, CP, W, C, GP, CP, W, C, GC. **Row 6:** W, C, GP, CP, W, C, GC, CP, W, C, GP, CP, W, C. **Row 7:** CP, W, C, GP, CP, W, C, GC, CP, W, C, GP, CP, W. **Row 8:** GC, CP, W, C, GP, CP, W, C, GC, CP, W, C, GP, CP. **Row 9:** Same as Row 1. **Row 10:** Same as Row 2. **Row 11:** Same as Row 3. **Row 12:** Same as Row 4.

3. Stitch the 12 rows of squares together to form the top of the tablecloth.

4. Cut out two 74 x 44-inch pieces of muslin for the tablecloth back. Sew the pieces together at a selvage edge and press the seam open. Smooth the tablecloth top over the muslin lining, right sides together, and pin the pieces together along the edges. Trim the muslin to match the edge of the patchwork top. Stitch around four sides, leaving a 6-inch opening for turning. Turn the tablecloth right side out. Turn under the open edges and slipstitch the opening closed.

5. Cut out 22-inch squares for the napkins. On opposite sides, turn under the raw edges ¼ inch, then turn under ¼ inch again and hem. Repeat on the remaining sides.

SPRINGTIME PILLOW SEATS

Materials: Square pillow forms to fit chair seats; green plaid and green check fabrics to match Springtime Tablecloth *(page 8)* for pillow top, bottom and ruffle; 2 yards of piping.

Directions (½-inch seams allowed):

1. Cutting: Wrap a tape measure all the way around the center of the pillow form, to find its girth. Divide this measurement by 2, and add 1 inch for seams. Cut two fabric squares of this dimension for the pillow top and pillow bottom.

2. Piping: Use purchased piping, or make your own: Cut a bias strip about 1½ inches wide, pieced as needed to the length required. Fold it over a ¼-inch-wide cord, raw edges even, and machine-stitch against the cord, using the zipper foot. Stitch the piping around the pillow top edges, seam lines matching. Clip the piping's seam allowance at each corner.

3. Ruffle: Cut two fabric strips, each 3 to 4 inches wide and 44 to 45 inches (the full width of the fabric) long. Stitch the strips together at the short ends to make a loop. Sew a ¼-inch hem at one long edge. At the opposite edge, sew a gathering row ½ inch from the raw edge, using the longest machine stitch. Pin the ruffle to the pillow top over the piping, right sides together, raw edges even and the loop seams at opposite corners. Pull up the gathers to fit the pillow top, distributing the fullness evenly. Stitch along the gathered row.

4. Pillow Seat: Pin the pillow bottom to the pillow top over the piping and ruffle, right sides together and raw edges even. Stitch around three sides and four corners. Turn the pillow right side out and insert the pillow form. Turn under the open edges and slipstitch the opening closed.

TIE-ON CHAIR BACKS

Materials: 1-inch-thick foam pad to fit across chair back for each chair; fabric to match Springtime Tablecloth *(page 8)*; 2 yards of piping.

Directions (½-inch seams allowed):

1. For each chair back, cut two fabric rectangles, each 2 inches wider and 2 inches longer than the foam pad. Cut two 3 x 15-inch fabric strips to make one pair of ties.

2. Use purchased piping, or make your own following the directions in Springtime Pillow Seats, Step 2 *(at left)*. Stitch the piping around the edges of one rectangle, seam lines matching. Clip the piping's seam allowance at each corner.

3. Fold the fabric strips in half lengthwise, right sides together. Stitch ½ inch from one short and one long edge. Turn the strips right side out and press. Turn under each strip's raw short edge and slipstitch the opening closed.

4. Fold one tie in half. Pin the folded tie edge to the top edge of one corner of the chair back ½ inch from a side edge, or as needed to fit the chair *(see photo, page 6)*. Stitch across the fold. Repeat at the opposite end of the top edge.

5. Finish the chair back following the directions for pillow assembly in Springtime Pillow Seats, Step 4 *(at left)*.

DOLLAR-WISE DECORATING

◆ Creative Kitchen Design ◆

◆ One of the easiest, and least expensive, ways to "redo" your kitchen is to give cabinets a facelift. Use panels of wallpaper or caning on drawers and door fronts, then trim them with molding.

◆ Painted borders around windows, doors, ceilings and floors add flair to any room.

◆ Use fool-the-eye techniques in a windowless kitchen. Paint a scene you'd like to see on the wall, complete with a window frame and curtains.

◆ If you're a little bored by a bare brick wall, paint a mural on it. A country scene with a white picket fence is a natural on this background.

Colonial Country

♦ A patterned cotton balloon shade in a warm red tone is a simple and elegant window treatment for a country dining room. It lets in the light as it softens the look of the handmade furniture.

♦ The look is colonial: rustic and utilitarian, reminiscent of an inn where weary travelers stopped for a hearty supper. Gone are the ornate ruffles and flounces of other period styles. In their stead are soft white walls, wood furniture in darker tones, and minimal accessories with the accent on practical. Underneath it all, a braided area rug adds warmth.

♦ A French wine-tasting table is teamed with American Windsor chairs as a dining set. Although the pairing is not historically accurate, the look works because the oval table and sturdy chairs with rounded backs complement each other in both shape and wood tone. To create a cozier atmosphere, add seat cushions in a fabric that matches or complements the window shade.

♦ What makes it country? Accessories that "work"—chandelier and fireplace tools straight from the blacksmith's shop . . . straw broom . . . two-handled wash basket . . . carved wooden bowl.

Eclectic Elegance

♦ The universal themes of food, wine and candlelight unite an art deco poster, contemporary candlesticks and turn-of-the-century furniture.

♦ A new look doesn't have to cost a bundle. Start by replacing heavy dining room drapes with inexpensive bamboo roll-ups that maximize natural light and echo the tones of the wide-plank wood floors and furniture.

♦ In a big sunny room like this, hunter green walls look fresh, not oppressive.

♦ A dining table and chairs don't have to match. Here, painted wooden armchairs mix with Bentwood chairs bought for a song at a local flea market.

♦ The 1890's hutch was spruced up with a fabric remnant behind the shelves.

♦ What makes it country? The "don't buy new, make do" attitude of mismatched furniture . . . the graceful hurricane lamp rewired as a unique—and functional—chandelier.

DOLLAR-WISE DECORATING

♦ *An Unmatched Set* ♦

All those individual chairs you've collected over the years can be reincarnated as a new set for your dining nook. Just paint them all the same color. For real pizzazz, paint each chair a different high-gloss shade. Or, if you'd prefer an updated country look, consider using pastel tones.

Dark Victory

♦ A rich, dark wallcovering won't overpower a room if it's tempered with light colors. Here, the light pine furniture, and the soft white wainscoting, trim and ceiling offset the burgundy floral paper on the upper half of the wall.

♦ The Oriental rug complements the wallpaper, and allows some of the wood floor to show through.

♦ Oversized pine furniture is a relaxed alternative to a more formal dining room. In another setting, the same furniture could have a Southwestern flavor.

♦ Whether it's reflecting sunlight or candlelight, a large mirror brightens a room.

♦ Keep fabrics and patterns to a minimum. If you use a tablecloth, choose a pale, solid color — steer clear of additional patterns.

♦ Don't over-accessorize! The walls are busy enough; too many knick-knacks would fight with the printed paper.

♦ What makes it country? Pine furniture . . . pretty accent lamps . . . a sturdy table big enough for lots of family and friends.

DOLLAR-WISE DECORATING

♦ *Mirror Images* ♦

Can't afford fine art? Decorate with mirrors. They make a small room seem spacious, and reflect light in dark corners. Frame one large mirror or arrange a collection of smaller mirrors on the wall.

♦ Shop around — you'll find hundreds of different styles in every price range. Older is not necessarily better, because many mirrors lose their reflective ability over time. As with any good decorative accent, a few carefully chosen pieces are preferable to a lot of rushed purchases. Don't buy a mirror collection at once; pick up each one along the way at local shops, craft fairs or auctions.

♦ Mix and match mirrors. Vary the shapes: round, oval, oblong, square — even hand mirrors and triptychs (three-paneled mirrors). Choose different frames for different rooms — rattan, ceramic, brass, wood, antique silver — but strive for a handcrafted look. Slick "frameless" mirrors would be out of place in this type of setting.

R·O·O·M·S T·O
L·I·V·E I·N

Federal Case

♦ Red, white and blue are the perfect colors for a Federal-style living room.

♦ In this historic sea captain's home, the accent is on nautical, with scrimshaw, nautical knots and even a fisherman's creel as wall decorations.

♦ The Oriental carpet recalls a time when traders sailed to the Far East for spices and other exotic fare.

♦ Sturdy, comfortable furnishings make this room very livable. The style of couch and chair are not representative of any particular era; it's the color and pattern of the upholstery that makes them work here.

♦ The upholstery-matching fabric swag hung over sheer lace curtains is a unifying element.

♦ What makes it country? Detailed molding around the door, window and fireplace . . . a weathered chest used as a coffee table (emphasizing that the room is meant to be used, not just looked at) . . . brass accents.

SHINING EXAMPLE

To keep brass knick-knacks free of tarnish longer, lightly spray them with extra-hold hair spray after polishing them. When they need repolishing, any hair spray residue can be washed off with soap and water.

Touch of the Orient

All rugs, carpets and kelims made in Persia, Turkey and China are considered to be Oriental rugs. Because Americans and Europeans have traded in the Far East for hundreds of years, Oriental rugs often are found in historic room settings. Before 1875, the utmost care was taken in the weaving of these rugs. Since that time, the demand for Oriental rugs has increased so greatly that their manufacture has become more commercialized, although some still are handmade on looms. The main types of Oriental rugs and their characteristics are:

Persian: These rugs are decorated with a large variety of flowers, leaves, vines and birds. They generally have a pattern stemming from a central medallion, and often are worked in soft colors.

Indian: Flowers, leaves and vines woven in a natural manner make these appear similar to Persian rugs. The colors of these rugs often are brilliant. Web fringes woven into squares, diamonds, octagons, stars and crosses are predominant in these carpets. The colors usually are shades of red.

Caucasian: These rugs are more elaborate in design. They have no fringes and are dyed many colors.

Turkish: These rugs have geometric and floral designs with bright, contrasting colors.

Chinese: Black backgrounds with blue designs predominate. Softer colors, such as pale yellow, salmon or tan, often appear in the designs.

East or west, home is best.
— English proverb

DOLLAR-WISE DECORATING

◆ *Stenciled Scatter Rugs* ◆

Make your own hand-painted scatter rug with cookie cutter "stencils." You'll need:

- ◆ an inexpensive solid color rag rug (available at most discount variety stores), or doormat-size carpet swatches
- ◆ cookie cutters in simple shapes, such as flowers, leaves, hearts or doves
- ◆ stencil paints for fabric (be sure the paints are water resistant)
- ◆ stencil brushes

Before you stencil, trace the *inside* of each cookie cutter onto a piece of paper. Experiment with the paper shapes to find a design you like. Borders and evenly-spaced repeating motifs work best.

With a pencil, lightly outline the boundaries of your design on the rug. Be sure you have enough space to complete the design you want.

Place a cookie cutter, sharp side down, firmly on the rug.

Using the stencil brushes and paints, dab paint onto the rug within the shape of the cookie cutter. Cover the entire area of the shape.

Carefully lift off the cookie cutter and proceed to the next shape.

Suggestions:

- ◆ For a nursery rug, use rocking horse, teddy bear or heart shapes.
- ◆ Use Christmas cookie cutters to make a holiday doormat. Holly leaves, gingerbread men or alternating trees and hearts are ideal.
- ◆ Play with color. Try yellow flowers with blue leaves, teal hearts with black leaves, or pink and blue motifs on a black rug.
- ◆ Create the illusion of an area rug on your floors. (Make sure the type of paint you use is appropriate for use on the floor's surface.) Rev up painted white floors or light-toned wood floors with brightly-colored, stenciled floral patterns or tropical ferns. This technique works well on plain window shades as well.

The New Frontier

♦ There are no limits to the versatility of country decor. A mix and match style of decorating makes this room both folksy and up-to-date.

♦ The rubblestone fireplace is a modern version of old-time fieldstone. As in early American homes, the fireplace is the centerpiece of the family living area.

♦ Big, beautiful windows and glass doors let air and light fill the room, allowing you to experience the changing seasons firsthand.

♦ The couch and chair, wicker chairs and lamp are new; the dining table and chairs are old-fashioned (perhaps reproductions of antique pieces). Other elements — polished wood floors, a rag rug, the open furniture arrangement — create a beautiful, and functional, living space.

♦ What makes it country? Rustic elements such as the large stone fireplace, knotty wood tables and cupboard . . . the use of natural colors in the furnishings and unpainted wood trim around the doors and windows . . . the open family room/dining room space reminiscent of a pioneer cabin.

Light, God's eldest daughter, is a principal beauty in a building.
— Thomas Fuller

The Four Seasons

◆ Coordinate room accessories with the seasons to keep your decor looking fresh all year round.

◆ The aqua couch is an ideal backdrop for seasonal accessories. It's equally at home with pastels in warm weather and with deep burgundy, rust and ultramarine in colder months.

◆ New throw pillows change the room's complexion. Buy them, or make your own from chintz fabrics, needlepoint or embroidery.

◆ Winter rooms call for darker colors, rich patterns and touchable textured fabrics.

◆ Throw an afghan over the back of the sofa. It changes the look of the upholstery, and comes in handy on chilly nights.

◆ In the spring, replace the heavy fabrics and colors of winter with polished cotton pastels, florals and lacy antimacassars over the sofa back.

◆ What makes it country? Plump pillows . . . the mixing of fabrics and prints . . . antique needlepoint.

DOLLAR-WISE DECORATING

◆ *Fresh Alternative* ◆

In winter, buying fresh flowers can be quite costly, but dried flowers also dress up a room — and they are less expensive, because they last longer. Follow our directions for drying and arranging your own flowers *(pages 122-123)*, or purchase arrangements from a florist, nursery or craft store.

Sitting Pretty Room

If you like to roll up your sleeves and do a decorating job yourself, this pretty room may provide just the right inspiration to help you create a wonderful country look. This type of decorating is made magically easy by the use of a glue gun—which often can do the work of a hammer and nails, a screwdriver or a heavy-duty stapler. The mixed and matched delicate floral patterns are what give this room its essentially "country" flavor.

STICK 'EM UP!

Glue guns, technically known as hot-melt glue guns, force solid sticks of glue through a heating element that melts the glue. The hot glue then is forced out of the nozzle and sets within 30 to 60 seconds.

•

Cordless glue guns are the newest version. They're ideal for ceiling-high or other hard-to-get-at areas.

•

Thumb guns are the lightest, smallest and most inexpensive version. They're best for small-scale and more detailed projects.

•

Trigger guns are larger—perfect for heavy-duty tasks that involve constant gluing, such as adhering sections of wall paneling.

FLORAL FABRIC SCREEN
(one panel is 16 x 80½ inches)

This custom-look floral screen is made up of "tiles" of fabric glued to squares of foam coreboard and attached to the screen with a thumb glue gun.

Materials: 1 x 2-inch pine lumber; ¼-inch-thick plywood; ¼ x 1-inch lattice; ⅞-inch-thick half-round rope molding *(see chart below for dimensions of wood pieces)*; 4 double-acting hinges; 6d finishing nails; ¾-inch-long brads; wood glue; ¼-inch-thick foam coreboard *(see chart below for coreboard tile dimensions and quantity)*; 5 yards of 54-inch-wide floral print fabric; glue gun; power saw; miter box; backsaw; power drill; hammer; screwdriver; scissors.

CODE Per Panel	PIECES	SIZE
A (1 x 2)	(2)	¾" x 1½" x 80½" Frame
A1 (1 x 2)	(2)	¾" x 1½" x 16" Frame
A2 (PLY)	(1)	¼" x 16" x 80½" Face
A3 (LAT)	(2)	¼" x 1" x 80½" Trim
B (MOLD)	(2)	⅞" Half-rnd. rope molding
B1 (MOLD)	(2)	⅞" Half-rnd. rope molding
C	(24)	¼" x 6" x 6" Foam core tiles

Directions:
See the diagram in Fig. I, 1 for the construction details of the screen. Drill holes for the 6d nails in the screen frame (pieces A and A1). Use the wood glue and brads to attach lattice piece A3 and molding pieces B and B1 (the hot glue from the glue gun dries too fast to use on stiff moldings). The individual flower bouquets for the tiles are cut from the same patterned fabric used to make the tablecloth for the Skirted Table *(page 20)*. Each flower bouquet fabric square is glued to a foam coreboard tile with the glue gun, which also is used to glue each tile to the screen. Only every other bouquet in the fabric can be used to make the fabric squares because of the tiles' size.

Home is a place you grow up wanting to leave, and grow old wanting to go back to.
—John Ed Pearle

Fig. I, 1 FLORAL FABRIC SCREEN

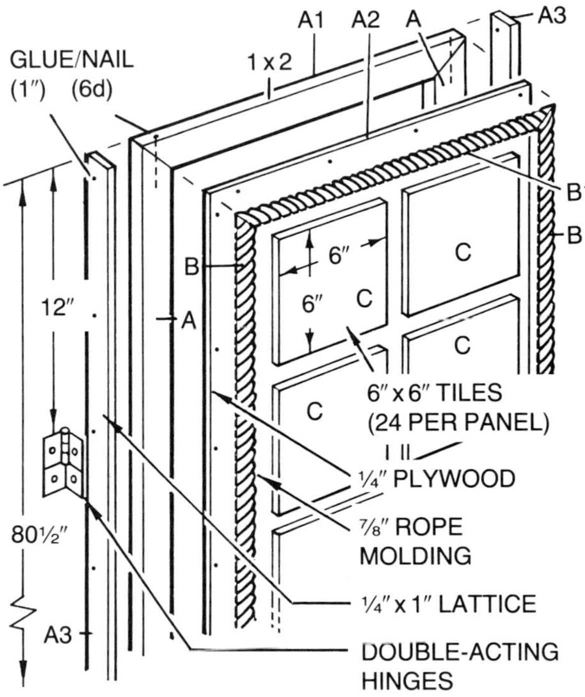

A1
A2
A
A3
GLUE/NAIL
(1") (6d)
1 x 2
B1
B
B
6"
6"
C
C
C
C
A
12"
6" x 6" TILES
(24 PER PANEL)
¼" PLYWOOD
80½"
⅞" ROPE
MOLDING
¼" x 1" LATTICE
A3
DOUBLE-ACTING
HINGES

SAFETY MEASURES

Glue guns are sold at home centers, hardware, crafts and discount stores, and even at some drugstores. Glue guns are not toys; they are electric tools. With the use of sensible safety precautions, glue guns perform without risk. Do not let children operate them unless closely supervised by an adult. Read the owner's manual carefully before using a glue gun. Never touch the nozzle area or the melted glue. Always set the gun on its stand between gluings. After each use, let the gun cool to room temperature. Store it out of children's reach.

SKIRTED TABLE
(48 inches round, with a 62-inch square tablecloth)

Materials: ¾-inch-thick 48-inch-diameter plywood circle; four 29-inch-long table legs with flared clinchnut plates; 5¾ yards of 54-inch-wide fabric for table skirt; 12¼ yards of velcro; 54-inch square of same floral print fabric used to make Floral Fabric Screen *(page 19)*, for tablecloth; 7¼ yards of 4½-inch-wide border fabric for trim; glue gun.

Directions:
1. Table: Join the legs to the plywood circle. Using the glue gun, glue the hook layer of the velcro around the table rim.
2. Table Skirt: Cut six 33½ x 54-inch lengths of the skirt fabric. Join three pieces along the selvage edges to make one panel. Repeat. At each end of each panel, turn 1 inch to the wrong side and stitch. At the top edge of each panel, turn under 1 inch and pin. Using the longest machine stitch, sew across the top of each panel along the fold, then ¾ inch below; break the stitching at each seam. Stitch a 3-inch bottom hem.
3. Gathered Edge: Pull up the gathers until each panel is 75 inches wide. Stitch the fuzzy layer of the velcro to the wrong side of each top edge. Press the panels to the table rim.
4. Tablecloth: Cut four 65 x 4½-inch borders. Using a ¼-inch seam allowance, join a border to each edge of the 54-inch square, ends extending equally. Diagonally sew adjoining borders from corners to selvages to form miters. Press.

TWIG BASKET
(3½ inches high, 9 inches in diameter)

Materials: ¾ x 9 inches of pine; wood stain or polyurethane; twigs; pruning shears; glue gun.

Directions:
Cut an octagonal shape from the pine for the basket base *(see* Fig. I, 2*)*. Stain or polyurethane the base. Using the pruning shears and making 45° cuts, cut the twigs to be 5½ inches long, an inch longer than the sides of the octagon. Alternately stack the twigs along the sides of the base, balancing the twigs as you work. Place thicker twigs near the bottom and thinner ones on top. Disassemble the twigs, laying them, in order, along each side of the octagon. Using the glue gun, glue the twigs in place in the same order as before.

FIG. I, 2 TWIG BASKET HALF PATTERN

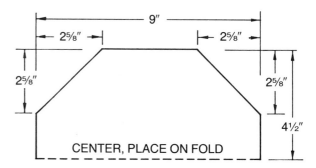

9″

2⅝″   2⅝″

2⅝″   2⅝″

4½″

CENTER, PLACE ON FOLD

GETTING ATTACHED

Almost anything can be attached to walls by using a hot glue gun. If you decide to remove the item, you can do so easily by reheating the glue for a few seconds with a hair dryer. This method avoids making surface marks and nail holes on walls.

PIER GLASS MIRROR
(24 x 44¼ inches)

Materials: ¼ x ⅞-inch lattice; ½ x 1⅞-inch lattice; ½ x 2¼-inch lattice; 1¼ x 1¼-inch corner molding *(see chart below for dimensions of wood pieces)*; 6 x 24-inch fretwork; ¼ x 23¾ x 36-inch mirror; two 3-inch-long finials *(see photo)*; twenty 1-inch-diameter wooden buttons; four #6 1-inch-long flathead wood screws; 6 screw eyes; clear polyurethane; paint brush; picture wire; heavy-duty picture hanger; fine-toothed saw; awl; screwdriver; staple gun; glue gun.

CODE	PIECES	SIZE
A (LAT)	(2)	½" x 1⅞" x 38¼" Side frame
A1 (LAT)	(1)	½" x 1⅞" x 20¼" Top frame
A2 (LAT)	(1)	½" x 2¼" x 24" Bottom frame
B (MOLD)	(2)	1¼" x 1¼" x 38¼" Corner mold.
B1 (LAT)	(2)	¼" x ⅞" x 36" Filler
C	(1)	¼" x 23¾" x 36" Mirror
D	(1)	6" x 24" Fretwork
E	(2)	3" Finial
F	(20)	1" Wooden buttons

Directions:

1. Cut the frame pieces A, A1 and A2 to size. Place the A pieces on a flat surface, and glue A1 between them at the top. Staple the joints to give them extra strength *(see Fig. I, 3)*.

2. Glue A2 to the front of the A/A1 assembly, flush with the A pieces at the bottom and sides. Strengthen the frame by attaching two wood screws to each side, through A into A2.

3. Place the mirror on the frame, with the bottom of the mirror resting on the top edge of A2.

4. Glue a B1 piece to the front inside edge of each B corner molding piece. The B1 pieces should be flush with the outside edge of the B pieces. Glue each B/B1 assembly to the A/A1/A2 frame, flush at the bottom of A2 *(see Fig. I, 3)*.

5. Glue the D fretwork piece to A1 and to each B/B1 assembly, at the top of the frame. Glue the E finials at the top corners, and the F wooden buttons to the front of the B pieces.

6. Using the paint brush, coat the entire frame with the polyurethane. Attach the screw eyes and run the picture wire as shown in Fig. I, 3. Hang the mirror from the picture hanger.

Fig. I, 3 PIER GLASS MIRROR

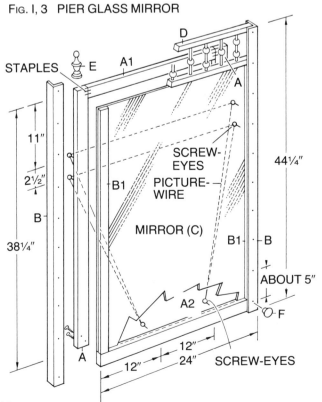

FLORAL CURTAIN POLE

Materials: ¾-inch-diameter wooden clothes pole; twelve 36-inch-long ¼-inch-diameter wooden dowels; 2 decorative wooden brackets *(see photo)*; 2 "L" hooks; 2 ball finials *(see photo)*; glue gun.

Directions:

Cut clothes pole 3 inches longer than outside width of trim around window where pole will be hung. Using the glue gun, glue dowels to the clothes pole *(see* Fig. I, 4*)*. If clothes pole is longer than 36 inches, butt ends of dowels; alternate joints for a better look. Glue each wooden bracket to an outside edge of the window trim, and to an "L" hook for insurance *(see photo)*. If necessary, remove dowels or screw stubs from ball finials. Glue a finial to each end of the curtain pole.

Fig. I, 4 FLORAL CURTAIN POLE

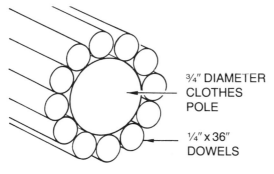

¾" DIAMETER CLOTHES POLE

¼" x 36" DOWELS

GREEN GLASS CHANDELIER
(23 x 32-inch frame)

Materials: ½ x ½-inch lattice; ½ x 1½-inch lattice; ½ x 2-inch lattice *(see chart below for dimensions of wood pieces)*; two 1½ x 11 x 11-inch quarter circle fan brackets *(see photo, page 23)*; twenty-six 1-inch-diameter wooden buttons; 10 feet of lamp cord (UL approved); 2 lamp sockets (UL approved); 2 wire nuts; ⅝ x ¾ x 12-inch brass lamp pipe; 22¾-inch-long ⅜-inch-diameter threaded tubing; two 2½-inch-long pieces of ⅜-inch-diameter threaded tubing; 1 threaded loop to fit ⅜-inch-diameter tubing; lamp chain; two 1-inch-diameter brass washers with ⅜-inch-diameter holes; 3 nuts to fit ⅜-inch-diameter tubing; 2 brass socket covers; two #7 1¼-inch-long flathead wood screws; clear polyurethane; paint brush; two 12-inch-diameter green glass lamp shades; fine-toothed saw; power drill, with ³⁄₃₂-inch and ⅜-inch bits; screwdriver; cutting pliers and wire stripper; hacksaw or tube cutter; glue gun.
Note: *Have your work checked by a licensed electrician before turning on the power.*

CODE	PIECES	SIZE
A (LAT)	(2)	½" x 1½" x 32" Arm
A1 (LAT)	(2)	½" x ½" x 32" Arm
A2 (LAT)	(2)	½" x 2" x 1½" Arm filler
B (LAT)	(2)	½" x 1½" x 12½" Post
B1 (LAT)	(2)	½" x ½" x 12½" Post

Directions:

1. Cut the lattice parts to size. Drill a ⅜-inch-diameter hole, centered between the side edges, 2 inches from each end of the bottom arm A piece. Drill a ⅜-inch-diameter hole, centered, in the top arm A piece *(see* Fig. I, 5, *page 23)*.
2. Glue the A1 pieces on top of the bottom arm A piece, flush at the ends and edges. Glue an A2 piece, between the A1 pieces, flush at each end *(see* Fig. I, 5*)*.
3. Glue the B1 pieces to a B piece, flush at the ends and sides. Glue the remaining B piece to the B1 pieces. Bevel the corners of the B pieces.
4. Push the 22¾-inch-long threaded tubing through the hole in the centers of the B/B1/B post and the A top arm. Screw a nut on the tubing below A, letting two threads show. Run a 5-foot-long piece of lamp cord through the tubing. Starting at the top, place a brass washer, a 9-inch-long piece of brass pipe, and the remaining brass washer on the tubing. Thread the

threaded loop on the pipe; tighten it. Check that the B/B1/B post is square with the A top arm *(see* Fig. I, 5*)*.

5. Cut the remaining lamp cord and 3-inch length of brass pipe in half. Attach one length of the lamp cord to one of the lamp sockets *(see* Fig. I, 5*)*. Pass the cord through one of the 2½-inch-long pieces of threaded tubing, and screw the tubing into the socket. Place a brass socket cover and one of the brass pipes over the tubing. Push the wire and tubing through the hole in one of the ends of the A/A1/A2 bottom arm. Run the wire through a nut and tighten the nut. Repeat for the opposite side of the bottom arm.

6. Attach the center post lamp cord to the bottom arm lamp cords with the wire nuts. Press the cords into the channel in the bottom arm. Glue the top arm and bottom arm together. Secure the arm with a wood screw in each end *(see* Fig. I, 5*)*.

7. Glue the fan brackets in place. Glue the wooden buttons to both sides of the arm and center post.

8. Using the paint brush, coat the chandelier with the polyurethane. Attach the lamp shades. Attach the lamp chain to the threaded loop, and weave the lamp cord through the chain. Attach the chandelier to the ceiling junction box.

Fig. I, 5   GREEN GLASS CHANDELIER

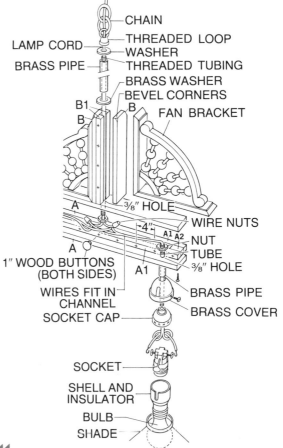

CHAIN
LAMP CORD — THREADED LOOP
WASHER
BRASS PIPE — THREADED TUBING
BRASS WASHER
BEVEL CORNERS
B1   B — FAN BRACKET
B
A   ⅜" HOLE
4"   A1 A2 — WIRE NUTS
A — NUT
TUBE
1" WOOD BUTTONS   A1   ⅜" HOLE
(BOTH SIDES)
WIRES FIT IN — BRASS PIPE
CHANNEL — BRASS COVER
SOCKET CAP
SOCKET
SHELL AND
INSULATOR
BULB
SHADE

VICTORIAN SIDEBOARD
(18 x 64½ x 60 inches)

Materials: ⅛-inch-thick birch plywood; ¾-inch-thick birch plywood; ¾-inch-thick quarter round molding; 1½-inch-diameter wooden dowels *(see chart below for dimensions of wood pieces)*; ¾-inch-diameter half round molding; #7 1¼-inch-long flathead wood screws; 6d finishing nails; 1-inch-long brads; eight 2½-inch-diameter ball finials *(see photo)*; four 7-inch-long 5½-inch-diameter ball feet *(see photo)*; four 2-inch butt hinges; 2 doorknobs; 8 shelf pins; wood glue; sandpaper; clear polyurethane; paint brush; power saw; miter box; back saw; power drill, with assorted bits; countersink; screwdrill set; screwdriver; hammer; glue gun.

CODE	PIECES	SIZE
A (PLY)	(4)	¾" x 17¼" x 29½" Sides
A1 (PLY)	(4)	¾" x 13½" x 17¼" Top/Bottom
A2 (PLY)	(2)	⅛" x 14¾" x 29¼" Back
A3 (PLY)	(2)	¾" x 13⅜" x 15¾" Adj. shelf
B (PLY)	(2)	¾" x 18" x 60" Top/Bottom
C (MOLD)	(2)	¾" qtr-rnd. x 15¾" Cleat
C1 (PLY)	(1)	¾" x 16" x 30" Shelf
D (PLY)	(2)	¾" x 13¼" x 27¾" Doors
E (DOW)	(8)	1½"-dia. x 9½" Pillars
E1 (DOW)	(4)	1½"-dia. x 12¾" Pillars
E2 (DOW)	(4)	1½"-dia. x 2½" Pillars
E3 (DOW)	(4)	1½"-dia. x 9½" Pillars
F (PLY)	(4)	¾" x 10" x 20" Shelves
F1 (PLY)	(1)	¾" x 10" x 24" Shelf

Directions:
See the diagram in Fig. I, 6, page 25, for the construction details of the sideboard. All the plywood edges, except the backs, are covered with the half round molding. The cabinets are glued with the wood glue and nailed with the 6d nails. They are attached to the B top and bottom with the wood screws. Drill undersized holes for the nails and screwdrill for the screws. Use the glue gun to glue all the other parts of the sideboard in place. When you have finished constructing the sideboard, sand it. Using the paint brush, coat the sideboard with the polyurethane.

FABRIC FACE-LIFT

To give rooms a personal touch even when you're not permitted to make permanent decor changes, cover the walls with fabric. You won't damage the walls, or upset the landlord. Sheets are best to use because they come in greater widths than most fabrics, and are less expensive per yard.

•

To adhere the fabric to the wall, use undiluted starch. It works like glue, yet is easy to remove. A half gallon of starch will cover about 8 feet of wall. Make sure the walls are clean before you start. Before proceeding, test a small swatch of the fabric with the starch mixture to see if it adheres properly.

•

Cut the fabric panels to the desired length, adding 1 inch extra for shrinkage and seams. Liberally sponge the starch onto the wall, starting at the top and working down. Smooth each fabric panel into place and trim it at the bottom. For extra adhesion, sponge starch on top of the fabric as well.

•

Curtains and pillows can be made from the same fabric to give your apartment a custom-decorated look. When you're ready to move, simply sponge down the fabric with water, pull down the panels, wash them out and wash down the wall.

FIG. I, 6 VICTORIAN SIDEBOARD

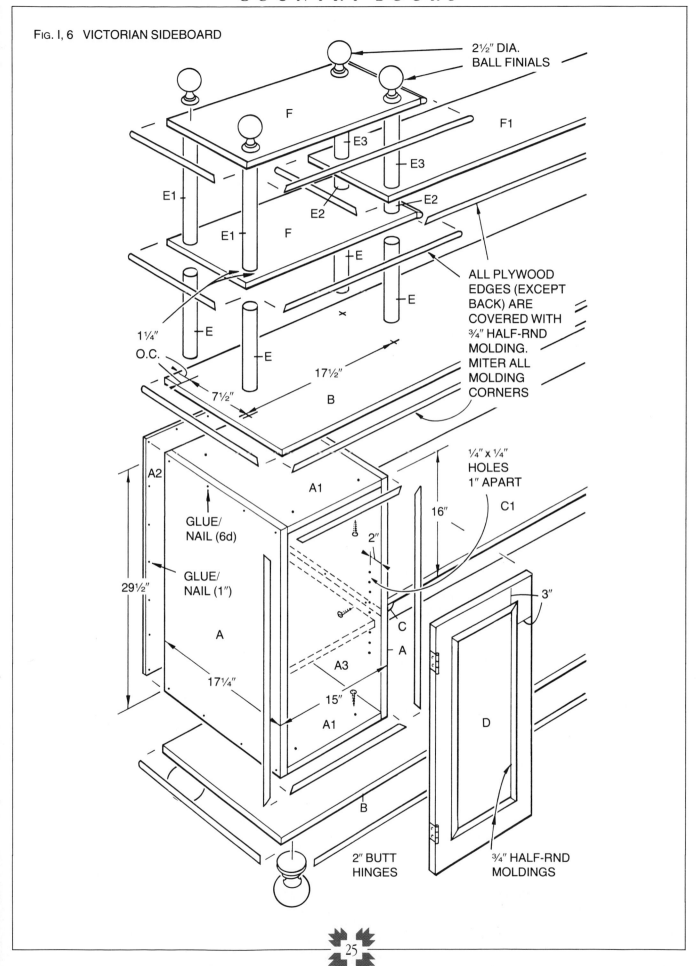

2½″ DIA.
BALL FINIALS

F

F1

E3

E3

E1

E2

E2

F

E1

E

E

E

ALL PLYWOOD
EDGES (EXCEPT
BACK) ARE
COVERED WITH
¾″ HALF-RND
MOLDING.
MITER ALL
MOLDING
CORNERS

1¼″
O.C.

7½″

17½″

B

¼″ x ¼″
HOLES
1″ APART

A2

A1

C1

16″

GLUE/
NAIL (6d)

2″

GLUE/
NAIL (1″)

C

3″

29½″

A

A

A3

17¼″

15″

A1

D

B

2″ BUTT
HINGES

¾″ HALF-RND
MOLDINGS

Light, welcoming and airy, this living room is all set for summer with pretty slipcovers made from painters' drop cloths. The country feeling is further enhanced by dressmaker details, such as pleated and ruffled skirts and looped green braid!

SUMMER WHITE SLIPCOVERED CHAIRS

Materials: Slipcover-weight canvas fabric or painters' drop cloths (available in paint and hardware stores in gray, natural, blue or pink); straight pins; yardstick; cloth tape measure; strong thread; double-faced masking tape; pencil; purchased piping *(optional)*; zipper, hooks or touch fasteners, if necessary *(see General Directions, Step 3)*; braid or other trim *(optional)*.

Note 1: *Painters' cloths must be pre-shrunk. See "Before You Begin," on page 29.*

Note 2: *The slipcovers are loosely fitted and consist of three basic sections — back, seat and skirt. We show you three variations. After the fabric has been washed, rectangles for the back, arm and seat sections are pinned, fitted, and cut directly on the chair. The skirt dimensions are determined with a tape measure.*

General Directions:

1. Try-On: After following the directions for the Chair Backs, Tuck-Ins, Arms, Seats and Skirts *(pages 28-30)*, carefully slip the pinned cover off the chair. In doing so, you will see whether or not you need to leave one seam open to get the cover on and off. If so, the back left corner (right corner when turned right side out) usually is made to be the open seam. Before you unpin this seam, mark the seamline along each pin on both layers of fabric. Then slip off the cover. If there are darts, stitch them first. Then baste all the seams. Turn the cover right side out and slip it back on the chair. Slight adjustments can be made in the seams in case the chair is not symmetrical. Turn the cover wrong side out again and, unless they are going to be piped, stitch the seams.

2. Piping (optional): If you wish to pipe the edges, slide piping between the two back cover fabric pieces, seamlines matching, removing the basting and repinning as you do so. Machine-stitch, using the zipper foot. Pin piping, finished edge inward, to the seat and stitch the piping.

3. Assembling: Right sides together, pin the skirts to the lower edge of the cover, matching the edges and centers. Draw up gathered edges to fit. Stitch. If there is an open seam, apply a zipper, hooks or touch fasteners to it. Trim the seams to ¾ inch.

4. Trims (optional): Braid was looped and tacked with thread to the seat edge of the chair on the right in the photo on pages 26-27.

5. Seat Pillow: A separate seat pillow may be added to a chair for extra height and softness. Make it following the directions for the Ruffles and Lace Pillows *(page 31)*, but apply piping to the pillow front before the lace edging and the ruffle.

Two-Piece Chair Back *(chair on left in photo, pages 26-27)*:

The simplest chair back is made of an inner and an outer back piece sewn together around the chair's top and side edges. Both pieces go from the chair's top to the seat. Sometimes the outer back piece goes all the way to the floor.

1. Measuring: For the length, measure the inner back from the top of the chair to the seat, and add 6 inches. Add another 4 inches for a tuck-in, if it is needed *(see Tuck-Ins, page 29)*. Measure the outer back from the top of the chair to the top of the skirt, or to the floor, and add 6 inches. For the width, wrap the tape measure all the way around the widest part of the chair back, and add 8 inches to that measurement. Divide the total in half.

2. Cutting: Using the length and width measurements, cut two rectangular fabric pieces, one for the inner back and one for the outer back. Be sure to cut on the grain (along the threads).

3. Marking: Press masking tape to the chair's inner back, with one edge of the tape along the chair's vertical center. Or, if the chair is padded, pin on the center. On the wrong side of both fabric pieces, lightly draw the vertical center. Tape the inner back fabric piece, wrong side up, to the chair's inner back, centers matching. Apply the outer back fabric piece in the same way.

4. Pin-Fit: With the edges matching, pin the two fabric pieces together around the chair frame; the row of pins will define the seamline. If there are chair arms, leave the edges of the fabric pieces open below the arms. Do not fit the cover too tightly; it should slide on and off easily. Cut off the excess fabric outside the pinned seamlines, leaving a 1-inch seam allowance on all four edges.

No house should ever be on any hill or on anything. It should be of the hill, belonging to it, so hill and house could live together each happier for the other.
— Frank Lloyd Wright

Darted Chair Back *(braid-trimmed chair on right in photo, pages 26-27):*
Use this method for thick or padded frames, to provide a better fit without adding a boxing strip.
1. Follow the directions in Two-Piece Chair Back, Steps 1 to 3 *(page 28).*
2. *Pin-Fit:* Smooth the inner back fabric piece over the top and side edges of the chair across the frame thickness. At each top corner, take up the extra fullness in a dart and pin its seamline. Pin the inner back fabric piece to the outer back piece in a seam that lies along the back edge of the chair frame. If there are chair arms, leave the fabric edges open below the arms.

Tuck-Ins *(chair on left in photo, pages 26-27):*
If there is space for your hand between the chair seat and the chair back, add about 4 inches to the length of the inner back and inner arm fabric pieces, and to the back and both side edges of the seat fabric piece.

Arms:
Arms often are covered as part of the total slipcover. If the chairs are padded, the arms can be exposed and covered with little sleeves.
1. *Slipcovered* *(sofa in photo, pages 26-27):* Pin-fit a pair of rectangular fabric pieces for each chair arm as you did for the chair back, without a dart as in Two-Piece Chair Back *(page 28)*, or with a dart as in Darted Chair Back *(above)*. Pin the back edges of the arm fabric pieces to the loose side edges of the chair back cover, shaping the inner seams as needed.
2. *Sleeved* *(chair on left in photo, pages 26-27):* Wrap fabric, wrong side up, around an arm and pin-mark the long seam; allow an extra inch at each end. Draw the seamlines on both layers over each pin. Unpin the fabric. Apply piping 1 inch from each end, turning under the seam allowance and topstitching along the piping. Apply a zipper to the seam.

Seats:
1. *Flat Seat* *(chair on left in photo, pages 26-27):*
On the grain, cut a rectangular piece of fabric 2 to 3 inches larger all around than the chair seat; add a tuck-in at the side and back edges, if they are needed *(see Tuck-Ins, at left)*. Wrong side up, mark the center of the seat fabric piece, and tape the seat fabric piece to the chair seat, centers matching. Pin the seat fabric piece in a seam together with the lower edges of the inside arm pieces and the inside back piece; leave a 1-inch seam allowance beyond the front edge of the seat fabric piece.
2. *Darted Seat* *(braid-trimmed chair on right in photo, pages 26-27):* The front seat corners can be darted in the same fashion as the chair back *(see Darted Chair Back, at left).*

Skirts:

Skirt pieces don't need to be pin-fitted. Take the following measurements and cut the skirt pieces.

1. *Gathered Skirt at Seat Level* *(braid-trimmed chair on right in photo, pages 26-27)*: Using the tape measure, measure around the seat and the back along the edges to which the skirt will be joined. Add half again to this measurement to create a 1½-times fullness. For the other dimension, measure from the chair seat to the floor and add 3 inches. Cut a fabric strip, pieced as needed, of this length and width, and stitch the short ends together. Sew a gathering row ½ inch from one long edge. Turn up 2½ inches at the opposite edge and press. Turn under its raw edge and stitch the hem.

2. *Pleated Skirt* *(chair on left in photo, pages 26-27)*: This chair back extends to the floor and includes 2½ inches for the hem. There is a separate front and two side skirts. The arms are exposed, and the cover zips down each back corner from the chair arm to the floor. To cut the skirt pieces, measure the length from the chair seat to the floor and add 3 inches. To find the other dimensions for each skirt piece, measure the edge of the seat cover to which it will be joined. Add 2 inches for each pleat and 2 inches for two side hems. Cut the three skirt pieces and stitch a 1-inch hem at each side. Turn up 2½ inches at each skirt piece's lower edge, press, turn under the raw edge and stitch the hem. Measure and press 1-inch pleats (three at each end of the front skirt, three at the front end of each side skirt), and baste them across the top edge.

SUMMER WHITE SEAT COVERS

Materials: *See Summer White Slipcovered Chairs, Materials and "Before You Begin," page 29*; purchased piping *(optional)*; bias tape or ribbon, for ties.

Directions (½-inch seams allowed):
1. On the grain, cut a rectangle of fabric 2 to 3 inches larger all around than the chair seat. Fold the seat fabric piece in half and mark the center. Spread out the seat fabric piece, wrong side up and centered on the chair seat. On it, draw the outlines of the seat. Cut 1 inch outside the drawn lines.
2. If you wish, stitch piping to the seat fabric piece, seamlines matching, and with the piping's finished edge facing the center of the seat piece.
3. The seat cover's short skirt is made of two pieces that tie together, behind the chair, at the back corners of the cover *(see chair near window in photo, pages 26-27)*. Cut two 6-inch-wide skirt pieces, one of them 2 inches longer than the width of the chair back, the second piece 2 inches longer than the sum of the other three sides.
4. Turn up 1 inch at one long and two short ends of each skirt piece. Stitch the hems. Sew the raw edges of the skirt pieces to the raw edges of the seat fabric piece, seamlines matching. Sew two 6-inch-long strips of bias tape or ribbon at each end of the skirt pieces, to tie behind the chair.

RUFFLES AND LACE PILLOWS

Materials: Preshrunk medium-weight muslin or lightweight canvas; lace edging; square pillow form in your choice of size, or fiberfill stuffing.

Directions (½-inch seams allowed):
1. Cut two fabric squares ½ inch larger all around than the pillow size you want to make. Cut a 2- to 3-inch-wide ruffle strip, pieced as needed, whose length is 1½ to 2 times the sum of the pillow edges' lengths.
2. Right sides together, sew the lace edging to the pillow front square, with the lace's finished edge facing the center of the square, and its seamline ½ inch from the raw edges of the square. At each corner, hold in enough fullness so that the edging will lie flat when it is turned outward.
3. Sew together the short ends of the ruffle strip to make a loop. Narrowly hem one long edge. On the other long edge, sew a gathering row ½ inch from the raw edge. Divide the ruffle into quarters and pin-mark them. Pin the ruffle to the pillow front over the lace, right sides together and raw edges even, with a pin mark at each corner. Draw up the gathers to fit the pillow front. Stitch along the gathering row.
4. Pin the pillow back to the pillow front, right sides together and raw edges even. Stitch around three sides and four corners.
5. Turn the pillow right side out. Insert the pillow form or stuffing. Turn in the open edges and slipstitch them closed.

Before most people start boasting about their family tree, they usually do a good pruning job.
— O. A. Battista

Sweet Dreams

♦ To create a rustic country look, a few well-chosen pieces are all that's necessary. Hard-working pioneers didn't own many frivolous items.

♦ Here, a bedroom draws its charm from original hand-hewn ceiling beams and wide floorboards, along with antiques and fresh flowers.

♦ For an authentic and inexpensive wall treatment, group together colorful bunches of dried herbs and hand-dipped candles.

♦ What makes it country? An antique quilt . . . faded colors that make the room look "lived in" . . . absence of frills that lets the architectural details shine through.

Serenade in Blue

♦ Slate blue walls set off the white sloped ceiling in an upstairs bedroom.

♦ A lighter shade of slate blue spiffs up a flea market armoire.

♦ One soothing color repeated throughout the room—bed, rug, walls, armoire—creates a restful atmosphere. You can achieve the same feeling with hunter green, cocoa brown or dusty rose.

♦ What makes it country? The simple blue and white color scheme . . . a brass headboard and calico prints on the bed . . . white lace at the window . . . . stoneware crockery on top of the armoire.

The Color Connection

♦ Checks, plaids, stripes, florals — how can all these patterns work in one area? By using color to tie them together. Here, cheery shades of red unite the different elements of this eclectic country look.

♦ A plain white wall in the bedroom, and white trim throughout, keep the bold red color from overpowering the room.

♦ Even though the patterns are busy, the lines are simple. Ruffles and frills would make the contrasting color scheme overwhelming.

♦ Amid the busy accents, the window provides relief to the eye with simple, clean lines and a plain white shade.

♦ A painted checkerboard floor covers flaws in the original planks, and adds depth to the room.

♦ In the hall, the use of petit-pattern wallpaper creates visual interest up close, and gives the illusion of a solid from a distance.

♦ The "log cabin" quilt on the wall, the old rocking chair with the stuffed duck and the pastel runner all contribute to the "homey" atmosphere.

♦ What makes it country? Traditional fabrics and patterns: buffalo plaid, checkerboard, quilt motifs . . . a diverse collection of wreaths, made from patchwork, grapevines, and dried flowers . . . a whimsical folksy feeling throughout.

SHIRRED CURTAINS

A shirred curtain has a deep heading to create a ruffle at the top. The wider the curtain fabric, the fuller and more dramatic the heading. If you wish to make a heading more than 2 inches deep, you should interface the heading so it will stand up well. A jumbo rod accents the gathering.

Directions:

1. Determine the amount of gather you'd like. Three times the length of the rod is the standard measure for the width of a shirred curtain. If you are using very light-weight fabric, you can use up to four times the rod's length for extreme fullness. For a mild gather in any weight fabric, double the length of the rod.

2. To determine the total length of the unfinished curtain, decide how deep you want the heading, and double that dimension. To that total, add: 1 inch for turning under; the circumference of the rod; the length from the rod to the floor, or the desired length; 3½ inches for the bottom hem; 1 inch for the drape.

3. Hem the sides by turning them under ½ inch, then 1 inch. Press, pin, and hem or topstitch.

4. To make the heading and rod pocket, turn under the top edge ½ inch and press. Along the top, fold back this total measurement: the depth of the heading plus ½ the circumference of the rod plus ½ inch. Press the top. Measure the depth of the heading and mark it with dressmaker's chalk by drawing a line across the curtain. Stitch across that line. To create the rod pocket, stitch across the turned-under edge very close to the edge.

5. Press under ½ inch along the bottom edge. Hang the curtain and mark it for the hem. You will lose up to 1 inch because of the drape of the fabric.

PINCH-PLEATED DRAPERIES

All the hard work is done for you because you create the pleats with slotted tape and pronged hooks. You sew the tape to the top back of the drapery and insert the hooks, ready-made for single, double or triple pleats, to pull the pleats together. A single pronged hook should be used at the corners to keep them neat. You can choose to use a traverse curtain rod, or a decorative rod with rings made to accommodate the hooks. Rods, hooks and tape are available at fabric stores or in drapery hardware departments.

Here's a guide to how much fabric you'll need: for single pleats, 1¾ times the length of the rod; for triple pleats, 2¼ times the length of the rod; the amounts will vary slightly according to the brand of tape you use.

Directions:

1. To determine the total length of the unlined curtain, measure the depth of the tape, double it and add 2 inches. Then add the curtain length desired plus 3½ inches for the hem.

2. Hem the sides by turning them under ½ inch, then 1 inch. Press, pin, and hem or topstitch.

3. Turn under ½ inch along the top edge and press. Fold back the depth of the tape plus 1½ inches and topstitch this down. Sew the tape to the back of the heading, leaving 1 inch of fabric along the top. Before cutting the tape, plan pleats in groups of two (single), three (double) or four (triple) slots, spaced evenly, and allow ½ inch at each end to turn under. Topstitch the tape on.

4. Press under ½ inch along the bottom edge. Hang the curtain and mark it for the hem.

DOLLAR-WISE DECORATING

◆ Windows on the World ◆

◆ White rice-paper window shades are a lovely and cost-effective way to dress up windows and still let the sun shine in. Try using them in the bedroom, bath, or an informal dining area. Many stores sell lampshades and other accessories to match these delicate shades.

◆ For a more colorful window treatment, make curtains from flat sheets. The pattern selection is limitless, and kids in particular will love curtains decorated with their favorite cartoon characters.

T·H·E B·A·T·H·I·N·G R·O·O·M

Splendor in the Bath

♦ Sloping ceilings get a lift with pretty patterned wallpaper. The print adds visual height, turning the wall into a buoyant floral canopy.

♦ The border, in a complementary pattern, gives a finished look to the room.

♦ A small chest of drawers tucked in the corner serves as a linen closet.

♦ What makes it country? A free-standing sink . . . the table lamp on the dresser instead of overhead lighting . . . a doily on the dresser top.

BATHING SCENT-SATIONS

Try soaking a large cotton towel in cool water and spraying it with your favorite cologne. Roll up the towel and use it to cushion your head while you relax in the bath.

•

When your muscles ache, drop a few handfuls of Epsom salts under hot running water. Add a touch of your favorite cologne.

•

Add a cup of brandy to your bath — it really helps to relax you, and smells divine!

Bathed in Nature

♦ Here the bathroom takes on a simple, rustic look that has the feel of an old farmhouse.

♦ The accents are straight from nature: a raw pine cupboard, a collection of baskets, a pine cone wreath.

♦ A new solution for towel storage — a sturdy wooden towel basket.

♦ What makes it country? A variety of wood tones . . . clean, simple lines accented with collectibles . . . a rag rug in pastel colors.

What is more agreeable than one's home?
— Cicero

A View from the Bath

Instead of a medicine chest, the pine cabinet atop the roomy bathroom sink counter holds the necessities — including a hand-held hair dryer that plugs into the wall.

Window shutters, stained to match the cabinets, let in light and ensure privacy.

The suede-colored carpet is a treat for the feet.

Brass trimmings — clock, towel bar, faucets, reproduction antique chart lamps — dress up an otherwise plain setting.

What makes it country? The window shutters . . . petit-pattern wallpaper . . . knotty pine cabinets with white porcelain knobs.

Bring ideas in and entertain them royally, for one of them may be the king.
— Mark Van Doren

B oudoir Bouquets

Pretty up an antique claw-foot tub with a hand-painted floral motif.

A big basket next to the tub is perfect for keeping a collection of natural sponges and a back scrubber close at hand.

The free-standing brass towel rack and the brass-stemmed lighting fixture above the bathtub add an air of elegance to the bathroom.

Humidity-loving plants will thrive in the steamy bathroom, and hide an unsightly radiator.

What makes it country? The old claw-foot bathtub . . . pastel color scheme . . . framed botanical prints . . . the potted flowering plants.

L·A·S·T·I·N·G
I·M·P·R·E·S·S·I·O·N·S

Close Up and Personal

The entry hall is the preview to your house, and the last glimpse of home when you leave.

♦ Here, a grouping of personal treasures—a framed photograph, spatterware jug brimming with freshly-cut flowers, a ceramic cat—sit atop a wicker side table.

♦ In the background, the tiny print wallpaper adds interest, but doesn't overwhelm the small space.

Lookin' Out My Back Door

What could be more evocative of country hospitality than a back porch that beckons your friends and neighbors to "come and set a spell"?

♦ Wicker furniture looks appealingly fresh and airy with a new coat of white paint.

♦ Colorful patchwork pillows, scattered about, cozy up the area.

♦ Potted and hanging plants bring Mother Nature right to your doorstep!

*True friendship's laws are by
this rule expressed,
Welcome the coming, speed the
parting guest.*
—Alexander Pope

The Stair Case

◆ The hand-painted folksy border brings visual interest to a well-traveled staircase.

◆ The details and colors of the painted-on "tiles" add spark to a white wall and bare wooden stairs.

◆ Use free-hand motifs such as the ones shown here, or try stencils or textured painting techniques.

◆ Can't paint a straight line? You can achieve the same effect with painted ceramic tiles, or an additional strip of painted molding.

◆ For a richer, more Victorian look, paper the walls with a finely detailed print, and run a bold companion border up the stairs along the bottom of the wall.

◆ What makes it country? The uncarpeted "character" of the stairs lets you imagine who might have climbed those steps 100 years ago . . . the slight variations in the colors from tile to tile, showing that the tiles were hand-crafted.

Welcome Home

◆ In the entry hall, finely detailed wallpaper makes even a tiny alcove seem spacious. Up close, the printed pattern adds interest *(see photo, page 40)*. But from a distance, the wallcovering is a neutral background for framed artwork and wall ornaments.

◆ Other small-print wallpapers would work well here too. Good alternatives for limited spaces include a fine stripe pattern and a mini-geometric print.

◆ Keep the background light for an airy look.

◆ What makes it country? The staircase with its unique banister . . . the natural motifs and materials: floral fabrics, botanical prints, wood floor, cotton rug, wicker table, fresh flowers in clay pots.

Simply Sensational

Make the most of your home's architectural details.

♦ Here, hunter green and ivory walls offset a burnished-red chair rail and ceiling molding.

♦ For a cozier look, try a delicate floral wallpaper on the upper walls. A light-toned background for the wallpaper is best.

♦ The unique pine chimney cabinet adds storage and height. It's an eye-catching vertical shape in a room with a strong horizontal focus.

♦ Bamboo "matchstick" roll-up shades on a curtainless window allows the maximum amount of sunlight to filter in.

♦ To create this look in a modern home, put up your own chair rail and moldings. You'll find dozens of different types of molding at your lumber yard or home center.

♦ What makes it country? Angular, utilitarian furnishings that capture the feeling of a simple farm house . . . lines that are clean but not high-tech . . . the earthy color scheme . . . equine accents.

DOLLAR-WISE DECORATING

♦ *Hidden Beauty* ♦

"Found art" is just that: everyday objects that become works of art when they are displayed decoratively. These treasures can add a fanciful touch to any corner of your house.

♦ Rethink the castoffs you find at flea markets and yard sales. A milk bottle with an interesting shape or decoration makes a great vase. The finely carved arm of a chair past its prime can become unique wall art, as can brass door knockers or drawer pulls, wood or iron architectural details, even an old wooden tennis racket with character.

♦ Keep your eyes open and you'll see what others can't: the beauty of the everyday objects we take for granted.

Peace be to this house.
— The Holy Bible: Luke

C O U N T R Y
S·T·O·R·A·G·E

*If you keep a thing seven years, you are sure to
find a use for it.*
— Sir Walter Scott

he Shakers had the right idea when they hung their ladderback chairs on the wall to keep them out of the way. We all could use extra storage space, and the best way to find it is to use some ingenuity.

In this chapter, you'll find pretty and practical space stretchers: tactics that make the most of kitchen cabinets, *faux* antiques that hold and hide everything (even a television), clever transformations for "wasted" space in your home. For instance, the photo at left demonstrates how a shallow shelf unit becomes an ideal showcase for a collection of well-loved porcelain plates. Each shelf has a ridge to hold the plates in place, and store-bought moldings protect the display. Ingenuity, yes—all with a country flair.

If you're a bit more ambitious, turn to "Faux Antiques" *(page 54).* With basic carpentry and painting skills, you can change ordinary unpainted furniture into one-of-a-kind pieces your friends will envy. Our space savers were designed by professionals, but they're easy to adapt if you have patience and a steady hand.

Use these ideas as a jumping-off point for rethinking your own needs. Remember, sometimes simple rearranging can open up usable space you never dreamed you had.

E·V·E·R·Y·T·H·I·N·G
I·N I·T·S P·L·A·C·E

Country in the City

Even the tiniest apartment kitchen can take on a country air with the right accents and storage ideas.

♦ Open shelving (just remove those clunky cabinet doors) creates an airy, country pantry feeling.

♦ Fruits and vegetables look like they're fresh from the garden when displayed in rattan baskets.

♦ Pretty platters and serving trays hung on the wall save valuable shelf space.

♦ Heart motifs, cutting boards and patchwork potholders give a small area instant charm.

♦ Dried flowers in a wall-mounted vase look appealing by the narrow window area.

Open, Sesame!

Give a room new dimension by making a cramped, old-fashioned closet part of the room.

♦ To do this, remove the closet doors and install shelves. Adding wallpaper to the rear wall and shelves of the closet ties this area into the room.

♦ A wicker chair plumped with pillows makes this area a "nook."

♦ To add the finishing touch to this cozy look, go for an eclectic display on the shelves—photos, books, pottery—anything that feels homey to you.

Upright and Out of Sight

Behind simple wooden cabinet doors lies a model of modern-day efficiency—no more digging through piles of pans!

♦ Vertical dividers in under-the-counter cupboards maximize the use of space and also provide easy access to bakeware.

♦ Pull-out shelves hold the countertop appliances you don't use everyday.

Island Ideas

A deep-angled cabinet extending down to the countertop is an eye-pleasing alternative to the standard square cabinet.

♦ The second sink on the kitchen island is the perfect spot for kitchen helpers to do "prep" work while the cook is in residence.

♦ Spices, decanted into bottles, are as colorful as they are useful.

Low Overhead

Use every inch of available space; in country style, "organized clutter" is part of the charm.

♦ An inexpensive shelf mounted over a doorway shows off a collection of ceramic serving pieces that is beautiful to look at, but hard to store in ordinary kitchen cabinets.

♦ The pristine white-on-white scheme is accented by a tiny country cottage alongside the pitchers.

GINGERBREAD-STYLE BATHROOM SHELF

Sections of gingerbread-like molding, painted white, can give architectural interest to bathroom shelving *(see photo, page 51)*. Stock moldings can be adapted easily to decorate any shelf. Have the lumberyard cut pieces of molding to size, paint or stain them and, if they are going to be used in the bathroom, protect them with a few coats of polyurethane.

Materials: 28½-inch-long 1 x 6 board for shelf top, or rip a 1 x 8 board to a 6¼-inch width and cut to a

28½-inch length (most lumber yards will do this for you); 26½-inch-long 1 x 3 board for shelf back; 4 feet of fancy molding (we used 3½-inch-wide Fleur Running Trim, available from Vintage Wood Works *(see Materials Shopping Guide, page 242)* in 4-foot lengths, leaving 3 inches for error)*; 6 feet of ¾-inch-wide cove molding; three 2-inch-long #6 flathead screws; two 3-inch-long #7 or #8 flathead screws; five 3½-inch-long Shaker pegs; 2 wood plugs to fit larger screw size *(see* Fig. II, 1A*)*; wood glue; wood putty; medium-grade sand paper; tack cloth; wood sealer, stain and sealer, or paint; miter box; back saw for mitering; drill, with countersink bit and appropriate-size bits for screws and pegs; rip saw; cross-cut saw.

Directions:

1. Carefully measure the exact inside (shorter) and outside (longer) lengths of fancy molding needed for the front of the shelf. Follow the diagram in Fig. II, 1, and check against the shelf top piece to be sure the molding fits exactly. Mark the exact lengths with a pencil on the fancy molding.

2. Using the miter box and the back saw, cut the fancy molding for the front of the shelf. Glue the molding to the front edge of the shelf top *(see* Fig. II, 1*)*.

3. Miter the corner ends of the side fancy molding, but do not cut the molding for length. Glue the fancy molding to the sides of the shelf top. Squarely trim off the back ends of the side molding to match the shelf width exactly.

4. Miter cove molding for the bottom and ends of the shelf back, and glue the molding in place.

5. Measure and mark the positions of the peg holes, and drill the holes.

6. Glue the shelf top to the shelf back. When the glue is dry, drill three evenly-spaced pilot holes, for the 2-inch screws, through the top of the shelf into the back. Install the screws. Fill the screw holes with wood putty and, when the putty is dry, sand it.

7. Cut a 26½-inch length of cove molding and glue it into the right angle formed by the shelf top and back *(see* Fig. II, 1A*)*.

8. Glue the Shaker pegs into the peg holes.

9. If any of the shelf's surfaces are rough, sand them smooth. Wipe off all the sawdust with the tack cloth. Seal, stain and seal, or paint the shelf.

10. Drill positioned holes *(see* Fig. II, 1*)* through the back of the shelf for the 3-inch screws. Drill larger holes for the wood plugs *(see* Fig. II, 1A*)*. Screw the back of the shelf into wall studs to secure the shelf or, if necessary, use toggle bolts. Glue the wood plugs into the screw holes to hide the screw heads or bolts.

Instead of a "no-frills" shelf, stock moldings transform a bathroom space saver into an eye-pleasing area.

FIG. II, 1   GINGERBREAD-STYLE BATHROOM SHELF

FANCY MOLDING PLACEMENT

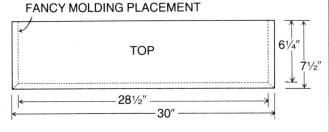

TOP

6¼"
7½"
28½"
30"

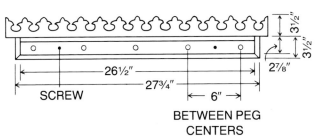

3½"
3½"
26½"
27¾"
2⅞"
6"
SCREW
BETWEEN PEG CENTERS

FIG. II, 1A   SHELF DETAIL

COVE MOLDING

WOOD PLUG

COUNTERSUNK SCREW

COVE MOLDING

⅝"

Contemporary Country

Here's a picture-perfect example of how modern "streamlined" and old-fashioned "country" looks can work together beautifully.

♦ The streamlined look: the recessed lighting fixtures, sleek cabinets and grids on the wall.

♦ The country look: the practical use of the wall to hold cooking utensils and gear too bulky to fit in drawers; the terra cotta mortar and pestle set; wood cutting boards on display.

Mix 'n Match

An eclectic collection makes a more interesting display—and can help you store odds and ends!

♦ Transform ironstone plates into free-form wall art using "invisible" wire plate hangers.

♦ Split up pairs of candlesticks and fill in the collection with novel singles.

♦ An assortment of covered picnic baskets are a smart country storage idea. Your guests see pretty wicker in interesting shapes; only you know about the paraphernalia stashed inside!

F·A·U·X
A·N·T·I·Q·U·E·S

Unfinished Symphony

◆ Paint the back and shelves of an unfinished hutch to showcase your decorative ceramics. You also can highlight your collectibles by using subtly patterned wallpaper or fabric applied with glue or staples. Either method is ideal to cover imperfections in the wood.

◆ Even though this hutch is in the dining room, the objects displayed are not limited to dining-related items. Other showcased items include pine cones in baskets, fresh flowers, a carved swan and tiny dolls.

Keeping Secrets

◆ This reproduction pine armoire looks like an antique—but it has all the right dimensions for modern storage. A television, VCR and videotape collection fit inside perfectly, with plenty of drawer space to spare.

◆ With its doors closed, the armoire becomes an inspired addition to a classic decor. It's really a Southwestern-style piece, but it's neutral enough to blend into any setting, from striking and spare to flowers and lace.

Treasured Chest

This Six-Board Chest is made, as its name implies, from just six pieces of wood. A staple of early American households, such chests originally were used to store linens and clothing. The colorful floral design stenciled on the front, top and sides of the chest was inspired by the Pennsylvania Dutch. Directions for the Six-Board Chest begin on page 58.

Rhapsody in Blue

Pretty and elegant, this console table began as a simple, unfinished table. With a few coats of latex paint and sponge dappling, it's transformed into a showcase piece of furniture, lovely enough for your living room. The final touch: a graceful painted ribbon. The same sponge painting technique was used to give the table lamps a quick makeover. Directions for the Rhapsody in Blue: Table and Lamp Shades are on page 59.

SIX-BOARD CHEST
(17½ x 21½ x 41 inches)

Materials: 1 inch x 18 inches x 18 feet of pine (tight knots); ⅜ inch x 1 inch x 7 feet of lattice; compass; ruler; medium-grade sandpaper; 2d and 6d finishing nails; nail set; two 1½ x 2-inch brass hinges; wood glue; wood putty; tack cloth; paint brush; blue wood dye powder *(see Materials Shopping Guide, page 242)*; rags; black fine-point pen; mylar sheets; utility knife; masking tape; acrylic paints or water-based stencil paints in your choice of colors *(see Materials Shopping Guide)*; stencil brushes; cross-cut saw; rip saw; saber saw; back saw for mitering; miter box; hammer; screwdriver.

Cutting Directions:

Code	Pieces	Size
A (1 x 18)	(2)	¾" x 17" x ⅝" Sides
B (1 x 18)	(2)	¾" x 17" x 38¾" Front/Back
C (1 x 18)	(1)	¾" x 17" x 38¾" Bottom
D (1 x 18)	(1)	¾" x 17" x 40" Lid
D1 (LAT)	(2)	⅜" x 1" x 17½" Trim
D2 (LAT)	(1)	⅜" x 1" x 40¾" Trim
E	(2)	1½" x 2" Brass hinges

FIG. II, 2 SIX-BOARD CHEST

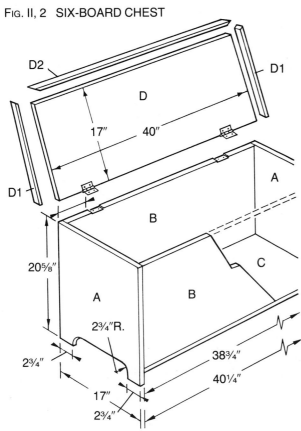

Directions:

1. Cut the pine to the lengths required for parts A, B, C and D, and rip the parts to 17-inch widths.
2. Using the compass and the ruler, lightly scribe the leg cutouts on the bottom of each A side *(see FIG. II, 2)*. Cut out the legs with the saber saw and sand the edges.
3. Using 6d nails, glue and nail the A sides to the ends of the B front and back, making the A and B pieces flush at the top and side edges.
4. Using 6d nails, glue and nail the C bottom to the bottom edges of the B front and back, between the A sides *(see FIG. II, 2)*.
5. Using the miter box and the back saw, miter the D1 and D2 lattice trim pieces following the directions for the Gingerbread-Style Bathroom Shelf, Steps 1 to 3 *(page 51)*. Using 2d nails, glue and nail the trim pieces to the edges of the D lid, making the trim pieces flush at the top edge of the lid. Set the nails, fill the holes with wood putty and, when the putty is dry, sand it.

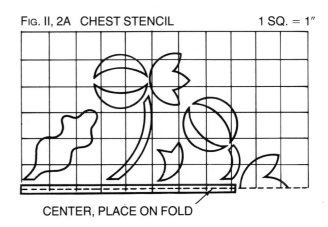

FIG. II, 2A CHEST STENCIL   1 SQ. = 1"

CENTER, PLACE ON FOLD

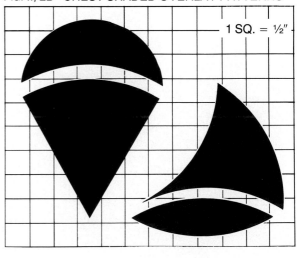

FIG. II, 2B CHEST SHADED OVERLAY PATTERNS

1 SQ. = ½"

6. Using the hinges, attach the lid assembly (D, D1 and D2) to the chest (A, B and C), placing a hinge 6 inches from each end of the D lid (see FIG. II, 2).

7. If any of the chest's surfaces are rough, sand them smooth. Wipe off all the sawdust with the tack cloth.

8. Add water to the blue wood dye powder following the manufacturer's directions. Brush a coat of the blue dye over the entire chest. Wipe off the dye with rags to achieve a grained antique look.

9. Enlarge the Pennsylvania Dutch chest stencil design in FIG. II, 2A, and the two shaded overlays in FIG. II, 2B, following the directions on page 241. Using the black fine-point pen, trace the chest stencil design and the two shaded overlay designs onto sheets of mylar. Make a separate traced mylar sheet for each paint color you plan to use in the Pennsylvania Dutch design. Cut out the stencils with the utility knife. Tape the stencils in place on the front, sides and lid of the chest (see photo, page 56). Stencil the designs using acrylic paints or water-based stencil paints, and stencil brushes. To paint the border, apply masking tape to mark the outline (see photo) or create your own design.

DOUBLE DUTY

Grandma's old steamer trunk can do double duty in your home. Depending on its size, use it as a wonderfully nostalgic coffee table in front of the sofa, or as an end table. Not only does it make a great table, it can provide terrific storage space for extra linens, books, magazines, even important papers.

Some other good uses for trunks: If you have a fireplace, set a trunk beside it and fill it with kindling or firewood. (Always be sure to set any piece of furniture a good distance away from a burning fire.)

A large trunk serves as a great place to store a component stereo system when it's not in use. If you have an empty corner in the living room, leave the trunk open and fill it with quilts or blankets that coordinate with your living room colors. Hang old family photographs inside the top.

•

Give your time-worn trunk a little refurbishing by shining up the brass hardware with a little polish. If the hardware is steel, give some extra visual interest by darkening it with liquid stove blacking (available at hardware stores). Freshen the trunk interior with wallpaper, scented paper drawer lining or fabric. If the trunk is an antique, keep in mind that any changes you make to it will reduce its value and diminish its authenticity.

RHAPSODY IN BLUE: TABLE AND LAMP SHADES

Materials: Unfinished pine console table in your choice of style (see photo, page 57); 2 lamps with black paper shades in your choice of style (see photo, page 57); medium-grade sandpaper; tack cloth; paint brushes; white latex paint; powder blue, medium blue and white acrylic paints; sponge; scrap paper; tracing paper; soft lead pencil; masking tape; 1-inch-wide artist's flat brush; satin-finish acrylic varnish.

Directions:

1. If any of the table's surfaces are rough, sand them smooth. Wipe off all the sawdust with the tack cloth.

2. Brush two coats of white latex paint on the table, allowing the paint to dry after each coat.

3. Place a small amount of the powder blue acrylic paint in a saucer. Tear off a small piece of the sponge and dip it into the blue paint. Dab the sponge on scrap paper to see the effect it makes. Adjust the size of the sponge piece or the quantity of paint on it until you achieve the desired effect. When you are satisfied, directly dab the powder blue paint over the table, letting the white paint underneath show through (see photo, page 57). Let the paint dry completely.

4. Directly sponge powder blue paint onto the outside surface of each lamp shade, letting the black color underneath show through (see photo, page 57). Let the paint dry completely.

5. Enlarge the ribbon design in FIG. II, 3 onto tracing paper, following the directions on page 241. Go over the design with the soft lead pencil. Center the design on the front of the table, with the penciled side against the wood, and tape the design in place. Rub over the design with the back of a spoon to transfer the design lines to the wood. Using the artist's flat brush, paint the ribbon design with the medium blue and white acrylic paints. Let the paints dry completely.

6. Brush or spray a coat of acrylic varnish over the entire table.

FIG. II, 3 RHAPSODY IN BLUE TABLE

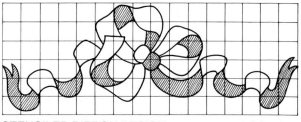

STENCILED RIBBON DESIGN   1 SQ. = 1"

A homemade "heirloom," this country hutch is made from shelf units, doors and decorative moldings.

RUSTIC HUTCH

Materials: Two unfinished pine shelf units (the stacked shelves in the photo measure 74 inches in height); molding; 2 lumber frames with hinges, or 2 unfinished, ready-to-hang doors (available at home centers, lumber stores and unfinished furniture stores); fine screening; 2 metal doorknobs; nails; medium-grade sand paper; tack cloth; fabric of desired colors and design; spray adhesive; satin-finish polyurethane; miter box; back saw for mitering; cross-cut saw; hammer; staple gun.

Directions:

1. Carefully measure the exact inside (shorter) and outside (longer) lengths of molding needed for the hutch front. Mark the exact lengths with a pencil on each type of molding you have selected for the top, middle and bottom of the hutch.

2. Using the miter box and the back saw, cut each type of molding to the length needed for the front of the hutch. Nail the moldings to the top and bottom of the hutch. Nail the molding for the middle of the hutch to the top of the lower shelf unit so that the molding forms about a ½-inch lip that will hold the upper unit snugly after it is slipped into place.

3. Miter the corner ends of the moldings for the sides of the hutch, but do not cut the moldings for length. Nail the moldings to the top and bottom of the hutch sides, and to the middle so it forms a ½-inch lip. Squarely trim off the back ends of the side moldings to match the shelf units' width.

4. If the surfaces of the shelf units and doors are rough, sand them smooth. Wipe all the sawdust off the units and doors with the tack cloth.

5. Cut the fabric to fit the inside back of the upper shelf unit, and attach the fabric to the back of the unit with spray adhesive.

6. To let the wood show through, leave the uncovered wood surfaces of the two shelf units and the doors unstained and unpainted. Give the surfaces two coats of polyurethane to keep the wood from absorbing stains. Allow the polyurethane to dry between coats.

7. If you are using lumber frames for the doors, measure and cut the screening to fit the center openings of the frames. Using the staple gun, attach the screening to the frames.

8. Attach the lumber frames or ready-to-hang doors to the lower shelf unit.

9. Attach the metal doorknobs to the doors. Slip the upper shelf unit into place on top of the lower unit.

JELLY CUPBOARD

Materials: Unfinished pine jelly cupboard; medium-grade sandpaper; tack cloth; paint brushes; white and blue acrylic paints; masking tape *(optional)*; green acrylic paint *(optional)*; checkerboard stencil *(optional)*; acrylic or water-based stencil paints *(optional)*; stencil brushes *(optional)*; sponge; 220-grade wet and dry sandpaper; cotton rags; black and raw sienna acrylic paints; acrylic extender medium; plastic container.

Directions:

1. If any of the jelly cupboard's surfaces are rough, sand them smooth with the medium-grade sandpaper. Wipe off all the sawdust with the tack cloth.

2. Brush on an undercoat of white acrylic paint, and let it dry. Brush on a coat of blue acrylic paint, and let it dry. Paint the door hinges *(see photo)*, if you wish, or let the black metal show, as was done centuries ago.

3. To make the harlequin design on the cupboard doors *(see photo)*, tape off triangular sections with masking tape, and paint the triangles in two contrasting colors (we used green and raw sienna). Or, if you prefer, stencil a checkerboard design on the doors, using acrylic or water-based stencil paints and a checkerboard stencil, or by taping off the checkerboard squares with masking tape.

4. To distress the jelly cupboard, apply water with a damp sponge to the surface of one section. Dampen the wet and dry sandpaper in clean water and gently rub the painted surface so that some of the white undercoat shows through. Rub off the colored paint in areas where wear normally would occur, such as the sides and doors. Distress one section at a time. When you have finished distressing a section, wipe the surface with a rag. When you have finished distressing the entire cupboard, wipe off any remaining sawdust with the tack cloth.

5. To antique the jelly cupboard so the painted color fades somewhat, prepare a wash of acrylic paints. Put one squeeze each of black and raw sienna acrylic paints in a plastic container. Stirring constantly, very gradually add water and a little acrylic extender medium to the acrylic paints until you have a very thin wash. Working one section at a time, brush on the wash. Then rub off the wash with a rag, leaving more wash near the edges and removing more wash as you approach the centers of the top, sides and doors. Allow the wash to dry completely.

This jelly cupboard looks as though it has given years of loving service. In reality, distressing techniques were used to give it that time-worn look.

B·A·S·K·E·T
B·O·N·A·N·Z·A

RUFFLE-AND-BOW BASKET

Materials: Basket with handle; ½ yard of fabric; acrylic spray paint; fabric stiffener; tacky glue; clear gloss acrylic spray varnish.

Directions:

1. Spray paint the basket, using two or three thin coats.

2. Cut two bow strips, each 5½ inches wide and 30 inches long. Cut two 3-inch-wide ruffle strips, each the same length as the circumference of the basket rim.

3. At all four edges of each ruffle strip, turn ¼ inch to the wrong side and stitch. At one long (top) edge, machine baste ¼ inch from the top, using the longest stitch. Pull up the threads to reduce the strip length by half, so it will fit between the handle ends on one side of the basket. Tie the thread ends. Distribute the gathers evenly and topstitch to keep them in place. Repeat with the second ruffle strip.

4. Fold each bow strip in half lengthwise, right sides together, and stitch ¼ inch from one short and both long ends. Turn each strip right side out. Tie it into a bow around one basket handle end and shorten the strip, if necessary. Untie the bow. Turn in the open edges of each strip and slipstitch.

5. Apply the fabric stiffener to one of the ruffles, following the manufacturer's directions. While the ruffle is wet, fold its gathered edge about ¾ inch inside the basket between the handle ends. Using a round-bladed knife, push the gathered edge into the weave of the basket; the ruffle will stay in place until it is dry. Repeat with the second ruffle on the other inside half of the basket.

6. Apply the fabric stiffener to one of the bow strips. Wrap the strip around a handle end and tie a bow. Repeat with the second bow strip around the other handle end. Place rolled-up wax paper or plastic wrap within the bows to shape them while they dry.

7. In two or three hours, when the fabric is dry but still pliable, check and correct the shaping of the bows and ruffles. Glue any part of the ruffle that may have come undone. Allow the glue to dry. For a glossy finish, spray the basket with clear gloss acrylic varnish.

A BUSHEL OF USES FOR BASKETS

In the Bathroom:

A pretty and ventilated laundry hamper.

•

To store guest towels or pretty soaps for visitors.

•

A potpourri container (pages 116-117).

•

A holder for toothbrushes and toothpaste.

◆

In the Kitchen:

To display fruit ripening on a windowsill.

•

To serve bread, rolls and biscuits at the table.

◆

In the Dining Room:

Stack silverware wrapped in linen napkins in a basket for easy buffet service.

•

As a centerpiece, filled with fresh fruit or flowers.

◆

In the Living Room:

As containers for nuts or candy.

•

Near the fireplace as a bin for firewood or kindling (keep the basket a good distance from a burning fire).

•

A collection displayed on the wall as a decorative element.

•

To stockpile magazines or keep needlework "in progress."

◆

In the Nursery or Childrens' Room:

To store lotions, powder and diaper pins.

•

To keep rolled up socks, t-shirts and "stretchies" for your infant at hand.

•

As a toy chest or a "nest" for stuffed animals.

•

To organize dresser or desk-top clutter.

◆

In the Hall:

A convenient holder for house and car keys.

•

By the phone to keep a pen and notepad handy.

•

A fishing creel or covered basket near the door as a mailbox.

•

On the floor near the door as a receptacle for wet galoshes and umbrellas.

◆

Around the House:

As a carry-all for gardening tools and gloves.

•

To camouflage modern pieces that clash with your country decor: audio cassettes and video tapes, computer equipment, cleaning or laundry supplies.

BEAUTIFUL BASKETS

Decorate your baskets with the same painting techniques you would use on furniture: stenciling, sponge painting, spatter painting, antiquing. To finish the baskets, spray them with a coat of clear acrylic varnish.

EXPLORE THE OPTIONS

Seek out unique basket shapes, textures and colors. The most common baskets are made from rattan or willow, but you'll find others made of woven grapevine, twigs, wood, palm, even banana leaves! Colorful cotton rag baskets — often imported from the Caribbean — make very cheerful accents for any room in the house.

BASKETS FULL OF LOVE

Make a gift basket for a special occasion.

◆

For the New Baby:

Stencil nursery motifs on a white painted basket or woven baby carrier and fill it with essentials: powder, lotion, moist baby wipes, a spare "stretchie" outfit, diaper pins, cotton balls and a rattle to occupy the little one at changing time.

◆

For the Bride:

Have each guest at a bridal shower bring a kitchen gadget — cheese grater, garlic press, ice cream scoop, mushroom brush — and a favorite recipe, typed on a pretty card, for which the gadget is to be used. Place all the gifts in a serving basket tied with a gold and white bow and present it to the bride-to-be.

◆

For a Friend:

Decorate a basket to match a friend's bathroom decor, and fill it with a bottle of bubble bath, a big squishy sponge, a fun novel, a small box of chocolates, and after-bath lotion in her favorite scent. Attach a card encouraging her to pamper herself after a hard day.

◆

For Christmas:

When a friend or relative has to spend the holidays far from home, send him or her a Christmas basket filled with homemade cookies or fruitcake, a pretty ornament, simmering potpourri with an evergreen or spicy scent, a photo, and a tape-recorded message or videotape from the whole gang.

C·O·U·N·T·R·Y
C·O·L·L·E·C·T·I·O·N·S

Antiques and Collectibles

Antiques and collectibles are the mainstays of country decor. Antiques generally are defined as items over 100 years old that have some intrinsic artistic or historical value. A collectible generally is a mass-produced item that is collected largely for nostalgic reasons. For example, an authentic Shaker ladderback chair is an antique; original recordings by the Beatles are collectibles.

Throughout this book you'll see a myriad of collections worked into a variety of room settings. The following section provides a few tips for building and displaying your own collections.

♦ **Take Stock** Take a good look around your home—you may have a collection that simply needs nurturing. The "tacky" souvenirs Aunt Harriet brought back from the World's Fair would make a wonderfully campy collection. Pretty trinket boxes take on new life when you display them as a group.

♦ **Make It Personal** Your collection should reflect your taste, personality and interests. Porcelain thimbles would suit an avid stitcher. Antique eyeglasses are a clear choice for an optician. Old-time primers and textbooks might amuse a teacher.

♦ **Have Fun** Build a collection that brings you joy. Disney memorabilia, baseball cards, novelty buttons and pins all are ideal collectibles.

♦ **Don't Spend A Fortune** Depending on what you collect, building a collection does not have to be costly. You may find treasures at yard sales or thrift shops as well as in antique stores. Part of the fun is hunting for bargains.

◆ *Love It Or Leave It* Unless you're a serious antique collector with lots of time and money to spend, don't buy pricey items you aren't prepared to live with. There's always a chance your collection will become more valuable over time, but the best collections are born from the heart, not the purse.

◆ *Give It Local Appeal* Use your hometown as the theme for an historic or nostalgic collection. Unite old maps, photos or drawings with souvenirs of local attractions and businesses. Then add your personal mementos from annual county fairs and celebrations, or even your high school prom favors!

◆ *Show It Off* Shelves in a bookcase or hutch are an ideal showcase for most collections. A fireplace mantel also is a natural, but there are plenty of other ways to display your collection.

Old printer's drawers work well for miniatures. Slide on a glass front to protect the collection, and hang the drawers on the wall. Or hunt down a knick-knack shelf at a flea market or antique show to give your curio collection an old-time flavor.

Inexpensive screw-in hooks attached underneath cabinets and shelves are great to display mugs, pitchers and hanging ornaments. Use windowsills to hold colored hobnail or depression glass — sunlight shining through the pieces really makes them sparkle. For more display space, mount narrow shelves within the frames of inset windows. Be sure to leave enough room for the window to slide freely.

Don't overlook the powder room, stairwells, foyer and dining room — they may offer unused space that suits your collection display to perfection.

IN THE KNOW ABOUT ANTIQUES

To learn more about antiques, contact:
The National Antique and Art Dealers Association of America, 15 East 57th Street, New York, NY, 10022, (212) 826-9707.
The association conducts workshops, lectures and exhibitions, answers inquiries and makes referrals for individuals who are interested in antiques and the decorative arts.

BOOK SENSE

Place musty smelling books — those great old ones you found in the attic or bought at a garage sale — in a paper bag filled with cat box litter. Close the bag and leave it for about a week. When you take the books out, no odor will remain!

If you carry your childhood with you, you never become older.
—Abraham Sutzeker

TAKE A BOW!

Draw attention to your favorite photograph or print by "hanging" it from a bow. Tack or hot glue a piece of ribbon so that it runs down the center back of the picture frame. Then tack or hot glue the ribbon to the wall. Make a bow from another piece of the ribbon. Hand stitch the center of the bow to keep it from coming untied, and tack or hot glue the bow to the top of the ribbon.

C O U N T R Y
T·O·U·C·H·E·S

*Whatsoever thy hand findeth to do,
do it with thy might.*
— Ecclesiastes

Crafting was born of necessity. The men and women who settled the New World had to learn to make for themselves—or to do without. Country crafting is a perfect marriage of the practical and the decorative: the quilts, pillows and wood crafts found in this chapter are as beautiful as they are useful. Many of these projects are based on designs handed down from parent to child.

Early needlecrafters developed quilting as a practical way to use up scraps of precious fabric. Our quilts are both sensible and spectacular, and just the thing to cuddle under on a cold winter's night. There are afghans to crochet and pillows to make from patchwork. Our Birds 'N Blossoms Hooked Rug, in the photo at left *(directions, page 90)*, will add warmth and beauty to any room in your house. And there are many other projects, from Americana cross stitch samplers to decorative pottery—all of them country classics.

The love of good materials and the satisfaction of making something beautiful has kept craftwork thriving for generations. Crafting is not just an echo from another time, when things were lovingly, patiently created. It is an art, and a hands-on link to the solid values of yesteryear.

Lovely and elegant, "Carolina Lily" was a favorite quilt pattern in the mid-1800's. This quilt, a reproduction of an antique, features patchwork flower petals and appliquéd stems. Directions for this project were written by studying the actual 19th-century quilt!

Q·U·I·L·T·S
A·N·D A·F·G·H·A·N·S

He hath no leisure who useth it not.
— George Herbert

SUNSHINE AND SHADOW QUILT
(about 81 x 102 inches)

Materials: Forty-five-inch-wide fabric in 4 different light shade calico prints (A, E, F and G), 4 different medium shade calico prints (B, D, H and Y) and 5 different dark shade calico prints (C, I, J, X and Z): ¼ yard each of B and Z, ½ yard each of G, H, X and Y, ¾ yard each of A, C and D, 1 yard of J, 1⅛ yard each of E and F, and 2¾ yards of I *(see Note, below)*; matching thread; 6 yards of 44-inch-wide fabric for quilt back and binding; synthetic batting; masking tape; darning or milliner's needle; crochet thread.

Note: *We have used thirteen different fabrics in this quilt. You may use more or fewer, if you wish. Choose the fabrics and arrange them in terms of their value (light, medium or dark), so that you will have a "sunshine and shadow" effect. To identify the lettered fabrics, compare FIG. III, 1 with the photo on page 70.*

Directions (¼-inch seams allowed):
1. Cutting: From Fabric I, cut two 4 x 95-inch borders and two 4 x 74-inch borders. On the wrong side of the fabrics, mark and cut the following quantities of 4-inch square patches: 59 (A), 16 (B), 44 (C), 52 (D), 82 (E), 86 (F), 24 (G), 28 (H), 32 (I), 72 (J), 40 (X), 28 (Y) and 8 (Z).

2. Patchwork: Sew 21 patches together to make horizontal Row 1 (*see* FIG. III, 1; the last ten patches are the same as the first ten, but in reverse order). Make Rows 1 to 13 twice, Row 14 once. Be sure to sew exactly ¼ inch from the raw edges. Sew the 27 rows together vertically, with Row 1 at the top and bottom, and counting toward Row 14, which is the center row (*see* FIG. III, 1).

3. Borders: Sew a 95-inch border to each side edge of the patchwork. Sew a light (F) square to each end of a 74-inch border, and sew the border to the top edge of the patchwork. Repeat at the bottom edge.

4. Quilt Back: Cut across the quilt back fabric to make two 44-inch x 3 yard pieces. Sew them side by side along a selvage.

5. Basting: If you have a quilt frame, fasten the quilt back, batting and quilt top to the frame and omit basting. If you don't have a quilt frame, spread the quilt back wrong side up on a clean floor. Tape down the corners to prevent the quilt back from moving. Cut the batting to be at least as long and wide as the quilt top and spread the batting, centered, over the quilt back. Spread the quilt top, centered and right side up, over the batting.

Using the darning or milliner's needle, start at the center of the quilt and baste through all three layers. Baste straight to each edge and diagonally to each corner. Add more vertical and horizontal rows of basting about 6 inches apart.

6. Binding: Trim only the batting to be flush with the quilt top. Trim the quilt back to extend 1¼ inches beyond the quilt top on all sides. Fold the raw edges of the quilt back over the quilt top to be the binding, and pin the binding in place. Pick up the quilt, turn under the raw edges of the binding and slipstitch them to the quilt top.

7. Tie Quilting: Thread the darning needle with crochet thread; do not knot the thread. Starting at the center square of the quilt top, take a short stitch in the center of the square through all three layers, leaving a tail of thread about 2 inches long. Take another stitch on top of the first. Cut the thread to be about 2 inches from the stitch. Tie the thread tails into a square knot and trim the ends to be about ½ inch long. Space more ties evenly across the quilt about 4 to 6 inches apart. Tie in the center of the first square and in the same place in the other squares. Remove the basting.

FIG. III, 1 SUNSHINE AND SHADOW QUILT COLOR CHART

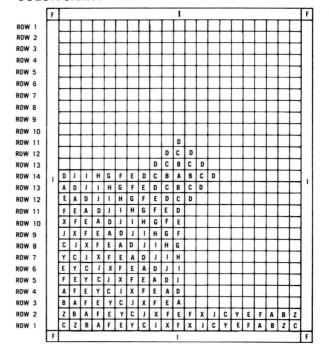

CAROLINA LILY QUILT
(about 88 inches square)

Materials: 14 yards of 45-inch-wide muslin; 1½ yards of 45-inch-wide red calico print; 2 yards of 45-inch-wide green calico print; matching thread; 90-inch square of synthetic batting; crisp cardboard or manila folders; sharp hard-lead pencil; ruler; masking tape; darning or milliner's needle; between needle; white quilting thread; quilting frame or large quilting hoop.

Note 1: *To cut a "pair" of a patch shape, trace the shape once with the pattern right side up, and once with the pattern right side down.*

Note 2: *Begin and end seams ¼ inch from the raw edges; this makes it easy to sew adjoining pieces to the inside corners.*

Directions (¼-inch seams allowed):

1. Patterns: On crisp cardboard or manila folders, draw or trace patterns A through M in FIG. III, 2 and III, 2A, and the curved stem and leaf in FIG. III, 2B.

2. Cutting: From the red calico, cut 144 pairs of patch A, and about 10 yards of a 1-inch-wide strip, pieced as needed, for the binding. From the green calico, cut 48 pairs of patch A, 16 pairs of curved stems, 16 pairs of leaves, sixteen 1 x 13-inch straight stems, and 108 J patches. From the muslin, cut one 45 x 94-inch and two 26 x 94-inch quilt back pieces, four 7½ x 74-inch border strips, 4 M patches, nine 12½-inch square quilt blocks, 12 K patches (half blocks), 4 L patches (quarter blocks), 48 B patches, 96 C patches, 32 each of patches D, E and F, 16 each of patches G, H and I, and 108 J patches.

3. Quilt Blocks: Sew together a pair of red A patches at one long edge. Make six sets. Sew one red A patch to one green A patch at a long edge. Make six sets. Sew two red sets and two mixed sets together at their pointed ends to make one lily (see FIG. III, 2C). Make three lilies. Sew one B patch, two C patches and one D patch to two of the lilies. Sew one B patch and two

C patches to the third lily. Sew two F patches and two E patches between the three lilies. Sew a G patch within the lilies. Draw a diagonal line across the G patch flush with the green patches' raw edges, and cut on the drawn line. Sew patch H to the assembly *(see* FIG. III, 2C*)*. Press the colored seams away from the muslin patches. Sew the whole assembly to patch I. Make 16 quilt blocks.

4. Appliquéing: Turn under ¼ inch at the long edges of a pair of curved stems and of one straight stem. Press. Turn under the top ends of the three stems and pin the stems to a quilt block *(see the dotted lines in* FIG. III, 2C*)*. Let the bottom ends of the curved stems run under the straight stem. Let the bottom end of the straight stem run out to the raw edge corner of the I patch. Turn under the edges of a pair of leaves ¼ inch and pin the leaves to the quilt block. Slipstitch all the turned edges to the block. Repeat on each quilt block.

5. Assembling: Sew together the patchwork blocks alternately with the 12½-inch square muslin blocks to make the diagonal rows in FIG. III, 2D. Add K patches (half blocks) or L patches (quarter blocks) to complete the rows. Sew the rows together, seams matching. Add the two remaining L patches to complete the block assembly.

6. Borders: Sew each green J patch to a muslin J patch at the long edge to make a square. Sew 26 squares together to make a row *(see photo, pages 68-69)*. Make four rows. Sew an extra green and muslin square to each end of two of the rows. Sew a short row to the top and bottom of the block assembly, raw ends even. Sew a long row to each side of the block assembly. Sew a 7½ x 74-inch muslin border strip to the top and bottom of the quilt top. Sew an M patch to each end of the two remaining muslin border strips. Sew these borders to the sides of the quilt top to complete the 88-inch square quilt top.

7. Marking: Using the hard-lead pencil and ruler, draw quilting patterns of your choice on the quilt top. On the quilt photographed, the muslin blocks were quilted in 1-inch squares. The patchwork blocks were quilted in lines parallel to the straight center stem 1 inch on each side of the stem, then ½ inch away, then repeated. The borders were quilted in the same way, parallel to the long edge of the green triangles.

8. Quilt Back: Sew one 26 x 94-inch muslin piece to each long edge of the 45 x 94-inch muslin piece. Press the seams to one side.

9. Basting: Spread the quilt back, wrong side up, on a clean floor. Tape down the corners to prevent the quilt back from moving. Spread the batting over the quilt

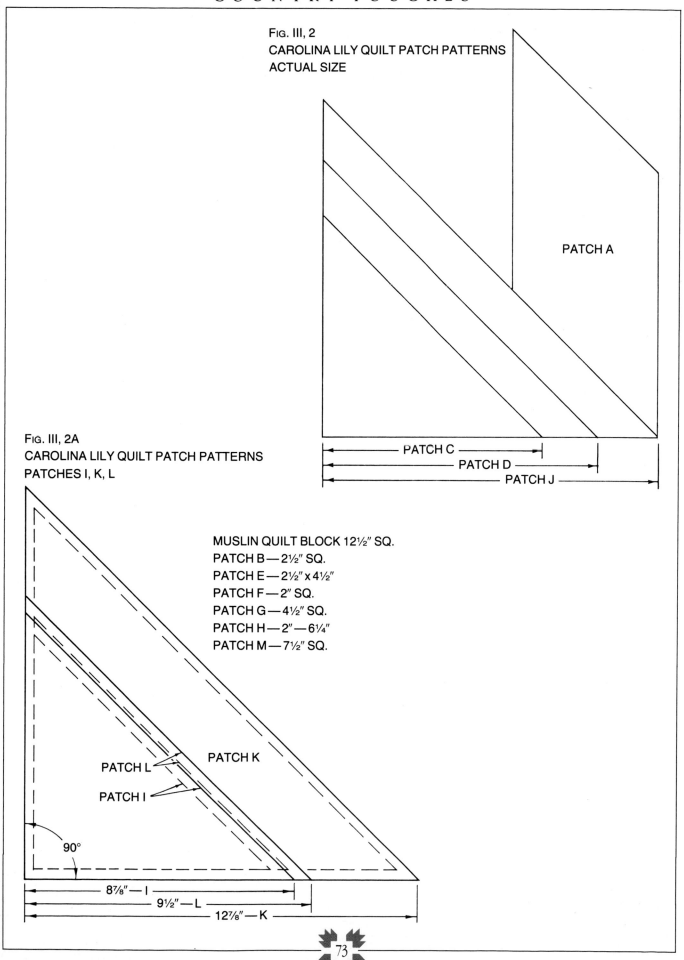

Fɪɢ. III, 2
CAROLINA LILY QUILT PATCH PATTERNS
ACTUAL SIZE

PATCH A

PATCH C
PATCH D
PATCH J

Fɪɢ. III, 2A
CAROLINA LILY QUILT PATCH PATTERNS
PATCHES I, K, L

MUSLIN QUILT BLOCK 12½″ SQ.
PATCH B—2½″ SQ.
PATCH E—2½″ x 4½″
PATCH F—2″ SQ.
PATCH G—4½″ SQ.
PATCH H—2″—6¼″
PATCH M—7½″ SQ.

PATCH K

PATCH L

PATCH I

90°

8⅞″—I
9½″—L
12⅞″—K

FIG. III, 2B CAROLINA LILY QUILT
STEM AND LEAF PATTERN

ACTUAL SIZE

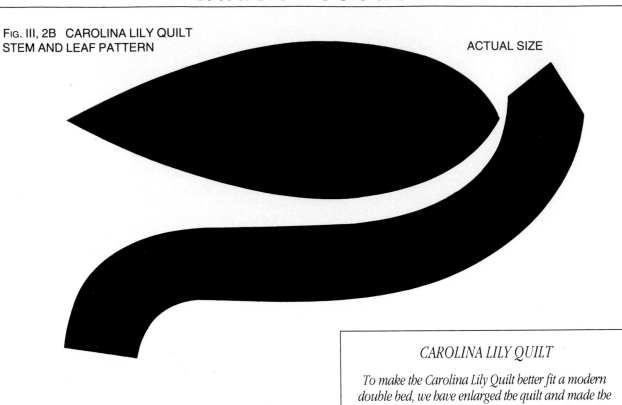

CAROLINA LILY QUILT

To make the Carolina Lily Quilt better fit a modern double bed, we have enlarged the quilt and made the muslin borders 4 inches wider than those shown in the photograph on pages 68-69.

FIG. III, 2C CAROLINA LILY QUILT
PATCHWORK QUILT BLOCK

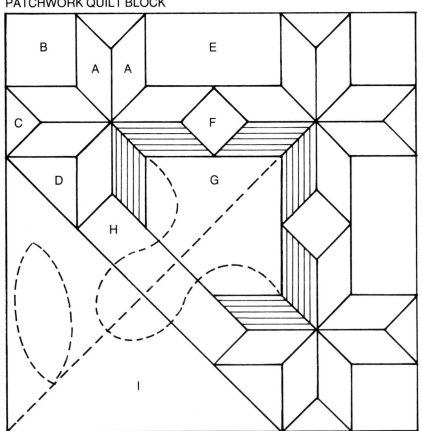

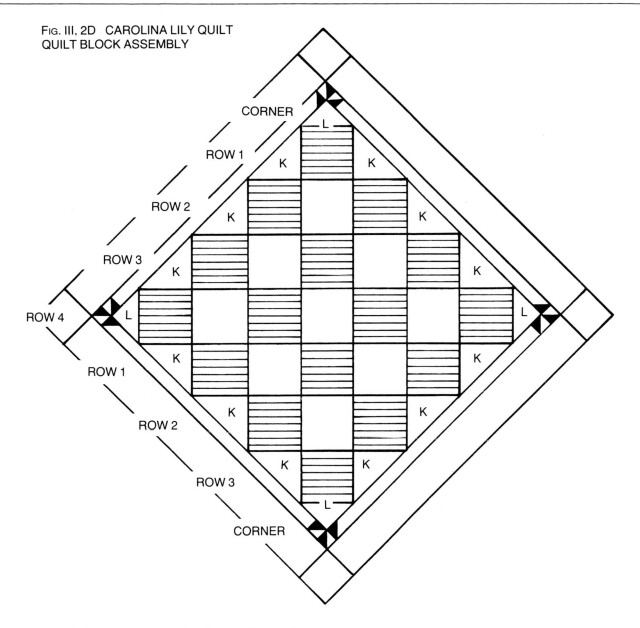

FIG. III, 2D CAROLINA LILY QUILT
QUILT BLOCK ASSEMBLY

CORNER

ROW 1

ROW 2

ROW 3

ROW 4

ROW 1

ROW 2

ROW 3

CORNER

K K K K K K K K K K K K
L L L L

back, smooth the batting outward and trim it flush with
the quilt back. Spread the quilt top, centered and right
side up, over the batting. Using the darning or
milliner's needle, start at the center of the quilt and
baste outward through all three layers. Baste with long
stitches straight to each edge and diagonally to each
corner. Add more vertical and horizontal rows of
basting about 6 inches apart.

10. *Quilting:* Place the quilt in a quilting hoop,
starting at the center of the quilt, or in a quilting frame.
Using the between needle and quilting thread, sew
small running stitches along the marked lines through
all three layers. Trim the quilt back and batting flush
with the quilt top and baste around the outer edges.

11. *Binding:* Bind the top and bottom of the quilt
with the 1-inch-wide red binding strip. Bind the sides
of the quilt, turning under the raw ends of the binding.

WHY DO WE QUILT?

*In addition to the decoration it provides, quilting has
two functions: to fasten the backing, batting and top
layers together, and to keep the batting from
developing holes or lumps after long use. Hand-
quilting a running stitch about ¼ inch from the
patchwork seams is the most secure method. If you
use synthetic batting, quilting rows can be as much as
3 to 4 inches apart.*

BED OF ROSES COMFORTER AND COVER

Materials: Enough muslin to make the top and back of a comforter in size of your choice, using a 1-inch seam allowance; same amount of muslin or solid-color linen for comforter cover, using a ½-inch seam allowance, and with 1 inch added to all sides for an easy fit; chintz fabric with well-delineated motifs for appliqués; matching colorfast thread; fiberfill stuffing; sharp scissors; spray starch; buttons or snaps.

Directions:

1. Comforter: Piece the muslin for the comforter top and back in the size you have chosen. Pin the top and back, right sides together. Stitch around three sides and four corners, using a 1-inch seam allowance; leave a 10-inch opening. Turn the comforter right side out; stuff to the desired fullness. Pin together the edges of the opening and machine-stitch close to the edges.

2. Piecing Comforter Cover: Piece the muslin or linen for the comforter cover top and back *(see Step 1)*, but do not sew the cover together yet.

3. Appliquéing: Using the sharp scissors, cut out the motifs from the chintz fabric and arrange them on the comforter cover top. Place the motifs around the outer edges of the cover; if you try to appliqué in the center of the cover, the cover fabric may bunch up as you machine-stitch the motifs. Allow the motifs from the chintz fabric to inspire your design arrangement. To create a three-dimensional effect with the design, slightly overlap the cutouts.

4. Pin the cutout motifs in the desired arrangement and lightly baste the motifs. Using a hot iron and the spray starch, press each cutout.

5. Using a sewing machine zigzag stitch on the appliqué setting, stitch around each cutout motif, simultaneously doing outline stitches of each color thread. Change the thread color to match the color of the cutout motifs' edges. Use larger stitches for bigger cutouts; vary the machine setting from #1 to #3½.

6. Using a hot iron and the spray starch, press the cutout motifs of each successive color group after the group has been machine-stitched down.

7. Assembling Comforter Cover: Pin the comforter cover top and back, right sides together, and stitch both sides and one end, using a ½-inch seam allowance. Turn the cover right side out. Turn under each open edge and topstitch it down. Add buttons with button holes, or snaps, spaced 10 inches apart. Slip the comforter into the cover and fasten.

ROSE PILLOW

Materials: Enough muslin to make the top and back of a pillow in size of your choice, using a ½-inch seam allowance; same amount of muslin or solid-color linen for pillow cover, using a ½-inch seam allowance; same chintz fabric used on Bed of Roses Comforter Cover, for appliqués; same chintz fabric, or fabric that picks up or contrasts with a color from the chintz appliqués, for ruffle; matching colorfast thread; fiberfill stuffing; sharp scissors; spray starch.

Directions:

1. Pillow: Measure and cut the muslin for the pillow front and back to make the pillow in the size you have chosen. Pin the front and back, right sides together. Stitch around three sides and four corners, using a ½-inch seam allowance, and leaving a 6-inch opening. Turn the pillow right side out and stuff it to the desired firmness. Turn under the open edges and slipstitch them closed.

2. Cutting Pillow Cover: Measure and cut the muslin or linen for the pillow cover front and back. Do not sew the cover front and back together yet.

3. Appliquéing: Cut out and appliqué a chintz motif design on the pillow cover front, following the directions in Bed of Roses Comforter and Cover, Steps 3 to 6 *(at left)*, centering the design on the cover front.

4. Ruffle: Double the finished measurement around the entire pillow cover for the length of the ruffle, or triple the measurement for a very full ruffle. The ruffle width can be 2 to 4 inches; cut out twice the width, plus a 1-inch seam allowance, so you can fold the ruffle strip in half. Cut and piece together the ruffle strip.

5. Sew together the short ends of the ruffle strip to make a continuous loop. Fold the loop in half, raw edges even, and sew a gathering row ½ inch from the raw edges. Gather the ruffle to fit the pillow cover. Pin the ruffle to the edges of the cover front, right sides together and raw edges even. Sew the ruffle to the cover along the ruffle's gathering row.

6. Assembling Pillow Cover: Pin the pillow cover front and back, right sides together and with the ruffle in between. Stitch along three sides. Turn the cover right side out and slip it over the pillow. Turn under the open edges of the cover and slipstitch them closed.

VICTORIAN NOSEGAY AFGHAN
(36 x 48 inches, including scalloped border)

Materials: For afghan, Tahki Imports "Laña" 100% Wool (3½-oz skeins): 10 skeins of Natural or White (MC); for cross stitch design, Paternayan Persian 3-ply yarn (8-yard skeins): 7 skeins each of Dark Green (A) and Light Green (B), 5 skeins each of Medium Pink (D) and Blue (F), and 2 skeins each of Dark Pink (C), Light Pink (E) and Yellow (G); size K afghan hook, OR ANY SIZE HOOK TO OBTAIN GAUGE BELOW; size I crochet hook; 7 yards of ¾-inch-wide blue satin ribbon; large-eye embroidery needle.
Gauge: In Afghan Stitch, 3 sts = 1 inch; 3 rows = 1 inch.
Note 1: *The cross stitch design is embroidered on the afghan after the afghan is completed.*
Note 2: *For the afghan's border scallops to work out evenly, the number of dcs on the sides of the afghan must be divisible by 12.*

Directions:
1. Afghan: Starting at the lower edge with the afghan hook and MC, ch 91. **Row 1:** Retaining all lps on hook, draw up a lp in 2nd ch from hook and in each ch across *(see FIG. III, 3, Step 1)*. There are the same number of lps on hook as there were ch sts. **Row 2:** Yarn over and draw through 1 lp, * yarn over and draw through 2 lps; rep from * across *(see FIG. III, 3, Step 2)*.
Row 3: Retaining all lps on hook, draw up a lp in 2nd vertical bar, and in each vertical bar across to within last vertical bar *(see FIG. III, 3, Step 3)*. Insert hook through last vertical bar and the st directly behind it *(see arrow in FIG. III, 3, Step 4)*, and draw up a lp. There are the same number of lps as on Row 1. Rep Rows 2 and 3 for afghan st until total length is 39 inches from beg. On last row, work one sl st in each vertical bar across. Fasten off.
2. Border, Rnd 1: With the crochet hook, work sc around outer edges and 3 sc in each corner st.
Rnd 2: Ch 5 (counts as 1 dc and ch 2 of corner). Working in corner sts, dc in 2nd of 3 sc, ch 2, dc in 3rd sc, * skip 1 sc, dc in next sc, ch 1 *; rep from * to * across to within next corner, in next corner work dc in first of 3 sc, ch 2, dc in 2nd sc, ch 2, dc in 3rd sc **; rep from * to ** 2 times more; then rep from * to * once. Join to 3rd ch of ch-5. **Rnd 3:** Ch 3 (counts as 1 dc), dc in first ch-2 sp, ch 3, 2 dc in next ch-2 sp, * 2 dc in each ch-1 sp across to within next corner *, in next corner work 2 dc in next ch-2 sp, ch 3, 2 dc in next ch-2 sp **; rep from * to ** 2 times more, then rep from * to * once. Join to top of ch-3. **Rnd 4:** Ch 3, in first ch-3 sp

(work 2 dc, ch 3, 3 dc), * dc in each dc across to within next ch-3 corner sp *, in corner-sp (work 3 dc, ch 3, 3 dc) **; rep from * to ** 2 times more, then rep from * to * once. Join to top of ch-3. **Rnds 5 and 6:** Rep Rnd 4. **Rnd 7:** Sl st in each of first 3 dc of corner, work 8 tr (yo 2 times) in ch-3 corner sp, * sk 3 dc, sc in next dc, ch 3, sk 3 dc, sc in next dc, sk 3 dc *, 6 tr in next dc; rep from * to within next corner-sp, work 9 tr in corner-sp **; rep from * to ** 2 times more, then rep from * to * once. Join to top of ch-3. **Rnd 8:** Ch 3, tr in first tr of corner, * 2 tr in each tr and in next sc, sc in next sc; rep from * around. Join to top of ch-3. Fasten off.

3. Cross Stitch Design: Find the center st on the afghan. Following the chart in FIG. III, 3B *(page 80)*, and using the embroidery needle and 18-inch lengths of yarn, work the design in cross stitch *(see FIG. III, 3A)*, starting at the center stitch. Each square in FIG. III, 3B equals 1 afghan stitch. Work 1 cross stitch over 1 afghan stitch.
4. Finishing: Cut two 50-inch lengths of the ribbon for the shorter sides of the afghan, and two 70-inch lengths for the longer sides. Weave the ribbons in and out of the ch-1 spaces of the Border, Rnd 2. Tie a bow at each corner.

FIG. III, 3 VICTORIAN NOSEGAY AFGHAN

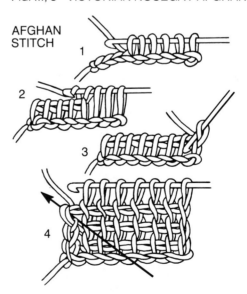

AFGHAN STITCH

FIG. III, 3A VICTORIAN NOSEGAY AFGHAN

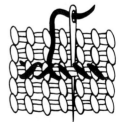

CROSS STITCH OVER AFGHAN STITCH

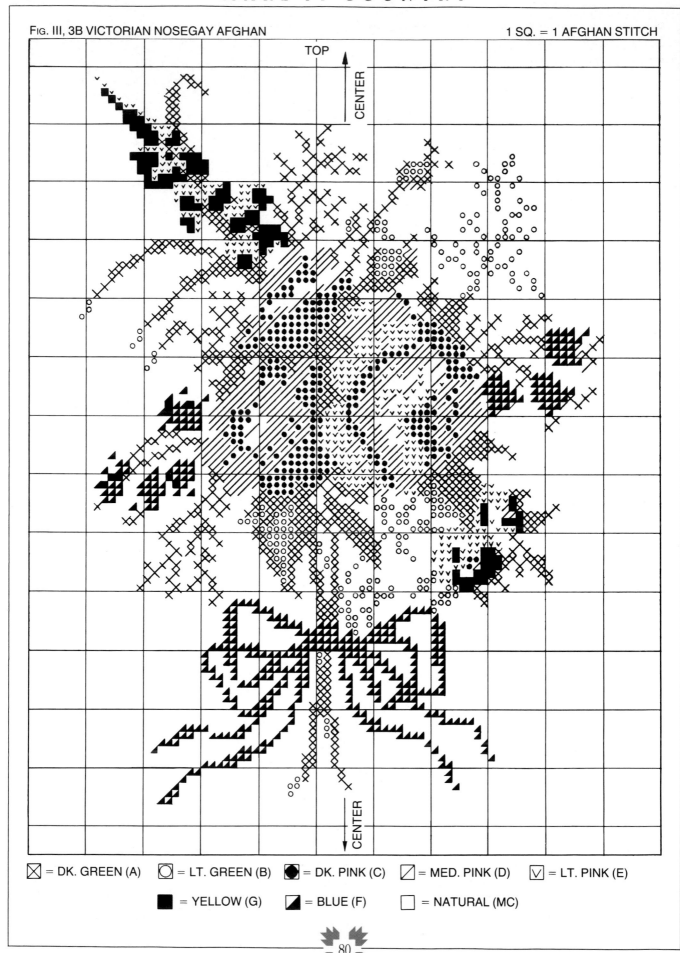

FIG. III, 3B VICTORIAN NOSEGAY AFGHAN

1 SQ. = 1 AFGHAN STITCH

TOP

CENTER

CENTER

⊠ = DK. GREEN (A)   ⊙ = LT. GREEN (B)   ⬣ = DK. PINK (C)   ◳ = MED. PINK (D)   ⱴ = LT. PINK (E)

■ = YELLOW (G)   ◤ = BLUE (F)   ☐ = NATURAL (MC)

COUNTRY CHARMS AFGHAN
(40 x 53 inches, plus fringe)

Materials: Bucilla Sport Yarn (50-gr balls): 16 balls of White (A), small amounts of Mauve (B), Pink (C), Green Heather (D), Light Blue Heather (E) and Dark Blue Heather (F); size E afghan hook, OR ANY SIZE HOOK TO OBTAIN GAUGE BELOW; size E crochet hook; tapestry needle; 5-inch square of cardboard.

Gauge: In Afghan Stitch, 11 sts = 2 inches; 5 rows = 1 inch; each square = 13 x 13 inches.

Note 1: *The afghan is made up of 12 squares that are crocheted together as you work them.*

Note 2: *The cross stitch designs are embroidered on the squares after the afghan is completed.*

Directions:

1. **Square 1:** With the afghan hook and A, ch 25.

Row 1: Retaining all lps on hook, draw up a lp in the 2nd ch from hook and in each ch across *(see FIG. III, 3, Steps 1-4, page 79, for the afghan stitch).* There are the same number of lps on hook as there were ch sts.

Row 2: Yarn over and draw through 1 lp, * yarn over and draw through 2 lps; rep from * across. **Row 3:** Retaining all lps on hook, draw up a lp in the 2nd vertical bar, and in each vertical bar across to within last vertical bar. Insert hook through last vertical bar and the st directly behind it, and draw up a lp. There are the same number of lps as on Row 1. Rep Rows 2 and 3 in afghan st for a total of 20 rows, working one sl st in each vertical bar across the last row. *Do not fasten off.* Now change to the crochet hook and work in rnds as follows:

Note: *Work 7 popcorn sts evenly spaced between corners. If necessary, skip 1 st rather than 2 sts as stated below.*

Rnd 1: Ch 3, 3 dc in corner-st, drop lp from hook, insert hook in top of ch-3, pick up dropped lp and draw through—***first popcorn st made (pcn st)***; working along the right hand side of the Square, * ch 2, sk 1 st, *work 4 dc in next st, drop lp from hook, insert hook in first dc of the 4-dc group, pick up dropped lp and draw through—**popcorn st made**; (ch 2, sk 2 sts, pcn st in next st) 6 times, ch 2, sk 1 st; in corner-st, work pcn st, ch 5, pcn st; working along the next side of the Square (ch 2, sk 2 sts, pcn st in next st) 7 times, ch 2, sk 2 sts; in next corner-st work pcn st, ch 5, pcn st; rep from * once working along the other 2 sides of the Square, ending with ch 2, sk 2 sts, pcn st in starting corner-st, ch 5. Join with sl st to top of the first pcn st. *Turn,* sl st in ch-5 corner-sp, *turn.* **Rnd 2:** Work first pcn st as stated above in same sp as sl st, * ch 2, pcn st

The charm of this lovely afghan is found in the quaint motifs recalling days gone by.

in next pcn st, (2 dc in next ch-2 sp, dc in next pcn st) 3 times, 2 dc in next ch-2 sp, to make a total of 11 dc, pcn st in next pcn st, (2 dc in next ch-2 sp, dc in next pcn st) 3 times, 2 dc in next ch-2 sp, pcn st in next pcn st, ch 2; in next corner-sp work pcn st, ch 5 **, pcn st *; rep from * to * 2 times more, then rep from * to ** once. Join with sl st to top of first pcn st. *Turn,* sl st in ch-5 corner-sp, *turn.* **Rnd 3:** Work first pcn st, * ch 2, dc in next pcn st, ch 2, pcn st in next pcn st, dc in each of next 8 dc, pcn st in next dc, ch 2, sk 2 dc, dc in next pcn st, ch 2, sk 2 dc, pcn st in next dc, dc in each of next 8 dc, pcn st in next pcn st, ch 2, dc in next pcn st, ch 2; in next corner-sp work pcn st, ch 5 **, pcn st *; rep from * to * 2 times more, then rep from * to ** once. Join with sl st to top of first pcn st. *Turn,* sl st in corner-sp, *turn.* **Rnd 4:** Work first pcn st, * ch 2, dc in next pcn st, ch 2, dc in next dc, ch 2, pcn st in next pcn st, dc in each of next 5 dc, pcn st in next dc, ch 2, sk 2 dc, dc in next pcn st, ch 2, dc in next dc, ch 2, dc in next pcn st, ch 2, sk 2 dc, pcn st in next dc, dc in each of next 5 dc, pcn st in next pcn st, ch 2, dc in next dc, ch 2, dc in next pcn st, ch 2; in next corner-sp work pcn st, ch 5 **, pcn st *; rep from * to * 2 times more, then rep from * to ** once. Join with sl st to top of first pcn st. *Turn,* sl st in corner-sp, *turn.* **Rnd 5:** Work first pcn st, * ch 2, dc in next pcn st, (ch 2, dc in next dc) 2 times, ch 2, pcn st in next pcn st, dc in each of next 2 dc, pcn st in next dc, ch 2, sk 2 dc, dc in next pcn st, (ch 2, dc in next dc) 3 times, ch 2, dc in next pcn st, ch 2, sk 2 dc, pcn st in next dc, dc in each of next 2 dc, pcn st in next pcn st, (ch 2, dc in next dc) 2 times, ch 2, dc in next pcn st, ch 2; in next corner-sp work pcn st, ch 5 **, pcn st *; rep from * to * 2 times more, then rep from * to ** once. Join. *Turn,* sl st in corner-sp, *turn.* **Rnd 6:** Work first pcn st, * ch 2, dc in next pcn st, (ch 2, dc in next dc) 3 times, ch 2, pcn st in next pcn st, ch 2, sk 2 dc, dc in next pcn st, (ch 2, dc in next dc) 5 times, ch 2, dc in next pcn st, ch 2, sk 2 dc, pcn st in next pcn st, (ch 2, dc in next dc) 3 times, ch 2, dc in next pcn st, ch 2; in next corner-sp work pcn st, ch 5 **, pcn st *; rep from * to * 2 times more, then rep from * to ** once. Join. *Turn,* sl st in corner-sp, *turn.* **Rnd 7:** Work first pcn st, * (ch 2, dc in next st) 19 times, ch 2; in next corner-sp work pcn st, ch 5 **, pcn st *; rep from * to * 2 times more, then rep from * to ** once. Join, ending as previous rnds. **Rnd 8:** Work first pcn st, * ch 2, dc in next pcn st, (2 dc in next sp, dc in next dc) 19 times, 2 dc in next sp, dc in next pcn st, ch 2; in next corner-sp work pcn st, ch 5 **, pcn st *; rep from * to * 2 times more, then rep from * to ** once. Join, ending as previous rnds. **Rnd 9:** Work first pcn st, * ch 2, dc in next pcn st, ch 2, dc in next dc, (ch 2, sk 2 dc, dc in next dc) 20 times, ch 2, dc in next pcn st, ch 2; in next corner-sp work pcn st, ch 5 **, pcn st *; rep from * to * 2 times more, then rep from * to ** once. Join, ending as previous rnds. **Rnd 10:** Work first pcn st, * ch 2, dc in next pcn st, (ch 2, dc in next dc) 23 times, ch 2, dc in next pcn st, ch 2; in next corner-sp work pcn st, ch 5 **, pcn st *; rep from * to * 2 times more, then rep from * to ** once. Join, ending as previous rnds. **Rnd 11:** Work first pcn st, * ch 5, sc in next sp, (ch 5, sk 1 sp, sc in next sp) 5 times, ch 6, sk 2 sps, sc in next dc, ch 6, sk 2 sps, sc in next sp, (ch 5, sk 1 sp, sc in next sp) 5 times, ch 5; in next corner-sp work pcn st, ch 5 **, pcn st *; rep from * to * 2 times more, then rep from * to ** once. Join. Fasten off.

Note: Work all joining from the right side, holding the squares so the afghan st faces in the same direction.

2. Square 2: Work Rnds 1 to 10 as for Square 1.

Rnd 11 (joining rnd): Work Rnd 11 along the first side of Square 2 to the corner-sp. In corner-sp work pcn st, ch 2, join to corresponding corner-lp of Square 1 with sl st, ch 2, work pcn st in same corner-sp of Square 2 as before, * ch 2, join with sl st to corresponding lp of Square 1, ch 2, sc in next sp of Square 2; rep from * along the side of Square 2, joining to each corresponding lp of Square 1, to within the next corner-sp of Square 2; in corner-sp work ch 5, pcn st; ch 2, sl st in corresponding corner-lp of Square 1, ch 2, pcn st in same corner-sp of Square 2, complete Square 2 as for Rnd 11 of Square 1. Fasten off.

3. Remaining Squares: Work the remaining squares as for Square 1. Join in the same manner as Square 1 is joined to Square 2 to form 4 horizontal rows of 3 squares each.

4. Edging: With the right side facing, attach the yarn to the upper right hand corner-sp of the afghan and work pcn st in same sp, * (ch 2, pcn st) 2 times in each sp to within next corner-sp of the same square and ch 2, pcn st in same sp; in first corner-sp of next square ch 2, pcn st; rep from * 2 times more across first side of afghan to corner-sp and work ch 2, pcn st, ch 5, pcn st in same sp **; rep from * to ** along remaining 3 sides, ending with ch 2, pcn st, ch 5 in upper right hand corner-sp. Join. Fasten off.

5. Embroidery: With a single ply of sport yarn and the tapestry needle, work a cross stitch design (*see* Fig. III, 4-4E) on each square in the following sequence: *first row,* house, tulip, bird; *second row,* flowers, heart, basket; *third row,* house, tulip, bird; *fourth row,* flowers, heart, basket.

6. Fringe: Wind A yarn several times around the cardboard square. Cut the yarn at one end to make 10-inch-long strands. Attach 3 strands of the yarn to each ch-2 sp across the top and bottom edges of the afghan. Trim the yarn ends evenly.

Art is long and life is short.
— Hippocrates

COUNTRY CHARMS AFGHAN

FIG. III, 4 HOUSE

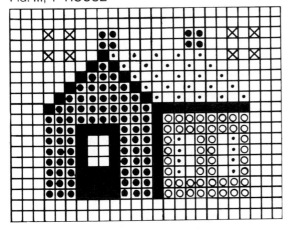

FIG. III, 4C FLOWERS

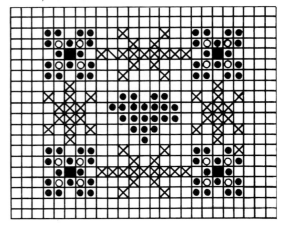

FIG. III, 4A TULIP

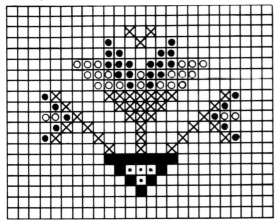

FIG. III, 4D HEART

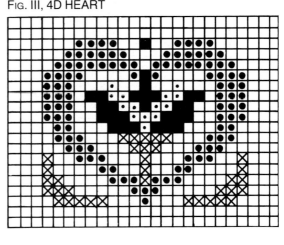

FIG. III, 4B BIRD

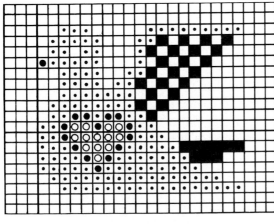

FIG. III, 4E BASKET

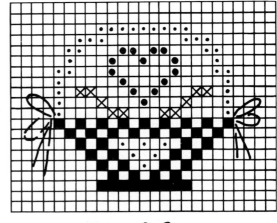

☐ = A   ◉ = B   ◎ = C   ⊠ = D   ⊡ = E   ■ = F   ⅔⅓ = C

P·A·T·C·H·W·O·R·K
P·I·L·L·O·W·S

*Beautiful patchwork pillows: Shining Star, Buttercup
(page 85) and Pretty Puzzle (page 86).*

SHINING STAR PILLOW
(10 inches square, plus ruffle)

Materials: Scraps of dark blue, medium blue, red, tan
and white fabrics; 10½-inch square of fabric for pillow
back; two 4½ x 45-inch strips for ruffle; stuffing; tracing
paper; dressmaker's carbon; tracing wheel.

Directions (¼-inch seams allowed):
1. Patterns: Trace patterns in Fig. III, 5 onto tracing
paper. Patterns give sizes of patches, without seam
allowances; outlines are sewing lines.
2. Cutting: Using carbon and tracing wheel, trace
patterns onto wrong side of fabrics. Cut patches ¼ inch
outside traced sewing lines. From tan fabric, cut 4 full
points. From dark and medium blue fabrics, cut 4 half
points each. From red fabric, cut 4 full points and 8
half points. From white fabric, cut 8 full points.

3. Quilt Blocks: Pin patches, right sides together,
along traced sewing lines, referring to Fig. III, 5A for
color placement. Sew 4 full points together at short
edges, stopping seams ¼ inch from edge at each end.
To complete quilt block, sew a half point at each edge,
using colors in Fig. III, 5A. Make 3 more quilt blocks.
4. Pillow Top: Sew 4 blocks together, with each dark
blue patch touching a medium blue patch.
5. Ruffle: Sew the 2 strips together at short edges to
make a loop. Fold loop in half lengthwise; press. Sew 2
gathering rows, one ¼ inch and the other ⅛ inch from
raw edges. Pin ruffle to pillow top, right sides together,
with ruffle seams at opposite corners of pillow top.
Pull up gathers to fit and stitch ruffle to pillow top.
6. Assembling: Pin pillow back to pillow top over
ruffle, right sides together. Sew around 3 sides and
4 corners. Turn pillow right side out; stuff. Turn in
open edges and slipstitch them closed.

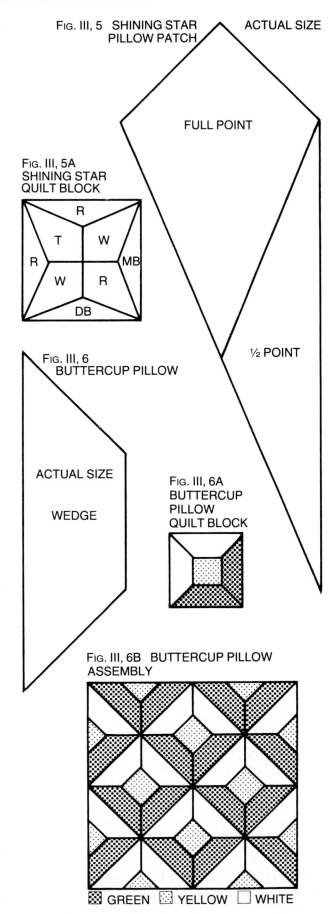

FIG. III, 5 SHINING STAR
PILLOW PATCH   ACTUAL SIZE

FULL POINT

FIG. III, 5A
SHINING STAR
QUILT BLOCK

½ POINT

FIG. III, 6
BUTTERCUP PILLOW

ACTUAL SIZE

WEDGE

FIG. III, 6A
BUTTERCUP
PILLOW
QUILT BLOCK

FIG. III, 6B BUTTERCUP PILLOW
ASSEMBLY

⊞ GREEN ⊡ YELLOW ☐ WHITE

BUTTERCUP PILLOW
(10 inches square, plus ruffle)

Materials: Scraps of light green, light yellow and white fabrics; matching thread; 10½-inch square of fabric for pillow back; 1¼ yards of 3½-inch-wide ruffled eyelet; synthetic stuffing; tracing paper; dressmaker's carbon; tracing wheel.

Directions (¼-inch seams allowed):
1. ***Patterns:*** Trace the wedge pattern in FIG. III, 6 onto tracing paper and cut it out. In addition, draw two 1⅜-inch squares on the tracing paper. Cut out one of the squares. Draw a diagonal line across the remaining square, between opposite corners. Cut out one of the resulting triangles and discard the other triangle. The three patterns give the finished sizes of the patches, without the seam allowances; their outlines are the sewing lines.

2. ***Cutting:*** Following the directions in Shining Star Pillow, Step 2 *(page 84)*, cut out the following patches: From the yellow fabric, cut four squares and eight triangles. From the green and white fabrics, cut 16 wedges each.

3. ***Quilt Blocks:*** Pin the patches, right sides together, along the traced sewing lines. Sew the short side of a green wedge to one edge of a yellow square *(see FIG. III, 6A)*, stopping the seams ¼ inch from the edge at each end. Repeat at an adjoining yellow edge. Sew white wedges to the remaining yellow edges. Make three more quilt blocks. Sew the blocks together to make the four-block diamond at the center of the pillow top *(see FIG. III, 6B)*.

4. ***Pillow Top Corners:*** Each corner is two half blocks sewn together *(see FIG. III, 6B)*. Sew a green wedge to each of the two short edges of a yellow triangle. Repeat. Sew a white wedge to each of the two short edges of a yellow triangle. Repeat. Sew one green wedge and one white wedge to the two short edges of a yellow triangle. Repeat three times.

5. ***Pillow Top:*** Sew two half blocks together to make each corner, referring to FIG. III, 6B for color placement. To complete the pillow top, sew a corner to each edge of the four-block center diamond.

6. ***Ruffle:*** Stitch the ruffled eyelet to the pillow top, right sides together and sewing lines matching. Sew together the raw ends of the ruffled eyelet.

7. ***Assembling:*** Follow the directions in Shining Star Pillow, Step 6 *(page 84)*.

PRETTY PUZZLE PILLOW
(10 inches square, plus ruffle)

Materials: Scraps of red, black and white fabrics; matching thread; 10½-inch square of fabric for pillow back; two 2½ x 45-inch red strips for ruffle; 1¼ yards of ½-inch-wide ruffled eyelet; 2½ yards of ¾-inch-wide eyelet edging; synthetic stuffing; tracing paper; dressmaker's carbon; tracing wheel.

Directions (¼-inch seams allowed):
1. Patterns: Draw two right triangles, one with 2½-inch legs and the other with 3½-inch legs, on tracing paper and cut them out. The patterns give the finished sizes of the patches, without the seam allowances; their outlines are the sewing lines.
2. Cutting: Following the directions in Shining Star Pillow, Step 2 *(page 84)*, cut four red and four black triangles from the larger triangle pattern. Cut 16 white triangles from the smaller triangle pattern.
3. Quilt Blocks: Pin the patches, right sides together, along the traced sewing lines. Sew a white triangle to each of the two shorter edges of every red and every black triangle *(see* FIG. III, 7*)*. To complete the quilt block, sew a red assembly above a black assembly *(see* FIG. III, 7*)*. Make three more quilt blocks.
4. Pillow Top: Sew the four blocks together, referring to the photo on page 84 for block placement. Stitch the ruffled eyelet to the pillow top, right sides together and sewing lines matching. Sew together the raw ends of the ruffled eyelet.
5. Ruffle: Sew the two red strips together at the short edges to make a loop. Fold over one raw edge ¼ inch, then ¼ inch again; press. Pin the eyelet edging over the folded ruffle edge, with the edging extending beyond the folded edge. Topstitch ¼ inch from the folded red edge *(see photo, page 84)*. Sew a gathering row ¼ inch from the other ruffle edge. Gather the edge and pin the ruffle to the pillow top, right sides together and raw edges even, with the ruffle seams at opposite corners of the pillow top. Pull up the gathers to fit and stitch the ruffle to the pillow top.
6. Assembling: Follow the directions in Shining Star Pillow, Step 6 *(page 84)*.

FIG. III, 7 **PRETTY PUZZLE PILLOW QUILT BLOCK**

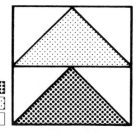

BLACK ▦
RED ▨
WHITE ☐

CRAZY QUILT PILLOWS
(13 inches square and 11 x 14 inches, plus ruffles)

Materials: ½ yard of 45-inch-wide velveteen or moiré; ½ yard of 36-inch-wide unbleached muslin; scraps of velvet, silk, taffeta and so on; matching thread; 1¾ yards of 2½-inch-wide ruffled lace; embroidery floss; embroidery needle; narrow lace or ribbon; tiny beads or pearls *(optional)*; two pillow forms (one square, one rectangular), or synthetic stuffing.

Directions (½-inch seams allowed):
1. Cutting: For the square pillow, cut a 14-inch square pillow back and 3½ yards of 2½-inch-wide strips (pieced as needed) for the ruffle from the velveteen or moiré. Cut a 14-inch square pillow top from the muslin. For the rectangular pillow, cut a 12 x 15-inch pillow back and 3½ yards of 2½-inch-wide strips (pieced as needed) for the ruffle from the moiré. Cut a 12 x 15-inch pillow top from the muslin.
2. "Crazy" Patchwork: Cut a roughly triangular patch from one of the fabric scraps and pin it over a righthand corner of the muslin pillow top. Trim the patch's two corner edges to match the muslin's edges and baste the patch and muslin together around the corner, turning under the patch's free edge. Slide a raw edge of two more scrap patches under the free edge of the first patch and pin the two new patches in place. Where the two new patches meet, turn under one raw edge and lap it over the other raw edge. Slipstitch the turned-under edges through all the layers of fabric. Continue adding patches across the muslin, always covering a raw edge with a turned-under edge. When you have finished covering the muslin with patches, stitch around the pillow top ¼ inch from the edges.
3. Embroidery and Trims: Outline the patchwork seams by sewing on strips of narrow lace or ribbon, or by working rows of embroidery with embroidery floss in the stitches of your choice *(see Stitch Guide, page 240)*, adding in tiny beads or pearls if you wish. Embroidery stitches also can be scattered on the patches. Or, enlarge the flower (see FIG. III, 8) onto tracing paper, following the directions on page 241. Embroider the flower in stem or outline stitch.
4. Ruffle: Sew the short edges of the ruffle strip together to make a loop. Turn under one long edge ¼ inch and stitch it with a zig zag stitch. Using the longest machine stitch, sew a gathering row ½ inch from the other long edge. Pin the ruffle to the pillow top, right sides together and raw edges even. Pull up the gathering thread until the ruffle fits the pillow top.

Opulent fabrics, lace and ribbons bedeck beautiful
Crazy Quilt Pillows (page 86).

Distribute the ruffle's fullness evenly around the pillow top, with a little extra fullness at the corners. Stitch the ruffle and pillow top together over the gathering row. Stitch a strip of the ruffled lace behind the fabric ruffle *(see photo)*, sewing together the raw ends of the lace.

5. Assembling: Pin the pillow back to the pillow top over the ruffle, right sides together and edges even. Sew around three sides and four corners. Turn the pillow right side out and insert the pillow form or stuff it. Turn in the open edges and slipstitch them closed.

A FINE MADNESS

Crazy quilts became popular in 19th century America. While quilt making began as a thrifty use of scarce fabric, crazy quilts reflected the splendor of the Victorian era. Originally they were made of silk in opulent jewel tones, and incorporated beautiful ribbons, laces and other materials that were produced specifically for use in crazy quilts.

FIG. III, 8 CRAZY QUILT PILLOW EMBROIDERY

1 SQ. = 1"

A·R·O·U·N·D
T·H·E H·O·M·E

*Home is where the heart is — with festive towels
and pillows (pages 88-89).*

A LITTLE LOVE PILLOWS
(6 x 7 inches and 8 x 12 inches)

Materials: ¼ yard of fabric; piping; fabric scraps for appliqués; fusible webbing; 3½ x 4-inch sheet of paper; dressmaker's carbon; tracing wheel; stuffing.

Directions:
1. Cut two 7 x 8-inch pieces of fabric, or two 9 x 13-inch pieces, for the pillow front and pillow back.
2. Fold the paper in half to 3½ x 2 inches; cut out a heart. With the carbon and tracing wheel, trace the heart pattern onto a fabric scrap. Pin scrap to fusible webbing; cut out heart through both layers. Fuse heart and webbing to pillow front with a hot iron. Cover raw edges of heart appliqué with a machine satin stitch.
3. Pin piping to the pillow front, right sides together and raw edges even. Using a zipper foot, stitch against the piping cord. Clip seam allowance at corners.
4. Right sides together, stitch pillow front to pillow back; leave a 2-inch opening. Turn pillow right side out; stuff. Turn in open edges; slipstitch them closed.

FIG. III, 9 COUNTRY KITCHEN TOWELS APPLIQUÉS

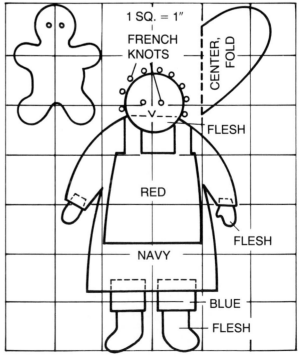

COUNTRY KITCHEN TOWELS

Materials: Dish towels; fabric scraps for appliqués; fusible webbing; tracing paper; dressmaker's carbon; tracing wheel; embroidery floss; embroidery needle.

Directions for Appliquéd Border:

1. Enlarge gingerbread boy pattern in Fig. III, 9 onto tracing paper, following directions on page 241. Enlarge heart half-pattern in Fig. III, 9 onto folded tracing paper, cut along traced lines and open the paper for full pattern. Using the dressmaker's carbon and tracing wheel, trace four boys and three hearts onto fabric scraps. Pin the scraps to fusible webbing and cut out the boys and hearts through both layers.
2. Pin the appliqués and webbing along edge of a dish towel, alternating boys and hearts. Fuse the appliqués and webbing to the towel with a hot iron. Stitch over raw edges of appliqués with a machine satin stitch.
3. Using embroidery needle and floss, take a stitch at the center of each gingerbread boy's neck, tie a bow and trim ends. Make a French knot for each eye.

Directions for Cook Appliqué:

1. Enlarge pattern pieces for the cook in Fig. III, 9 onto tracing paper, following directions on page 241. Using dressmaker's carbon and tracing wheel, trace two hands, two feet, two pantaloon legs, one dress, one apron and one face, with hair and eye dots, onto fabric scraps. Trace the lap-unders (the broken lines) onto the fabric as well. Pin fabric scraps to the fusible webbing and cut out the pieces through both layers.
2. Pin appliqués and webbing to the center of a dish towel, starting about 5 inches from towel's lower edge. Overlap pieces following the lap-under lines (*see* Fig. III, 9). Fuse appliqués and webbing to dish towel with a hot iron. Edgestitch appliqués to prevent peeling.
3. Using the embroidery needle and embroidery floss, make a French knot at each hair and eye dot. Stitch two straight stitches for the mouth.

FIG. III, 10   HEART IN HAND POTHOLDER

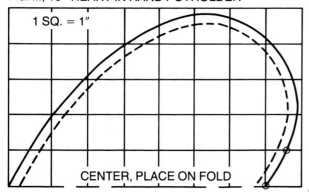

1 SQ. = 1"

CENTER, PLACE ON FOLD

HEART IN HAND POTHOLDER

Materials (for two potholders): ¼ yard of 45-inch-wide sturdy red fabric; ¼ yard of fleecy interfacing; scraps of purple and green cotton-broadcloth weight fabric; dressmaker's carbon; tracing wheel.

Directions for One Potholder (¼-inch seams allowed):

1. Patterns: Enlarge heart half-pattern in Fig. III, 10 onto folded paper, following directions on page 241. Trace pattern onto other side of paper; open paper for full pattern. Also, draw a 2-inch square on the paper.
2. Cutting: Using the dressmaker's carbon and tracing wheel, trace and then cut two red fabric hearts, two interfacing hearts, five purple squares and four green squares. Cut a 2½ x 5-inch red fabric strip for a hanger.
3. Patchwork: Sew one green square between two purple squares. Repeat. Sew one purple square between two green squares. Sew together the three rows, seams matching, to make a larger square with purple at the center. Turn under ¼ inch at each outside edge of the larger square and press.
4. Assembling: Pin an interfacing heart to wrong side of a red heart and machine-baste them together ¼ inch from edges. Repeat. Place one red heart on top of the other, right sides together. Stitch around the hearts; leave an opening between the circles. Trim interfacing close to the stitching; turn potholder right side out.
5. Hanger: Fold hanger strip in half lengthwise, right sides together, and stitch ¼ inch from the long raw edges. Turn hanger strip right side out. Fold it in half and sew it to the heart front at top center, right sides together and raw edges even. Turn loop upward. Turn in open edges of potholder; slipstitch them closed.
6. Appliquéing: Center green and purple patchwork square on the front of the potholder; slipstitch turned-under edges of patchwork square to the potholder.

BIRDS 'N BLOSSOMS HOOKED RUG
(about 40 x 60 inches)

Materials: 2 yards of 45-inch-wide Scottish Rug Burlap; size 6 rug punch needle or tufting tool; waterproof black fine-point pen; dark-colored dressmaker's carbon; tracing wheel or dry ballpoint pen; rug frame; staple gun; 2 quarts of rug latex; cardboard; Aunt Lydia's Heavy Rug Yarn: 22 skeins of Rust #325 (R), 17 skeins of Wood Brown #425 (WB), 8 skeins of Antique Gold #565 (AG), 6 skeins of Light Avocado #635 (LA), 4 skeins of Grass Green #615 (GG), 3 skeins each of Coral #310 (C), Gold #559 (G) and Copper #323 (CR), 2 skeins each of Bronze Gold #560 (BG) and Turkish Teal #720 (TT), 1 skein each of Bright Orange #320 (BO), Amethyst #0015 (A), Chestnut #150 (CT), Wild Rose #125 (WR) and Beige #405 (B).

Directions:

1. At each of the burlap's two cut edges, pull a thread and cut along it to straighten the edge. Turn the edge under ½ inch and machine-stitch it to prevent fraying.

2. ***Pattern:*** Enlarge the five designs in FIG. III, 11A-11E following the directions on page 241.

3. ***Marking:*** With the black fine-point pen, draw a line 7½ inches from each selvage edge, leaving 30 inches between the two lines. Draw two more lines to divide the 30-inch space into three 10-inch-wide vertical rows. Draw a line 11 inches from one short end of the burlap. Then draw five lines parallel to it and 10 inches apart. You now have drawn the center section of 3 x 5-inch blocks. Draw a ¾-inch-wide border around the center section, then a 3-inch-wide border and another ¾-inch-wide border. Using the dressmaker's carbon, and the tracing wheel or dry ballpoint pen, trace the designs onto the burlap following the chart in FIG. III, 11. Go over the tracings with the black fine-point pen. The marked side of the burlap will be the wrong side of the rug.

4. ***Frame:*** With the design centered, spread the burlap, marked side up, over the frame and staple it to the frame from the center of each side toward the corners. The burlap must be taut. If it sags while working, remove the staples, tighten the burlap and restaple it.

5. ***Punching:*** Roll the skeins of yarn into balls. Using ½-inch-long yarn loops, and following the manufacturer's directions for the rug punch needle or tufting tool, hook the rug. Begin by working the border and block outlines with two rows of hooked yarn. Fill in the border, including the copper

squiggles. Outline the design shapes. Fill them in by working back and forth in straight rows, or by following each shape's contours toward its center. Use the colors below, indicated by pattern block number, pattern shape number and yarn color number. Then fill in the background colors as indicated on the chart in FIG. III, 11.

A-1: 1-BG; 2-C; 3-G; 4-LA.
B-2: 1-GG; 2-TT; 3-B; 4-G; 5 and 6-CT.
C-3: 1-LA; 2-BO; 3-G; 4-AG; 5-C.
D-4: 1-LA; 2-WR; 3-BO; 4-AG; 5-CT; 6-WR.
E-5: 1-G; 2-C; 3-BG; 4-AG; 5-LA.
A-6: 1-C; 2-A; 3-G; 4-LA.
B-7: 1-GG; 2-B; 3-TT; 4-G; 5-BO; 6-TT.
C-8: 1-GG; 2-G; 3-C; 4-TT; 5-A.
D-9: 1-LA; 2-AG; 3-TT; 4-BO; 5-G; 6-AG.
A-10: 1-BG; 2-G; 3-C; 4-LA.
E-11: 1-BO; 2-TT; 3-G; 4-CT; 5-LA.
B-12: 1-GG; 2-BG; 3-WR; 4-AG; 5-TT; 6-TT.
C-13: 1-LA; 2-AG; 3-WR; 4-TT; 5-A.
D-14: 1-GG; 2-BG; 3-TT; 4-CT; 5-BO; 6-BG.
A-15: 1-AG; 2-G; 3-C; 4-LA.

6. ***Latex:*** Before applying the latex, check the right side of the rug to correct or add loops, if necessary. If the whole rug has been stretched on the frame at once, leave it on the frame. If the rug is larger than the frame, spread a plastic drop cloth on the floor of a well-ventilated place, remove the rug from the frame and lay the rug on top of the plastic, right side down. Apply the latex to the rug back. Cover the back of every yarn loop by using a small piece of cardboard to force the latex into the yarn. Let the latex dry overnight.

7. ***Finishing:*** Trim 4 inches off the top and bottom edges of the burlap. Diagonally trim each burlap corner 2 inches from the yarn. Using a small piece of cardboard, spread latex on one burlap corner. Diagonally fold the corner toward the yarn so the corner's raw edge is ½ inch from the yarn. Let the folded burlap soften for a moment, then fingerpress it smooth. Apply more latex to the corner burlap and fold the burlap, at the rug edge, over the rug back. Repeat at each corner. Spread latex on the burlap at one side edge, fold the raw edge ½ inch toward the rug and press down on the fold. Add more latex to the folded burlap and fold again, at the rug edge, to complete the hem. Repeat at each side edge. Place a weight over each corner and let the rug dry overnight. When the rug is dry, turn it over and clip any long yarn ends to match the nap.

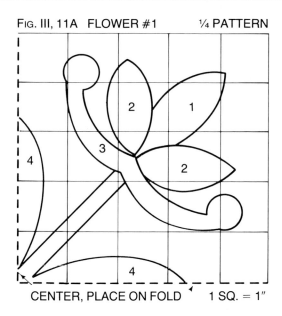

Fig. III, 11A   FLOWER #1   ¼ PATTERN

CENTER, PLACE ON FOLD   1 SQ. = 1″

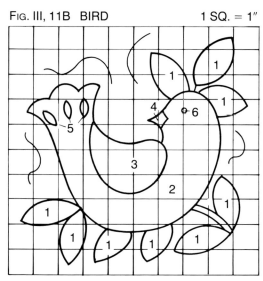

Fig. III, 11B   BIRD   1 SQ. = 1″

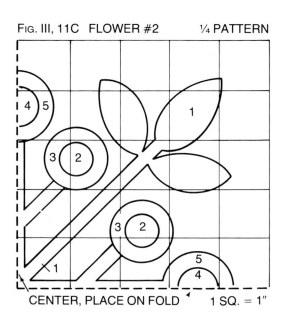

Fig. III, 11C   FLOWER #2   ¼ PATTERN

CENTER, PLACE ON FOLD   1 SQ. = 1″

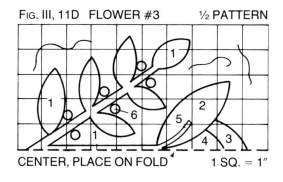

Fig. III, 11D   FLOWER #3   ½ PATTERN

CENTER, PLACE ON FOLD   1 SQ. = 1″

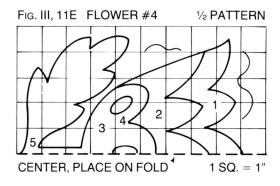

Fig. III, 11E   FLOWER #4   ½ PATTERN

CENTER, PLACE ON FOLD   1 SQ. = 1″

Fig. III, 11   RUG MOTIF PLACEMENT—
WRONG SIDE UP

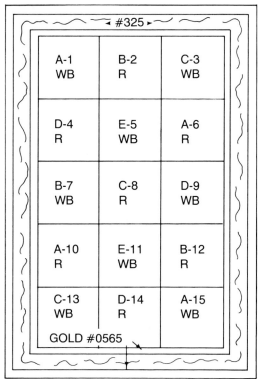

#325

A-1 WB	B-2 R	C-3 WB
D-4 R	E-5 WB	A-6 R
B-7 WB	C-8 R	D-9 WB
A-10 R	E-11 WB	B-12 R
C-13 WB	D-14 R	A-15 WB

GOLD #0565

PENNSYLVANIA DUTCH TIN PUNCH

Materials: 8 x 19 inches of tin (available at craft stores or, as roofing tin, from hardware stores); picture frame with 7½ x 18½-inch opening; push points; awl or nail; hammer; tracing paper; cardboard; masking tape; sawtooth hanger or picture wire.

Directions:
1. Enlarge the half-pattern for the Pennsylvania Dutch design in Fig. III, 12 onto folded tracing paper, following the directions on page 241. Trace the half-pattern onto the other side of the paper, and open the paper for the full pattern.
2. Cover an old table with at least a ½-inch thickness of cardboard, and tape cardboard in place. Find center point of the tin. Match center of the pattern to center of the tin, and tape pattern to the tin. Using the hammer and the awl or nail, punch holes along pattern lines.
3. Repeat the design at each side of the tin, leaving 6 inches between the centers.
4. Place the punched tin piece in the picture frame and secure it with the push points. Attach a sawtooth hanger or picture wire to back of frame for a hanger.

Fig. III, 12 PENNSYLVANIA DUTCH TIN PUNCH

1 SQ. = 1"

CENTER, PLACE ON THE FOLD

"WELCOME FRIENDS" TIN PUNCH

Materials: 9-inch-diameter tin pan; awl or nail; hammer; cardboard; masking tape.

Directions:
1. Enlarge the pattern in Fig. III, 13 following the directions on page 241. Draw a circle around the enlarged pattern that is the same size as the pan's bottom. Cut out around the circle and tape the pattern to the inside bottom of the pan.
2. Cover an old table with at least a ½-inch thickness of cardboard, and tape the cardboard in place. Using the hammer and the awl or nail, punch holes along the pattern lines.

Fig. III, 13 WELCOME FRIENDS TIN PUNCH

1 SQ. = 1"

WELCOME

FRIENDS

A TOUCH OF AMERICANA SAMPLERS

Materials For One Sampler: 16 x 20 inches of 11-count Pearl Aida cloth; embroidery floss: White, Pink, Red, Dark Red, Light Blue, Royal Blue, Dark Blue, Yellow, Gold, Light Green, Dark Green, Light Tan, Dark Tan, Brown, Light Gray, Dark Gray and Black; size 24 tapestry needle; embroidery hoop; picture frame with 14 x 18-inch opening; cardboard to fit picture frame opening; straight pins; masking tape; sawtooth hanger or picture wire.

Directions:

1. Outside Border: Pin mark the outside border, on the grain and centered on the Aida cloth, so it encloses a space of 147 x 190 blocks. Following the directions in Step 4 *(page 95)*, work a cross stitch in each block of the marked border until you come to a corner. Work the corners of the border using the photo on page 94 as a guide. Baste a vertical center line halfway between the side edges of the outside border.

2. Horizontal Placement: Using the photo below of the picture of your choice, measure the space between the side edges of the outside border. Draw the vertical center line right on the photo page. The line will fall either halfway between a pair of motifs, or halfway through one motif. The vertical center line also will show you the center of each line of words.

3. Vertical Placement: Pin mark the top of each row's center motif over the basted vertical center line, counting downward from the first empty block under the outside border's top edge. B stands for empty blocks. The numbers in parentheses are the number of cross stitch rows for each center motif, with the numbers given for word rows including any empty rows between them. Basic sampler designs:

A Friend: 14B, brown border (1); 10B, 3 rows of words (49); 10B, brown border (1); 8B, squirrels (18); 3B, cherries (18); 3B, bunnies (22); 3B, birds (23); 7B, bottom border.

My Heart: 7B, hearts (15); 3B, birds (23); 3B, flowers (19); 3B, red border (1); 6B, 4 rows of words (69); 4B, border (1); 11B, cherries (18); 7B, bottom border.

May Peace: 7B, bouquet (25); 8B, 2 rows of words (29); 11B, flag (28); 10B, flowers (19); 9B, bottom border.

Happy Is: 5B, house (24); 5B, red row (1); 3B, flowers (19); brown row (1); 7B, hearts (15); 3B, red row (1); 5B, 4 rows of words (69); 7B, squirrels (18); 7B, bottom border.

I Hear: 6B, hearts (15); 3B, blue row (1); 3B, house (24); 4B, blue row (1); 8B, 1 row of words (9); 10B, eagle (27); the white part of the eagle's head is outlined in Light Tan backstitches *(see Stitch Guide, page 240)*; 7B, trees (23); 6B, bottom border.

In God: 16B, blue row (1); 4B, flag (28); 8B, 1 row of words (9); 8B, flower (19); 7B, trees (23); 7B, blue row (1); 16B, bottom border.

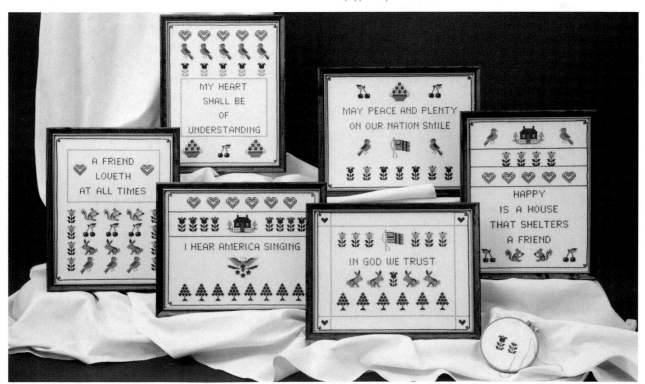

FIG. III, 14   AMERICANA SAMPLERS ALPHABET CROSS STITCH

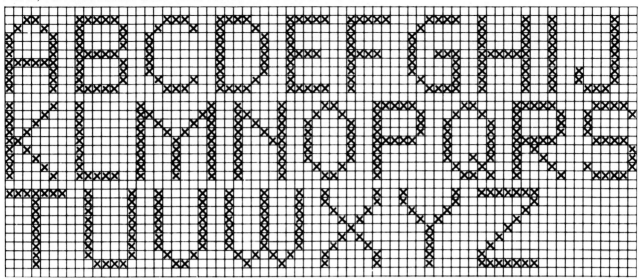

4. Embroidering: Using the tapestry needle, embroidery hoop, and three strands of embroidery floss in the colors shown in the photo on page 93, work the cross stitches; one completed cross stitch covers one block. Begin with the words, starting from the basted vertical center line and following the alphabet chart above. Leave two squares empty between each letter, seven squares empty between each word, and 11 blocks empty between each row. Work the inside borders and horizontal lines next; those that appear to be dotted have a cross stitch in every other square. Work the pictorial motifs last, using the photo on page 93 as a guide. Reverse the order of motifs as necessary, and add motifs as desired. Space the motifs from the basted vertical center line so that the left and right sides are symmetrical.

5. Finishing: Place the finished sampler face down on a towel and lightly press it. Center the sampler on the cardboard, fold the fabric edges to the back of the cardboard and tape them down. Insert the sampler in the picture frame, and tape it to the back of the frame with masking tape. Attach a sawtooth hanger or picture wire to the back of the frame for a hanger.

Homemade, homemade! But aren't we all?
— Elizabeth Bishop

A faithful reproduction of a 19th century
English motif.

OLD ENGLISH CORNUCOPIA

Materials: 18-inch square of 10-mesh needlepoint canvas; tapestry or Persian yarn: Light Beige for background, other colors as indicated in chart key *(page 97)*; tapestry needle; picture frame; cardboard to fit picture frame opening; masking tape; sawtooth hanger or picture wire.

Directions:
Following the chart on page 97, work the needlepoint design using the continental stitch *(see Stitch Guide, page 240)*. Block the needlepoint following the directions on page 239. Mount and frame the needlepoint following the directions in A Touch of Americana Samplers, Step 5 *(page 95)*.

COLOR IT BEAUTIFUL

Coloring a counted cross stitch pattern or needlepoint pattern with corresponding colored pencils makes the pattern easier to follow, and helps avoid missing stitches in each color used.

Keep your eyes wide open before marriage, half shut afterwards.
— Benjamin Franklin

MAKE IT CROSS STITCH!

This charted needlepoint design can be adapted for counted cross stitch. Work the design on 10-count ecru Aida cloth, and do not fill in the background. See A Touch of Americana Samplers, Step 5 (page 95) for blocking instructions.

FIG. III, 15 OLD ENGLISH CORNUCOPIA

■ = DARKEST COLOR IN EACH AREA - LEAVES: DARK GREEN FRUITS: DARK NAVY	□ = LIGHTEST COLOR IN EACH AREA - FRUITS: LIGHT BEIGE CORNUCOPIA: GREY (VERY DARK) CORNUCOPIA TOP: PALE BLUE CORNUCOPIA BASE: LIGHT GREY LEAVES: PALE GREEN	▼ = DARK GREY ▽ = LIGHT GREY ◪ = DARK GREEN ◺ = MEDIUM GREEN ⊞ = BROWN ▧ = RED ▨ = LIGHT PEACH	▣ = GOLD ⊡ = LIGHT YELLOW ▧ = MID BLUE ▨ = LIGHT BLUE ⊠ = PALE PINK ◪ = LIGHT GOLDEN BROWN

PATCHWORK TABLE RUNNER
(about 25 x 75 inches, including 2-inch-wide binding)

Materials: Scraps of print and solid fabrics; 4 yards of blanket binding; 4 yards of braid; graphite paper or carbon paper; stylus or dry ball point pen; firm cardboard.

Directions (¼-inch seams allowed):

1. Using the graphite or carbon paper, and the stylus or dry ballpoint pen, enlarge the triangle pattern in FIG. III, 16 onto firm cardboard, following the directions on page 241. The pattern outlines are the cutting lines. Cut 240 triangles from the mixed scraps of fabric.

2. Sew two triangles of contrasting colors and fabrics, right sides together, along their longest edge. Open the triangles to form a square, and press the seam in one direction. Repeat to make 120 squares.

3. Sew the squares into 20 horizontal rows of six squares each. Sew one row below another to make a runner top of 6 x 20 squares.

4. Cut, or piece from large scraps, a runner back that is 2 inches longer all around than the patchwork runner top. Wrong sides together, center and pin the patchwork top over the runner back. Topstitch through both layers ¼ inch from the patchwork edges.

5. Enclose the runner's short edges in the blanket binding, lapping the binding edge to the topstitching. Edgestitch, and cut the ends of the binding flush with the patchwork. Repeat at the runner's long edges, turning in the raw ends of the binding.

6. Stitch the braid along the inside edge of the binding.

FIG. III, 16   PATCHWORK TABLE RUNNER

4″

90°

4″

Come, let's to bed,
Says Sleepyhead;
Tarry awhile, says Slow;
Put on the pot,
Says Greedy-gut,
We'll sup before we go.
— Nursery Rhyme

OLD SANTA FE PLATES

Materials: Wooden plates; terra cotta and orange glossy latex paint; sponge brush; artist's brush; 3-inch square of sturdy cardboard; clear polyurethane spray.

Directions:

1. Using the sponge brush, paint the plates terra cotta and let the paint dry.

2. Decorate the painted plates in one of two ways: Using the artist's brush, make orange squiggles and dots across the plates *(see photo, page 100)*.

3. Or make a "comb" out of the cardboard square by cutting ⅛-inch-long teeth, with ⅛-inch spaces between them, along one edge of the square. Using the sponge brush, paint the plates orange, over the terra cotta, and quickly draw the comb across the wet paint to make wavy patterns.

4. When all the paint is dry, spray the plates with clear polyurethane.

Note: *The plates are purely decorative. Do not place food directly on them. If you wish to use a painted plate as a serving platter, place a clear glass plate on top of the painted plate to hold the food.*

FIG. III, 17 ANIMAL FARM   1 SQ. = 1"

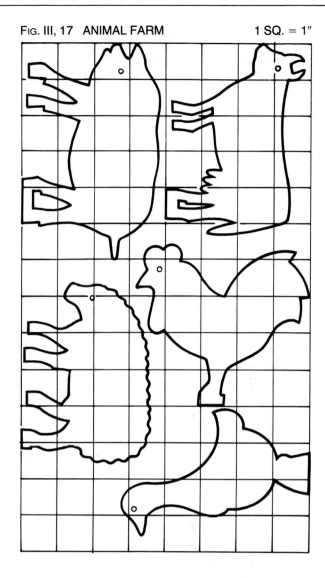

ANIMAL FARM
(about 5½ x 25 inches)

Materials: Sheets of thin tin or aluminum (animals average 4 to 6 inches in size); tin snips or scroll saw; Rustoleum® auto primer; 25 inches of 1 x 1 wood for base; masking tape.

Directions:

1. Enlarge the patterns in FIG. III, 17 following the directions on page 241. Using the tin snips or scroll saw, cut out the animals from the tin or aluminum. Spray the animals with the primer.

2. Cut a ¼-inch-deep saw kerf (groove) lengthwise down the center of the wooden base, as the groove in which to stand the animals. Wrap the feet of the animals with narrow strips of masking tape so the animals fit into the groove snugly.

3. Heads: At the neck edge, sew each Blouse piece to a Head piece. Sew together the two resulting pieces around the Head and across the shoulders. Sew the Shirt and the remaining Head pieces together in the same way.

4. Sleeves: Gather the top edge of each Blouse Sleeve piece and draw it up to fit an armhole of the Blouse. Repeat with the Shirt Sleeves and armholes. Sew the Sleeves and armholes together. Lap one edge of each knit cuff piece over the top edge of a Hand piece. Gather the lower edge of each Blouse Sleeve piece to fit the top edge of one of the remaining Hand pieces. Repeat with each of the Shirt Sleeves and cuff pieces. Sew the Sleeves to the Hands or cuffs on the gathered lines. Fold a Shirt Sleeve in half lengthwise, right sides together and armhole seam matching. Pin and sew around the Hand, up the Sleeve and down the underarm edge. Repeat. Fold and sew one of the Blouse Sleeves the same way. Leave the other Blouse Sleeve unseamed.

5. Skirt: At one long (top) edge of the skirt, sew two gathering rows ¼ inch and ½ inch from the edge. Draw up the gathers to fit the waist edge of the Blouse. Sew the skirt to the waist of the Blouse, open edges

AMISH FOLK DOLLS
(about 16 inches and 17 inches tall)

Materials: ⅓ yard of 44-inch-wide purple fabric for woman's dress; scrap of purple knit fabric for man's shirt; 9 x 12 inches of black felt; scraps of white, flesh and black fabrics; matching thread; fiberfill stuffing; tapestry, worsted or similar yarn; ½ yard of black grosgrain ribbon; scrap of cardboard; fabric glue; fabric scraps for baby's quilt.

Directions (¼-inch seams allowed):
1. Patterns: Enlarge the patterns in FIG. III, 18 following the directions on page 241.
2. Cutting: From the flesh fabric, cut one pair of Head and two pairs of Hand pieces for each doll. From white fabric, cut one pair of Knickers pieces for each doll, and a 5-inch-diameter circle for the woman's bonnet. From black fabric, cut two pairs of Boot pieces for each doll, and one pair of Slacks pieces. From purple fabric, cut one pair each of Blouse and Sleeve pieces, and a 10½ x 32-inch rectangle for the skirt. From purple knit fabric, cut one pair each of Shirt and Sleeve pieces, and two ⅞ x 2⅝-inch strips for cuffs. From black felt, cut one pair of Hat Brim pieces, one Crown Top piece and two ¾ x 10⅜-inch strips for crown sides. From the cardboard, cut one Hat Brim piece.

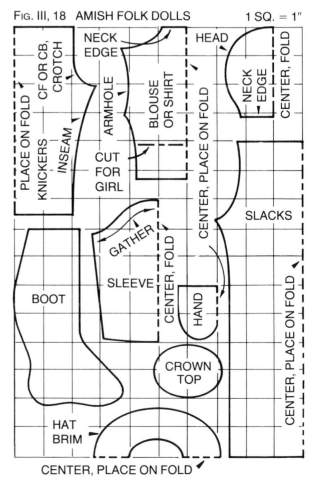

FIG. III, 18 AMISH FOLK DOLLS   1 SQ. = 1"

PLACE ON FOLD · CF OR CB, CROTCH · KNICKERS · INSEAM · NECK EDGE · ARMHOLE · CUT FOR GIRL · BLOUSE OR SHIRT · CENTER, PLACE ON FOLD · HEAD · NECK EDGE · CENTER, FOLD

GATHER · SLEEVE · CENTER, FOLD · CENTER, PLACE ON FOLD · HAND · SLACKS · CENTER, PLACE ON FOLD

BOOT · CROWN TOP · HAT BRIM

CENTER, PLACE ON FOLD

matching. Hem the lower edge of the skirt. Sew the open edges of the unseamed Hand, Sleeve, underarm and skirt.

6. Knickers: For each doll, unfold two Knickers pieces and sew the curved edges at the crotch front and crotch back. Refold the Knickers, on the broken lines, so the crotch seams match at the inner legs. Sew the inseam down each leg. At the lower edges, turn ½ inch to the wrong side and baste. Turn the Knickers right side out and stuff them.

7. Boots: Sew each pair of Boot pieces together; leave the top edges open. Trim the seams to ⅛ inch. Turn the Boots right side out and stuff them. Tuck a Boot ½ inch inside the lower edge of each Knickers leg, and pin. Securely slipstitch the Knickers over the Boots.

8. Waist Seam: Turn down the woman's bodice and pin the edge of one of the stuffed Knickers to the doll's waist seam inside the skirt, seams and centers matching. Stitch. Stuff the Hands, Sleeves, Head, and Blouse or Shirt of each doll. Turn under ½ inch at the waist edge of the Shirt, tuck the remaining stuffed Knickers ½ inch inside the Shirt, seams and centers matching, and pin. Securely slipstitch the Shirt over the Knickers.

9. Slacks: Sew the Slacks pieces together the same way as the Knickers in Step 6. Turn under ½ inch at the waist and ankle edges, and stitch. Pull the Slacks over the man doll. Cut two 9-inch strips of the ribbon. Slide their ends under the Slacks, cross the ribbons in the back to make suspenders, and sew them in place.

10. Woman's Hair: Arrange twelve 36-inch-long strands of yarn side by side, with the ends even, to make a bundle. Tie a piece of thread around the center of the bundle. Tack the center of the bundle to one side of the woman doll's Head, about ½ inch above the neck seam; and ½ inch behind the Head seam. Bring all the yarn up to the center front, about ½ inch in front of the Head seam and, stitching across the bundle, sew the yarn to the Head. Bring the yarn down the other side and sew it behind the Head seam in the same position as on the first side. Divide part of the yarn into three groups of four strands each, and braid the three groups together. Wrap the braid 2½ times around the Head and tack the braid to the Head at the center front. Fold the remaining yarn, unbraided, into a top knot at the center, and tack it to the Head.

11. Man's Beard: Arrange five 12-inch-long strands of yarn side by side, with the ends even, to make a bundle. Sew one side of the bundle, 1 inch from the yarn ends, to the seam on one side of the man doll's Head, about ½ inch above the neck seam. Sew down the bundle again about ½ inch away, leaving 2 inches

of yarn in a loop between the stitches. Repeat four more times to reach the opposite Head seam, making the two center stitches, around the "chin," a little lower to curve the beard. Clip through the yarn at the center of each loop.

12. Bonnet: Turn under ⅜ inch around the edge of the bonnet circle, and sew a gathering row ¼ inch from the fold. Draw up the gathers to fit the woman doll's Head and tie the thread ends together. Pin or sew the bonnet to the Head in three or four places.

13. Hat Brim: Draw ⅛ inch inside the outer edge of the cardboard Brim, and cut off on the drawn line. Glue the cardboard Brim between the two black felt Brim pieces, inside edges even. Let the glue dry, and set the brim on the man doll's Head.

14. Hat Crown: Using an empty cardboard bathroom tissue roll, cut off a ¾-inch-wide cardboard ring. Run a bead of glue along one of the black felt crown side strips, and wrap the strip smoothly around the cardboard ring. Wrap the other crown side strip the same way. Set the crown side on the man doll's Head and squeeze the crown side gently to fit the Brim. Without getting glue on the Head, glue the Brim to the crown side. Glue the felt Crown Top on top of the crown side.

15. Baby: From the flesh-colored fabric, cut a pair of Head pieces and a pair of Sleeve pieces. Sew the Head pieces, right sides together, ⅜ inch from the round edges; leave the neck edge open. Turn the Head right side out. Turn under ¼ inch at the neck edge and baste. Sew the Sleeve pieces, right sides together and raw edges even, at the armhole and underarm edges to make the baby's Body. Turn the Body right side out and gather around the open straight edges. Pull up the gathers to fit the neck edge of the Head. Stuff the Head and Body. Slide the gathered edge of the Body under the neck edge and slipstitch them together. Sew a few wisps of yarn for hair at the top of the Head.

16. Baby's Quilt: Sew together six rows of six 2-inch patches *(see photo)*, for the quilt top. Cut a 10½-inch square quilt back. Center quilt top over the quilt back, wrong sides together. At each edge, turn up the quilt back ¼ inch twice and slipstitch it over the quilt top.

CORN HUSK DOLLS

Materials For One Doll: Package of corn husks with corn silk; 12-inch-diameter half circle of pliable cardboard; stapler; straight pins; husk-colored thread; 1-inch-diameter Styrofoam® ball; scrap of lightweight wire; fabric dye *(optional);* 2 cotton balls; craft glue; clear enamel spray.

Directions:

1. Husks: Soak the corn husks in warm water to soften them. Unwrap them carefully so they won't break. Save the silk for hair. If you wish, dye some of the husks for the dresses and bonnets, following the dye manufacturer's directions *(see photo).*

2. Skirt Cone: Roll the cardboard into a cone about ½ inch wide at the small end. Overlap the straight edges and staple them. Hold a 5- to 6-inch-wide husk with its smooth side facing you. At the bottom, bend a 3-inch-long flap away from you. Insert the cone into the husk with the flap on the outside, and staple. Repeat, overlapping the husks until the cone is lined.

3. Skirt: Hold a husk that is 6 inches wide or wider with its rough side facing you. Bend a 2-inch-wide flap to the back along the right hand edge. Place the husk over the cone with the narrow end a little above the cone tip. Staple only the flap to the cone. Keep the rest of the husk in place with a straight pin to the left. Repeat, overlapping the husks until the cone is completely covered.

4. Skirt Blocking: Push a circle of straight pins through the husks into the cone about 3 inches from the tip. Just below them, loop thread several times around the cone. Gently pull the thread to anchor the husks, shaping the skirt. Trim the top ends of the husks flush with the cardboard. Glue and pin the husks flat to the waist. Trim the skirt bottom even so the skirt will stand. Blow-dry the skirt, or let it dry naturally overnight. Remove the pins and thread. Glue each folded edge and replace the pins until the glue is dry. Set the skirt aside.

5. Head: Gently push a 6-inch-long wire into, but not through, the Styrofoam ball. Wrap thread several times around the middle of a 3- to 4-inch-wide undyed husk and pull the thread tight. Carefully open both ends of the husk, rough side up. Place the foam ball on one half, against the thread, and cover it with the husk. Gently place the other end over the ball, too. Gather up the husk at the bottom of the ball, wrap it with thread and tie it securely, leaving the husk ends extending. Set the head aside.

6. Arms: At each end of an 11-inch-long wire, bend a teardrop-shaped hand about ⅝ inch long and ¼ inch wide. Into each hand, insert a ⅝-inch-wide corn husk strip. Wrap the husk around the hand and about 2 inches up the arm. Wrap the husk's end with thread, and tie.

7. Sleeves: Spread out a 4-inch-wide corn husk, rough side up, horizontally in front of you. Place a doll's hand on the husk about 2 inches from one end; the remaining wire doesn't touch the husk. Gather up the husk around the wrist, overlapping the long edges. Wrap the wrist with thread and tie it securely. Fold the husk back up over the gathered ends and onto the center of the wire, making a puffed sleeve. Wrap the husk, with thread, to the wire center. Repeat for the other hand, trimming off the husk end, if necessary, so it doesn't extend down the first sleeve.

8. Head: Gently push the head wire under the arm's center. Bring the extending husk ends down, shorter end at the front, and wrap them with thread just below the arms, keeping the arms close to the head. Tie securely.

9. Chest *(see the undyed V neck on the dark blue dress in the photo):* In the center of a 4-inch-wide husk, place two cotton balls side by side. Fold the long sides of the husk up over the balls. Fold the husk in half crosswise just above the balls. Wrap thread tightly around the husk ends and tie a tiny waist. Push the balls upward. Place this chest on top of the arms about ⅛ inch below the head. Lash the chest and arms together by crisscrossing thread over each shoulder and around the waist several times.

10. Bodice: Use two corn husk strips, each about 1 x 6 inches, to match the dress or apron. Crisscross a strip over each shoulder like the thread in Step 9. Wrap thread tightly around the waist and tie it. Continue wrapping thread down the rest of the husk and wire to keep the bodice narrow. Cut an ⅛-inch width of undyed husk. Wrap it over the thread under the head to make a neck. Tie it at the back and trim the ends.

11. Assembling: Gently push the doll's torso into the waistline until it sits snugly. Put a pin through the skirt front into the torso. Pin the torso again through the skirt back.

12. Apron: Glue the narrow end of a 7-inch-wide husk to the doll's waist, trimming the husk to fit. Then cut a curved bottom apron edge. Wrap a 1 x 8-inch strip of same-color husk around the doll's waist. Tie the ends in a square knot to cover the straight pin in back. Bring the extending ends together and pin them in place until they are dry.

13. *Pose:* Gently bend the arms to the desired position; this is done more easily if the arms are still damp. Be careful to keep the sleeve's puff at the wrist.

14. *Shawl:* Place a 3 x 7-inch strip of undyed husk across the doll's back and upper arms, centers matching, and cross the ends at the center front. Wrap a ⅛-inch-wide strip of husk around each end. Gather it up so it is narrow, and tie a bow. Pin each end, under the bow, into the torso.

15. *Hair:* Cut several strands of 1-inch-long corn silk and glue them to the top front of the head. Trim them to make bangs. Cut 3-inch-long strands of corn silk and glue them to the head behind the bangs. Or make braids by moistening 3-inch-long strands of corn silk with water and separating them into two sets of three strands each. Wrap thread around the top ends of the strands and place a weight over the thread. Braid each set of strands and tie it off at the end. Glue a braid to each side of the head.

16. *Ponytail Bonnet* *(see the pink and undyed dolls in the photo):* Moisten a 3- or 4-inch-wide husk and bend its narrow end back to make a 3-inch-deep brim. Pin it to the doll's head, shaping it to fit. Gather up the husk ends to make a ponytail. Wrap the gathers and tie them close to the head with a ⅛-inch-wide strip of husk. Trim the ponytail to be about 2 inches long and pin it to the back of the doll until it is dry.

17. *Cap Bonnet:* Fold a 3 x 4-inch moistened husk in half crosswise. Gather up the open back ends. Wrap and tie them tightly with thread. Trim the ends and

turn them to the inside. Place the cap on the doll and shape it to fit the head. Pin the cap in place until it is dry. Tie a ⅛-inch-wide strip of husk into a bow and glue it to the back of the cap.

18. *Both Bonnets:* When the bonnet is dry, remove the pins and carefully lift the bonnet off the doll's head. Squeeze a thin line of glue across the top of the head. Replace the bonnet and push a pin through it into the head until the glue dries. Then carefully remove the pin.

19. *Finishing:* Let the doll dry thoroughly. Then spray it with several coats of clear enamel, following the manufacturer's directions, and letting the enamel dry between coats. This will prevent the husks from cracking or curling.

20. *Corn Husk Child:* Use a ¾-inch-diameter Styrofoam ball for the head, about a 7-inch length of wire for the arms and an 8-inch-diameter cardboard half circle for the skirt cone. Make the doll like the adult doll, but the chest husk needs to be only 5 inches long, to make a chest about 1¼ inches long. Trim the skirt to be about 4 inches long. Omit the shawl.

21. *Corn Husk Baby:* Omit the skirt. Use a ½-inch-diameter Styrofoam ball for the head in Step 5, and a wire about 6 inches long for the arms in Steps 6 and 7. After Step 7, wrap the baby in a husk. Glue a corn silk topknot to the top of the head and tie it with a ⅛-inch-wide husk bow.

22. *Optional Accessories:* Add tiny wax candles, a broom, a ball of yarn or any other accessories you choose *(see photo, page 104, for guide).*

HOME SWEET HOME WREATH

Materials: Grapevine wreath (ours is 17 inches in diameter); balsa wood; scroll saw or coping saw; acrylic paints; Spanish moss or dried grass; hot glue gun; 1½ yards of 1½- to 2-inch-wide ribbon.

Directions:
1. Draw a house and three trees on the balsa wood (our house is about 3½ inches tall and 4 inches wide; our trees range from 2½ inches to 4 inches tall). Cut out the wood shapes, paint them and let the paint dry.
2. Using the hot glue gun, fasten some Spanish moss or dried grass over the bottom of the wreath. Glue the house and trees to the moss *(see photo for placement)*.
3. Tie a double bow through a vine at the bottom center of the wreath.

"OUR TOWN"

Materials: Unpainted wooden houses, barns and candlesticks; white latex paint; red, green, yellow and blue acrylic paints; sponge brush; artist's brushes; masking tape; fine-grade sandpaper.

Directions:
1. Paint the candlesticks any color. Using the sponge brush, paint an undercoat of white latex paint on all the buildings. When the undercoat is dry, paint the buildings' sides and chimneys red. When these are dry, tape the red edges and paint the roofs green. When they are dry, lightly draw doors, windows, grass and shrubs on the buildings. Paint them yellow and green with the artist's brushes *(see photo)*. When the windows are dry, outline them in blue.
2. After all the paint has dried, sand the edges of the buildings and candlesticks a little to make the pieces look old.

PRETTY PADDED HANGERS

Materials: Wooden coat hanger: full size or child's 10-inch; ¼ yard of 45-inch-wide fabric; matching thread; glazed batting; ½ yard of about ⅜-inch-wide decorative ribbon.

Directions:

1. Gathered Hook: Cut a 1½ x 14-inch strip of fabric. Turn each long edge ¼ inch to wrong side; press. Also turn under ¼ inch at one short end. Fold whole strip in half, wrong sides together; pin. Topstitch ⅛ inch from folded edges. Slide strip over hanger hook with topstitched edges to the outside, gathering slightly. Hand sew against outside curve of hook to keep the pushed-up gathers in place.

2. Padding: Wrap the batting around half the hanger, starting at the hook, until its girth measures about 4¼ inches. Sew along batting edges, especially over

the end, so it will stay in place while slipping on the cover. Repeat with the other hanger half.

3. Cover: Cut four 3-inch-wide strips of fabric, two of them 10 inches long and two 15 inches long. (For the child's hanger, cut four 2¾-inch-wide strips, two 6 inches long and two 9 inches long.) With the longest machine stitch, sew ⅜ inch from the two long edges and one short end of a 15-inch piece (9-inch piece for the child's hanger), rounding the two corners at the short end. Pin this piece to a 10-inch piece (6-inch for the child's), right sides together, raw edges even, pulling up gathers so edges will match. Distribute fullness evenly, then stitch on gathering row. Turn sleeve right side out; slide it over one end of the hanger. Repeat for the other half. Turn under raw edges at the center; slipstitch the sleeves together, catching in the hook cover.

4. Bow: Tie the ribbon into a double bow and tack it at the base of the hook.

PORTUGUESE POTTERY

Materials: Terra cotta pots, bowls and dishes; 1 roll each of 1-inch- and ¼-inch-wide masking tape; Krylon® spray paints: True Blue (1910), Bright Yellow (1804) and Antique White (1503); Krylon crystal clear spray finish; plastic Lazy Susan, for turntable; brown paper; rubber cement; pencil; scissors.

Directions:
1. Roughly sketch a design for a terra cotta pot, bowl or dish onto brown paper. Incorporate ¼-inch-wide or 1-inch-wide strips into the design; they are easy to mark on the pot using masking tape strips of the same width. Cut out the other shapes in the design from brown paper or tape. Label each shape cutout by color.
2. Place the pot on the Lazy Susan in an open area that is free of wind. Lightly spray the entire pot with the

blue paint, avoiding paint runs. Let the paint dry for at least two hours before applying tape strips and shapes, or the paint underneath may come off when the tape is removed. Fasten strips of tape to the pot where you want blue strips to be. Fasten the brown paper shapes marked blue to the pot with rubber cement.
3. Spray the entire pot with the second color: white for the two-color vase, yellow for the three-color bowl. Let the paint dry for at least two hours. For the three-color bowl, fasten the tape and brown paper shapes marked yellow to the pot; do not remove the blue patterns. Spray the entire pot white and let the paint dry.
4. Remove all the tape and paper patterns to uncover the colors that were taped over. Spray the entire pot with clear spray finish.

Note: *These pottery pieces are purely decorative. Do not place food directly on them. Do not clean them in a dishwasher.*

C O U N T R Y
S·C·E·N·T·S

*It is a mild, mild wind, and a mild-looking sky;
and the air smells now as if it blew from a
faraway meadow.*
— Herman Melville

Spicy cinnamon, cloves and nutmeg . . . sweet rose . . . crisp pine and eucalyptus . . . fresh citrus.

Fragrances are the invisible, intangible sensory delights that complete the country scene. The slightest hint of a special scent transports us to another time and place: a walk in the garden after a rainfall; cocoa and cookies in the kitchen after school; early morning on a camping trip.

In this chapter, you'll find recipes for potpourri masterpieces that bring the most wonderful scents of nature indoors. The aromatic concoctions in this chapter are beautiful in their natural state, displayed in baskets or decorative bowls. But you also can tie them up with ribbons and lace, create fragrant wreaths, sew them into sachets or fill your home with simmering spicy scents.

You'll also learn how to dry and arrange home-grown or store-bought flowers to preserve nature's beauty. Experiment with your own arrangements, or try one of our lovely creations. For instance, the wreath at left is created with strawflowers, hydrangeas, silvery artemesia, golden yarrow and statice, and clusters of globe amaranth, white ammobium and pink larkspur. With such exquisite "materials" to work with, you can create works of art that will beautify your home for years to come.

And, if you long for "flowers that last forever," we show you how to craft beautiful blossoms from simple cotton organdy. Between nature's glory and your creativity, you can fill your country home with all the sweetness of a country garden.

P·L·E·A·S·I·N·G
P·O·T·P·O·U·R·R·I·S

Fragrant Memories

Porcelain bowls heaped with colorful blooms, baskets filled with sweet-smelling herbs and spices, old-time tins and cut-glass ashtrays holding fragrant concoctions . . . what you choose for your potpourri, and how you display the mixes, can be as varied as you like. Pictured above is our Country Garden Potpourri *(page 116)*, which features a dusky blend of rose hips, pine cones, rosemary leaves, rosebuds and cornflowers. Other good flowers for potpourri: daisies, bachelor buttons, baby's breath, tiger lilies, marigolds, nasturtiums, hollyhock and aster.

Scent-sational Sachets

Remember Grandma's linens and how they smelled so sweetly of the lavender she tucked in with them? Recapture that old-fashioned fragrance with this collection of whimsical figures covered with lavender potpourri *(pages 116, 118)*. Or make a Cornucopia, Sweet Heart or Stocking Sachet *(pages 118-119)* redolent of Herbs and Spice or New England Spice Potpourri *(page 116)*. These fragrant fancies make wonderful gifts, too.

ROSE AND EUCALYPTUS WREATH

Materials: 20-inch-diameter grapevine wreath; 5 to 6 eucalyptus branches (any variety; the familiar "silver dollar" eucalyptus *(Eucalyptus cinerea)* will give the wreath a more formal look); branches of rosemary and sage; 1 to 1½ dozen short-stemmed roses (carnations can be substituted for the roses); floral wire; 1 to 1½ dozen floral water picks.

Directions:

1. Insert the ends of the eucalyptus branches into the grapevine wreath so that the branches cover the wreath. Tie any errant stems to the grapevine with floral wire.

2. Insert small bunches of the rosemary and sage branches into the wreath, tying them to the grapevine with floral wire, if necessary. Place more branches at the bottom of the wreath than at the top.

3. Fill each floral water pick with water, replace the rubber cap, insert a rose stem in the pick and poke the pick through the wreath. Place the roses around the wreath to make a pleasing and balanced arrangement *(see photo)*.

ROSE AND EUCALYPTUS POTPOURRI

You can combine the ingredients used to create the Rose and Eucalyptus Wreath, above, to make a potpourri. Mix together 12 crushed eucalyptus leaves, 13 sage leaves, 2 broken-up rosemary stems, ¾ cup of rose petals or carnation petals, ½ teaspoon of orris root powder and 3 drops of rose oil. Stir occasionally to release the scent.

CITRUS POMANDERS

Materials: Oranges; lemons; limes; whole cloves; orris root powder; pencil *(optional)*; skewer; light tack hammer; citrus peeler *(optional)*; ribbon *(optional)*.

Directions:

1. If you wish, use a pencil to outline a design you like on each fruit rind. Remove the rind with a citrus peeler, following the design. Poke pilot holes along the design with the skewer. Insert one clove into each hole with the tack hammer.

2. Or, if you prefer, leave the fruit intact and use the skewer and tack hammer to cover the entire rind with whole cloves.

3. Roll the finished fruit in the orris root powder to help preserve it. The fruit will darken and shrink a little as it dries.

4. When the pomanders have dried , display them in baskets, if you wish. Or individually tie the pomanders with ribbon, make a ribbon loop at the top of each, and hang the pomanders.

Nothing awakens a reminiscence like an odour.
—Victor Hugo

COUNTRY GARDEN POTPOURRI

Materials: 2 cups dried rosemary leaves; 1 cup dried rose hips; 1 cup dried red flowers: hibiscus, rose, geranium, cosmos, snapdragon or zinnia; 8 to 10 tiny cones: cedar, pine, hemlock or redwood; 1 teaspoon orris root powder; bright rose-colored and yellow-colored strawflowers *(optional)*; dried rosebuds *(optional)*; holly berry or potpourri oil *(optional)*.

Directions:
Mix together the rosemary, rose hips, red flowers, cones and orris root powder. For more colorful accents, add brightly-colored strawflowers, or dried rosebuds. To intensify the fragrance, add 1 or 2 drops of holly berry or potpourri oil. Also add a drop or two of the oil to renew the fragrance when it fades. Display the potpourri in an uncovered decorative container as a room freshener.

LAVENDER POTPOURRI

Materials: 2 cups dried lavender leaves; 1 cup dried lavender flower buds; ½ cup dried rosemary leaves; ½ cup dried cornflowers or other blue flower; 1 teaspoon orris root powder; ½ cup dried purple berries: bayberry or juniper *(optional)*; lavender oil.

Directions:
Mix together the lavender leaves and buds, rosemary, cornflowers or other blue flower, and the orris root powder. If you wish to display the potpourri in an open bowl, add dried purple berries for more bulk and color. To renew the fragrance when it fades, add 1 or 2 drops of the lavender oil. Display the potpourri in an uncovered decorative container as a room freshener, or use it to make the Lovely in Lavender Tree, Wreath and Ball and the Lavender Teddy Bear *(page 118)*.

NEW ENGLAND SPICE POTPOURRI

Materials: 2 cups dried rose geranium leaves; 1 cup dried sweet woodruff leaves; ¼ cup whole cloves; ¼ cup whole allspice; ⅛ cup freshly grated cinnamon; 7 whole nutmegs; ½ cup dried berries: pink pepper tree, juniper, bayberry or firethorn *(optional)*.

Directions:
Mix together the rose geranium, woodruff, cloves, allspice, cinnamon and nutmegs (cloves are a natural preservative, so no additional fixative is needed). If you wish to display the potpourri in an open bowl, add dried berries. To renew the fragrance, slightly crush a nutmeg. Display the potpourri in a container, or use it to fill the Stocking Sachet *(page 119)*.

OLD-FASHIONED ROSE POTPOURRI

Materials: 2 cups rose petals; ½ cup rose geranium leaves; ¼ cup lavender buds; ¼ cup carnation petals; 2 tablespoons dried and crumbled lemon or orange peel; 2 tablespoons sweet marjoram leaves; 1 tablespoon whole cloves; 1 crumbled bay leaf; 1 teaspoon orris root powder or 1 tablespoon orris root chips; 3 drops rose oil *(optional)*.

Directions:
Mix together the rose petals, rose geranium, lavender, carnation petals, orange and lemon peel, marjoram, cloves, bay leaf and orris root powder or chips. If you wish, add the rose oil. Place the potpourri in a self-sealing plastic bag and age it for at least four weeks.

HERBS AND SPICE POTPOURRI

Materials: 1 cup dried rosemary leaves; 1 cup dried peppermint leaves; ½ cup dried lemon thyme; ¼ cup whole allspice; 1 teaspoon orris root powder; 1 cup dried red berries: holly, firethorn or sumac *(optional)*; holly berry or bayberry oil.

Directions:
Mix together the rosemary, peppermint, lemon thyme, allspice and orris root powder. If you wish to display the potpourri in an open bowl, add dried red berries. To renew the fragrance when it fades, add 1 or 2 drops of the holly berry or bayberry oil. Display the potpourri in a decorative container, or use it to fill the Cornucopia and Sweet Heart Sachets *(pages 118-119)*.

SIMMERING SCENTS

General Directions:
1. Mix together the individual potpourri ingredients. Store the potpourri in a closed container.
2. To simmer the potpourri, place 1 tablespoon in a pot of water, or 1 teaspoon in a cup of water, bring the water to boiling and simmer the potpourri over low heat until the entire house is scented. Turn off the heat. If you wish to save the potpourri to use again, strain and dry it, and store it in a closed container.

SIMMERING APPLE SPICE

Materials: ½ cup carnation petals; ¼ cup dried sweet woodruff leaves; 3 tablespoons unpeeled dried apple; one 3-inch-long cinnamon stick or 2 tablespoons crumbled cinnamon; 1½ teaspoons grated nutmeg (1 whole nutmeg); 1 tablespoon whole cloves; 3 drops cinnamon- or vanilla-scented oil; long strands of lemon, lime and orange peel *(optional)*.

Directions:
1. To dry the apple, slice it paper-thin and place the slices in a single layer on a baking sheet. Dry the slices in a 150° oven for 30 minutes.
2. Follow the General Directions for Simmering Scents *(above)*.
3. If you wish to display the Apple Spice potpourri in an open bowl, decorate it with a bow of lemon, lime and orange peels: Starting at the top of each fruit, peel off the rind with a citrus peeler, going around the fruit in one continuous motion. Gently tie together the long strands of the peels into a loose bow.

SUMMER BREEZE SIMMERING SCENT

Materials: ¼ cup marigold or calendula petals; ¼ cup honeysuckle flowers; ¼ cup lemon-scented leaves: lemon verbena, lemon balm, lemon geranium, or lemon thyme; 3 tablespoons dried and crumbled lemon peel; ½ vanilla pod, chopped, or 1 tonka bean, chopped; 2 drops lemon or orange-blossom oil.

Directions:
Follow the General Directions for Simmering Scents *(above)*.

SIMMERING BOUQUET

Materials: ¼ cup rose petals; ¼ cup jasmine flowers; ¼ cup lavender buds; 2 tablespoons whole cloves; 2 tablespoons whole allspice; 10 rose hips; 2 drops rose oil.

Directions:
Follow the General Directions for Simmering Scents *(at left)*.

CEDAR BALLS

Materials: Cedar shavings (available at pet shops); clean discarded nylon stocking.

Directions:
Fill the foot of the nylon stocking with the cedar shavings until a baseball-size shape is formed. Tie two knots in the stocking. Continue filling and tying the stocking until the entire stocking is filled. Clip between each pair of knots to separate the cedar balls. Use the fragrant balls in place of moth balls in drawers, or pinned to stored woolen garments, to protect clothing during the summer.

LINGERING SCENT-SATIONS

In deciding where to display potpourri, keep in mind that warmth, even that given off by the light bulb of a table lamp, helps release the fragrance.

•

The fragrance of potpourri diminishes when the potpourri is exposed to the air for long periods of time, so keep the containers covered when not in use.

•

When making potpourri to display in an open bowl, include some dried whole flowers and buds to add bulk and make the display more attractive.

LOVELY IN LAVENDER: TREE, WREATH AND BALL

Materials: 4-inch-high Styrofoam® tree; 4-inch-diameter Styrofoam wreath; 3-inch-diameter Styrofoam ball; white or tacky glue; Lavender Potpourri *(page 116)*; ¼-inch-wide pale green velvet ribbon; small dried flowers; tiny cones; small silver leaves; silver star sequins; 3 straight pins *(optional)*.

Directions:
1. Completely cover the Styrofoam shapes with glue.
2. Roll the shapes in the Lavender Potpourri until they are completely coated. Gently pat potpourri on the inner part of the wreath. Let the shapes dry overnight.
3. Glue ribbon bows and streamers, flower clusters, cones, leaves and sequins to shapes *(see photo, page 113)*. Glue or pin a ribbon loop to each for a hanger.

LAVENDER TEDDY BEAR

Materials: 7-inch-high ceramic teddy bear; white or tacky glue; Lavender Potpourri *(page 116)*; small dried flowers; ¼-inch-wide pale green velvet ribbon.

Directions:
1. Using the ceramic bear, follow the directions in Lovely in Lavender, Steps 1 and 2 *(above)*.
2. Make a bouquet of the dried flowers and glue the bouquet in place *(see photo, page 113)*.
3. Tie a ribbon bow around the bear's neck.

FLORAL FAN

Materials: 9½ x 11 inches of scented paper drawer liner; white or tacky glue; ¾-inch-wide silver lace; wire or tape; small dried flowers; ¼-inch-wide pale green velvet ribbon; small silver leaves; silver star sequins.

Directions:
1. Fold the drawer liner in half lengthwise. Fold both short edges ¼ inch to the inside, and glue together the "finished" edges.
2. Glue the lace along one edge of the liner. When the glue is dry, pleat the liner with ½-inch-wide pleats.
3. Gather one edge of the pleated liner and wrap wire or tape around it to secure it.
4. Glue the dried flowers and silver leaves to the fan *(see photo, page 113)*. Make a double bow with the ribbon, and glue it to the fan, near the bottom. Glue the star sequins to the ribbon.

CORNUCOPIA SACHET

Materials: ⅓ yard of fabric (this amount also will make Sweet Heart and Stocking Sachets *(page 119)*); tracing paper; graphite paper; stylus or dried-out ball point pen; thin cardboard; dressmaker's carbon; tracing wheel; white or tacky glue; silver tassel; 1 yard of ruffled silver lace (this amount also will decorate Stocking Sachet *(page 119)*); 1 yard of silver trim; 1 yard of ¼-inch-wide velvet ribbon; silver star sequins; 5-inch square of nylon net; Herbs and Spice Potpourri *(page 116)*.

Directions:
1. Draw or trace a 13-inch-diameter circle on the tracing paper. Cut a wedge from the circle that is 9 inches in circumference (measuring along the outer edge of the circle) to make a pattern.
2. Using the graphite paper and the stylus or ball point pen tip, trace the wedge onto the cardboard. Cut out the cardboard pattern. Trim ½ inch off one straight edge and ¼ inch off the outer curved edge of the cardboard pattern.
3. Using the dressmaker's carbon and tracing wheel, trace the pattern onto the fabric. Cut out the fabric wedge and glue it to the cardboard piece, with the fabric extending ½ inch beyond one of the cardboard straight edges, and with the fabric curved edge extending ¼ inch beyond the cardboard curved edge. Fold the fabric overhangs over the cardboard straight and curved edges, and glue the overhangs in place.
4. When the glue is dry, form the wedge into a cone shape, with the fabric-covered straight edge on the outside of the cone. Glue the cone together along the straight edge.
5. Glue the tassel to the bottom point of the cone, the lace around the curved top edge of the cone, and the trim around, and slightly overlapping, the bottom edge of the lace *(see photo, page 113)*. Cut an 8-inch length of the ribbon and glue the ends to opposite inside edges of the cone for a hanger. Make a double bow with the remaining ribbon and glue the bow on top of the trim. Glue the star sequins to the ribbon.
6. Place 3 tablespoons of the potpourri in the center of the nylon net square. Tightly twist together the corners of the square to form a ball, and glue the ball in the center of the cone *(see photo, page 113)*.

SWEET HEART

Materials: Fabric remaining from Cornucopia Sachet *(page 118)*; tracing paper; scrap of nylon net; 17 inches of ruffled silver lace; synthetic batting; Herbs and Spice Potpourri *(page 116)*; scrap of silver trim; 20 inches of ¼-inch-wide velvet ribbon; silver star sequins; white or tacky glue.

Directions (¼-inch seams allowed):
1. Enlarge the heart half-pattern in Fig. IV, 1, following the directions on page 241. Trace the half-pattern onto folded tracing paper. Cut out the half-pattern and open it to make a full pattern. From the center top, draw a diagonal line to the center of each side edge *(see dotted line in* Fig. IV, 1*)*.
2. Cut out two fabric hearts. Cut off the curved segments above the diagonal lines on one of the hearts. Leave the second heart whole. Use the cut-off segments as patterns to cut two pieces of the nylon net. Topstitch the net pieces to the straight edges of the cut fabric heart, barely overlapping the edges.
3. Edges matching, sew the straight edge of the lace to the right side of the whole heart.
4. Right sides together, and the lace in between, sew the two hearts together, leaving a 2-inch opening. Turn the heart right side out. Stuff the bottom of the heart with the batting and the top of the heart with the potpourri. Slipstitch the opening closed.
5. Glue a piece of silver trim and a piece of ribbon over each seam line on the front of the heart. Make a bow, with a 3-inch loop for a hanger, from the remaining ribbon, and glue the bow to the top of the heart. Glue the star sequins to the bow.

STOCKING SACHET

Materials: Fabric and 10 inches of ruffled silver lace remaining from Cornucopia Sachet *(page 118)*; 14 inches of ¼-inch-wide velvet ribbon; synthetic batting; New England Spice Potpourri *(page 116)*; sharp razor; silver star sequins; white or tacky glue.

Directions (¼-inch seams allowed):
1. Enlarge the stocking shape in Fig. IV, 2, following the directions on page 241, and cut out the shape to make a pattern. Fold the fabric in half, and cut out the pattern on the double thickness of fabric for the stocking front and back.
2. Right sides together, sew the front and back pieces of the stocking together around the sides, leaving the top edges open. Clip the curves and turn the stocking right side out.
3. Edges matching, glue the straight edge of the lace, in one continuous length, to the open top edge of the stocking, following the top edges' shaping. Turn under the top edges ¼ inch so that the rippled edge of the lace is pointing out of the stocking *(see photo, page 113)*. Finger press the turned-under edge. Cut a 4-inch length of the ribbon and fold it in half to make a hanging loop. Glue the ends of the loop to the inside of the back top edge, over the lace and near the heel-side seams. Stuff the stocking with the batting and the potpourri. Glue together the open top edges, enclosing the lace straight edge and the loop ends.
4. Using the razor, cut two ¼-inch-long slits in each side of the stocking. Pull the remaining ribbon through the slits, with the ribbon ends even over the toe-side seam *(see photo, page 113)*. Tie the ribbon into a double bow and glue the star sequins to the bow.

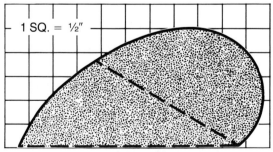

Fig. IV, 1 SWEET HEART HALF PATTERN

1 SQ. = ½"

PLACE ON FOLD

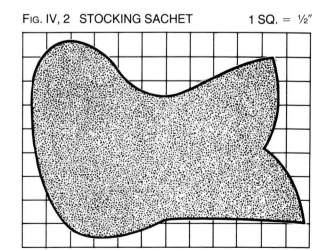

Fig. IV, 2 STOCKING SACHET   1 SQ. = ½"

Y·E·S·T·E·R·D·A·Y'S
B·L·O·S·S·O·M·S

Lovin' Spoonful

Create a tiny treasure for your kitchen or dining room wall! To make a Lovin' Spoonful, cut floral foam to fit inside the bowl of a soup ladle or other deep-bowled spoon. Glue the foam in place with craft glue. Insert dried flower stems into the foam. Pictured above are clustered *Helichrysum*, but "Bikini" strawflowers, globe amaranth or tansy can be substituted. Wrap craft wire around the ladle handle for a hanger. Tie a colorful ribbon bow around the ladle handle to conceal the wire.

Summer's Glow

Golden memories of summer afternoons in the sun will linger through the chilly days of winter if you fill a wooden pail with a mass of sunny dried flowers. Pictured here are yarrow, roses, globe amaranth, strawflowers and pearly everlastings *(Anaphalis)*. Some other wonderful containers include an old milk bucket, a wide-mouthed ceramic pitcher, an old glass bottle or, for larger blooms such as sunflowers, an antique butter churn.

A Dried Flower Palette

Choose your flowers for drying as an artist would, picking the best specimens, varying the textures and shapes of the flowers for interest.

♦ If you use flowers from your own garden, pick them at midday.

♦ Most flowers can be picked when they are open. Delphinium and larkspur should be picked when about half the florets along a stem are open, love-in-a-mist *(Nigella)* when the flowers have died and the seed pods are open slightly, roses when the buds are closed or just beginning to open, and strawflowers before the buds open.

DRIED TO PERFECTION

AIR DRY:	DRY IN MEDIUM:
Cockscomb	"The Fairy" rose
Strawflower	Zinnia
Ammobium	Queen Anne's lace
Globe thistle	Aster
Salvia farinacea	Marigold
Artemesia	Clarkia unguiculata
Statice	Black-eyed Susan
Larkspur	Feverfew

Air-Drying Flowers

Air drying is the easiest way to dry fresh flowers.

♦ Tie six to ten stems together with string or a rubber band. Hang the bunches of flowers upside down in a dark, dry spot where air circulates freely— an attic, spare room, shady kitchen corner, or closet with the door left open a crack. Flowers dried in the dark last longer and maintain a truer color.

♦ The dried stems of some flowers, such as strawflowers and globe amaranth, are too brittle to work well, so replace them with wire before drying the flower heads. Pinch off each stem close to the bottom of the fresh bud or flower. Push a length of 16-gauge wire midway into the flower head. Place the flowers upright in a container. As they dry, the flowers will open and adhere to the wires.

♦ To prevent seeds from dropping onto the floor, cockscomb (crested *Celosia*) and salvia flowers, and the seed pods of love-in-a-mist *(Nigella)* should be taped inside an open paper bag to dry. Save the seeds to plant next year.

♦ Most flower varieties will air dry in two to three weeks unless the weather is very humid.

♦ Leave bunches of air dried flowers hanging until you are ready to use them, or untie and store them, loosely packed, in a covered box.

♦ Some flowers, such as annual and perennial statice, oregano blossoms, strawflowers, hydrangea, baby's breath, globe amaranth and yarrow, can be dried upright; simply place them in a vase. Be sure to strip the leaves from yarrow after picking it.

Drying Flowers in Medium

There are two excellent mediums in which to dry flowers: sand or silica gel. Whichever method you choose, remember to include buds and half-opened flowers to give your arrangement a natural look. Trim the stems on flowers, leaving enough stem to work with in flower arranging (about 1 to 2 inches).

The Sand Method

This method drys flowers in 3 to 5 weeks. Flowers are placed in open containers, then completely covered with sand. The sand does not draw moisture from the flowers; it only holds flowers in place while they dry out. When using this method, remember:

♦ The sand must be clean and dry. To clean sand, place it in a container and pour water on it. Stir it so any particles rise to the top. After the sand settles, pour off the dirty water. Repeat until the sand is clean. Dry sand in the sun, spread out in a shallow container.

♦ Sturdy containers are a must. Good choices include shoe boxes, cake tins or plastic containers.

♦ Flowers with a single row of petals, such as wild carrot, can be dried face-down in the sand; "cupped" flowers such as roses and tulips must be dried face-up. In either case, begin with a 2-inch layer of sand. For face-down flowers, petals should be in a natural position and in contact with the sand. The flowers should not touch each other. For cupped flowers, settle the flowers in the sand and gently pour more sand over them, until all the petals are covered.

♦ When the flowers are dry, remove them from the container and gently brush off any remaining sand with a small paint brush.

The Silica Gel Method

Silica gel dries flowers by absorbing moisture from them. The process takes only 3 to 7 days, but you must carefully monitor the flowers as they dry, as overdried flowers will disintegrate when touched. Silica gel is blue and sandlike, and as it absorbs moisture, it turns pink. Silica gel must be redried before using again.

♦ Use a covered, airtight, preferably lightproof container to dry the flowers.

♦ As in the sand method, "cupped" flowers should be dried face-up; flatter flowers can be dried face-down. (See details, above, for placement of flowers.)

♦ Check the flowers daily, as thinner petals (ie., daisies) dry more quickly than thicker petals (ie., tulips). When dry, flowers should feel crisp. Handle flowers carefully: remove them with a slotted spoon. Brush off excess gel with a small paint brush.

Preserving Greens

Leaves and leafy branches that have been preserved in a glycerin solution are more pliable and easier to work with than air-dried leaves and branches.

♦ Beech, forsythia, crab apple, pear, spirea, laurel, eucalyptus, peony, weigela and magnolia branches are good candidates for treating with glycerin.

♦ Cut branches no longer than 2 feet.

♦ Pound the bottom 3 inches of the stems with a hammer so that they will take up the glycerin solution more easily.

♦ Thoroughly mix 1 part glycerin, which is available in drugstores, to 2 parts hot water. Place the branches in the glycerin solution and let them soak for 7 to 10 days. Add more solution as it is needed.

♦ When the branches have absorbed the solution, the leaves will have changed color slightly but they still will be pliable. Dry the branches with paper toweling and hang them upside down in bunches until you need them. You can reuse leftover glycerin solution if you store it in a jar with a tightly-fitting lid.

♦ Glycerinized branches will last indefinitely; when they become dusty, gently clean them with a soft damp cloth or moist paper toweling.

Flowers can be lovely the second time around! Here, a colorful Dried Flower Wreath and a Dainty Wreath made of lavender sprigs (directions for both are on page 127), surround a bouquet of rosebuds, yarrow, clustered Helichrysum and tansy with raffia.

Preparing Dried Flowers for Display

♦ Wrap dried flowers in damp newspaper the night before arranging them; they will be less brittle.

♦ To make clusters of small flowers, wrap a bit of spool wire around three to five of the flowers. Wire the cluster to a single length of 16- or 18-gauge stem wire.

♦ To lengthen a 1- to 2-inch-long stem, wrap floral tape around the tip of 18-gauge stem wire. Place the wire next to the dried stem and wrap the stem and wire together with floral tape. Continue wrapping tape around and down the stem wire until the wrapped wire is the length you wish. Snip off excess wire.

♦ Protect dried flowers from dust with two coats of clear acrylic spray varnish or with two applications of hair spray.

Arranging Dried Flowers

Dried flowers, like fresh ones, look beautiful just by massing them in a vase, basket, pitcher or other container. If you wish to display dried flowers more formally, the following advice will help you create a beautiful arrangement. These suggestions apply both to arrangements meant to be viewed from the front only and to those, like centerpieces, meant to be viewed from all sides.

♦ Cut a piece of dry floral foam large enough to fill the container and reach 1 inch above the rim. If you're using a fairly shallow container, you may need to secure the foam to the container with a narrow strip of green adhesive floral tape.

♦ Hide the foam and tape with sheet moss.

♦ Start the arrangement by creating an outline: insert spiky flowers, such as liatris, delphinium, larkspur or artemesia, or use leafy branches.

♦ Place a few larger flowers near the center of the container to act as a focal point.

♦ Gradually add smaller dried flowers and filler flowers. Baby's breath, statice or ageratum are ideal for this purpose. Filler flowers belie their name; they give an airy quality to a full arrangement that otherwise might seem too heavy and dense.

FLORAL NOTES

Use pressed flowers to decorate stationery and notecards, or as a decorative device for pictures. Flower presses are available in most craft stores, or by mail from Lillian Vernon, 510 South Fulton Ave., Mount Vernon, NY 10550.

•

Ten flowers to press: coreopsis, dianthus, geranium, marigold, nasturtium, petunia, Queen Anne's lace, rose, salvia, yarrow.

MAKING A DRIED FLOWER WREATH

Materials: Flower heads: peony, larkspur, yarrow, statice, cornflower, lily, iris, lavender, hollyhock, rose or globe amaranth; floral greens; lemon leaves; silica gel; straw or Styrofoam® wreath form (available at most craft stores or garden centers; when choosing the size of the wreath form, remember that the finished wreath will be 2 to 4 inches larger than the form itself); 22- or 24-gauge wire; ¼-inch-wide self-adhesive floral tape; fast-drying craft glue; decorative ribbon *(optional)*.

Directions:
1. Dry the flower heads, floral greens and lemon leaves in the silica gel, following the directions on page 123.
2. When you are ready to make the wreath, layer the dried greens around the front of the wreath form, wrapping and anchoring them with wire so they overlap. Add another layer of greens to cover the form. Tuck the stems of the second layer under the tops of the first layer of greens. If any stems still show, wrap them with floral tape.
3. Experiment with placing individual dried lemon leaves around the greens, varying the leaves' directions and their depths in the greens, until you have a pleasing arrangement. Apply glue to the base of each lemon leaf and gently press the leaf onto the greens.
4. Do the same experimenting with placing the dried flower heads until you have the most pleasing arrangement. Apply glue to the base of each flower head and gently press the flower onto the greens. Lift the greens slightly as you press on the flowers so the flowers nestle into the greens and look natural.
5. Add decorative ribbons, if you wish.
6. Make a wire loop and attach it to the back of the wreath for a hanger.

DAINTY WREATH

Materials: Dried lavender branches (dried baby's breath or artemesia can be substituted); spool wire; fast-drying craft glue.

Directions:
Bind together eight to ten lavender branches with uncut spool wire. Place a second, unwired, group of lavender branches over the first so the flowers cover the wired area. Wire together the two groups of branches. Repeat until a circle is formed. Glue loose lavender flowers over any exposed wire on the inner edge of the wreath.

BLOSSOMING BRAID

Materials: Raffia; short-stemmed dried flowers (we used delphinium *(Carthamus)*, lady's mantle *(Alchemilla)* and love-in-a-mist *(Nigella)*, but German (perennial) statice, larkspur (annual delphinium) and hydrangea can be substituted); white or tacky glue.

Directions:
Make a raffia braid that is 3 feet long and 3½ to 4 inches wide. Dip the flower stem ends into the glue and insert them into the alternating curves of the braid. (If you use dried hydrangea, you can use the flower head whole, or separate it after drying into floret clusters.) Tie a raffia bow at the top of the braid.

B·E·A·U·T·I·F·U·L
A·R·R·A·N·G·E·M·E·N·T·S

A Basketful of Roses

If you're a novice to floral arranging, start with a small basket, and be careful of the rose thorns!

◆ Fit a handled basket with a plastic container and insert a wet block of floral foam.

◆ Poke holes in the foam with a pencil and insert the stems of multi-flowered roses all over the foam.

◆ Insert the ends of ivy strands into the foam and trail the strands out of the basket.

Alternative flowers: Peonies; tulips.

B rilliant Disguise

Mustard crocks masquerade as costly earthenware in a lovely arrangement of snapdragons and wax flowers.

◆ Mass nine snapdragons very low in one crock.

◆ Insert five long snapdragon stems in a second crock, using a flower frog.

◆ To camouflage the snapdragon stems, add a few sprigs of wax flower *(Stephanotis floribunda)*.

Alternative flowers: Larkspur or delphinium with stock (a type of mustard flower).

Bring the beauty of your garden indoors. To make the most of fresh bouquets, follow these simple guidelines.

Pick flowers early in the day or late in the evening. Bring a bucket of water with you so you can submerge the stems immediately after cutting them.

Recut the stems before arranging the flowers. Use a sharp knife or pruners and make an angled cut across the bottom; stems with straight cuts may lodge against the bottom of the vase and be unable to take up water.

Strip off all the leaves that would be covered by water in the vase or other container.

Add a floral preservative to the vase water.

If you are using floral foam as the base for an arrangement, first soak the foam in preservative-treated water.

If you are arranging fresh roses, condition them by placing them in a container of warm water deep enough to cover the stems and flowers. Let the roses soak for two hours before arranging them.

Freshly-cut Queen Anne's lace can be colored easily by putting the stems in a solution of water and vegetable dye.

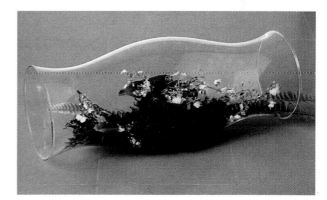

FILL IT WITH FLOWERS

Everyday items can do double-duty as showcases for your prettiest garden blooms.

- ◆ *Glass or ceramic pitchers*
- ◆ *Old-fashioned beer steins*
- ◆ *Decorative serving bowls*
- ◆ *The canister set you retired years ago*
- ◆ *Interesting gourmet food jars and bottles*
- ◆ *Collectible tin containers*
- ◆ *Everyday "pop art": mayonnaise jars, coffee cans, wine bottles, olive oil cans*
- ◆ *Baby bottles (a great pick-me-up gift for a new mother or mother-to-be)*
- ◆ *Umbrella holders*
- ◆ *Perfume and cosmetic bottles*
- ◆ *Garlic keeper*
- ◆ *Oil and vinegar cruets*

A Touch of Glass

- ◆ Turn a large hurricane lamp chimney on its side. To steady it, place a votive candleholder, filled with water, in the center.
- ◆ Camouflage the candleholder with a layer of moistened sphagnum moss. Place the stems of galax leaves in the holder.
- ◆ Insert three short stems of Dendrobium orchids in the candleholder.
- ◆ Place one or two Boston fern fronds in small flower picks filled with water, and add an orchid stem. Lay the picks inside the chimney.
- ◆ Camouflage the picks with pieces of moss.

Alternative flowers: Pansies or violets (including potted miniature African violets); any type of fern; begonia or piggyback plant leaves in place of galax.

Teatime Centerpiece

Insert a cluster of grape hyacinths in the opening of a teapot.

Add a few shorter hyacinths around the rim.

In the center, insert "airy" stems in a contrasting color — we used *Buddleia*.

Alternative flowers: Violets with lily-of-the-valley; white miniature roses with blue or red salvia.

Tumbling Tulips

Although we show just one vegetable basket, you can use a trio of baskets for a more spectacular effect.

♦ Line a wire hanging basket with moistened sphagnum moss.

♦ Fit the basket with a plastic container and insert a wet block of floral foam.

♦ Poke holes in the foam with a pencil and insert tulip stems upright, as well as at an angle so the tulips "droop" over the sides of the basket.

♦ Group tulips of a deeper shade to one side.

Alternative flowers: Roses; daffodils.

Spice Jar Medley

♦ Wash several empty spice jars and dry them well.
♦ Line the jars with aluminum foil to waterproof them, and place a flower frog in each; holders aren't needed in glass jars with narrow openings.
♦ Insert the stems of asters in a few of the spice jars. If you wish, use a different color aster in each jar. Add eucalyptus stems as filler.
♦ In the remaining jars, place veronica, blue lace flower *(Trachymene)* and liatris.
Alternative flowers: Carnations; salvia; scabiosa; love-in-a-mist *(Nigella)*.

Tangerine Dream

♦ Set a bowl inside a colander to hold a wet block of floral foam.
♦ Insert two stems of curly (corkscrew) willow into the foam.
♦ Follow the lines of the willow with yellow-flowered acacia, and add some acacia around the base of the arrangement.
♦ For spots of color, place calendulas among the feathery foliage.
♦ Fill the base with tangerines.
Alternative flowers: Any twisted branches; marigolds; Gerbera daisies; asters; zinnias.

Mary, Mary, quite contrary,
How does your garden grow?
With silver bells and cockleshells,
And pretty maids all in a row.
—Anonymous

F·O·R·E·V·E·R
F·L·O·W·E·R·S

Delightful Daffodils

Like all the flowers in this section, these magnificent daffodils are fashioned from cotton organdy colored with fabric dye. To create the delicate shading for these daffodils, the edges are colored with a felt-tip marker, then smudged with nail polish remover. Directions for the daffodils are on page 136.

Forever Young

It's always spring when you have beautiful fabric flowers in your home. These roses bloom in bright yellow, deep red and pretty pink, and are accented by baby's blossoms; the lilies, nestled in a basket on the windowsill, look as delicate and beautiful as nature's own. Directions for the white baby's blossoms are on page 137; directions for the roses are on page 138; directions for the lilies are on page 141.

FLOWERS THAT LAST FOREVER

General Directions:

1. All the flowers are made with 100% cotton organdy that has been colored with fabric dye, ironed dry and sized.

2. Dying Fabric: Cut the fabric into 18-inch squares. Mix about 1 tablespoon of fabric dye with 1 gallon of very hot tap water, adding more dye, if necessary, to attain the desired color. To get different shades of the same color, leave some fabric squares in the dye longer than others. Dip each fabric square in the dye, remove it and place it on several pieces of paper toweling. Squeeze out the excess water. Set an iron for "cotton" and iron the fabric dry.

3. Sizing Fabric: Place the dyed fabric squares on clean paper. Spray the squares with several coats of clear acrylic spray varnish. Allow the fabric to dry completely between coats.

4. Dying Covered Wire: Some flowers call for gluing covered wire to petals. Cut 26-gauge or 28-gauge white-covered wire into the specified lengths, dip the wire into the specified dye, and set aside the wire to dry.

5. Cutting: The direction of the arrow on each pattern piece (see Figs. IV, 3 and 3A) must match the direction of the fabric grain.

6. Wrapping: Wrap stamen bunches and petal wires together with masking tape before attaching them to a stem wire with floral tape. Then wrap the stem wire, and any other exposed wire, with floral tape. To wrap with floral tape, hold the tape at a slant at the flower base and press the tape in place. Wrap the tape in a spiral around the stem, stretching the tape as you wind to keep it taut and smooth. Add leaves to the stem as you wrap.

> *I wandered lonely as a cloud*
> *That floats on high o'er vales*
> *and hills,*
> *When all at once I saw a crowd,*
> *A host, of golden daffodils . . .*
> —William Wordsworth

DAFFODILS

Materials: White organdy, some of it dyed yellow, and all of it sized (see General Directions, Steps 2 and 3, at left); yellow and orange wide felt-tip markers; small watercolor brush; nail polish remover; white glue; needle; thread; 26-gauge covered wire dyed yellow (see General Directions, Step 4, at left); 22-gauge wire; 16-gauge stem wire; green floral tape; masking tape; 3-inch-wide green satin floral ribbon.

Directions:

1. Pattern: Enlarge the half-pattern piece marked "Petal" in Fig. IV, 3 on folded paper, following the directions on page 241. Cut out the pattern and unfold it.

2. Cutting: For each daffodil, cut twelve petals and one 1¾ x 3½-inch trumpet strip (see Fig. IV, 3A); use both the white and yellow fabrics to make the daffodils. Also cut two 9-inch lengths of the floral ribbon for each daffodil. Gently stretch the petal edges between your thumb and forefinger to ripple the edges. Fold the trumpet strip in half twice and cut a rippled edge through all the layers.

3. Trumpet: Lightly touch the rippled edge of the trumpet with the yellow marker if the fabric is white, or the orange marker if the fabric is yellow. Touch the marked area with the watercolor brush dipped in the nail polish remover, so the color will run and soften. Overlap the short ends of the strip and glue them together. Using the needle and thread, sew a running stitch ¼ inch from the straight bottom edge. Pull the thread tight and fasten the end.

4. Stem: Bend one end of a length of 16-gauge stem wire to make a small hook. Wrap the hook with floral tape, making a small green ball at the end. Push the straight end of the hooked stem into the trumpet and pull the stem through until the hooked end is inside the trumpet. Fasten the gathered edges of the trumpet to the stem with masking tape. Using the same color marker that was used around the trumpet edge, color the inside of the trumpet around the green ball. Touch the marked area with the watercolor brush dipped in the nail polish remover, to soften the color. Gently stretch the rippled trumpet edge.

5. Petals: Cut six 4-inch lengths of the yellow-covered wire. Dip 1½ inches of one end of one of the wires into the glue. Sandwich the glue-coated wire, centered, between two petals, letting the uncoated end of the wire extend beyond the bottom of the petals as a stem. Make five more petals the same way. When the petals are dry, touch their edges with the same color marker that was used on the trumpet. Touch the marked areas with the watercolor brush dipped in the nail polish remover, to soften the color. Let the petals dry.

6. *Leaves:* Using the 22-gauge wire, follow the directions in Lilies, Step 5 *(page 141).*

7. *Assembling:* Place the six petals around the base of the trumpet. Twist all the petal wires around the stem and wrap them with masking tape. Wrap the entire stem with floral tape, adding the leaves near the bottom as you wrap. Bend the daffodil head at an angle to the stem, and shape the petals.

BABY'S BLOSSOMS

Materials: Sized white organdy *(see General Directions, Step 3, page 136)*; 28-gauge covered wire dyed green *(see General Directions, Step 4)*; 19-gauge stem wire; green floral tape; small cloth leaves (available at most craft stores); green pastel chalk; small watercolor brush; rubbing alcohol.

Directions:

1. *Pattern:* Enlarge the half-pattern piece marked "Blossom" in FIG. IV, 3 on folded paper, following the directions on page 241. Cut out the pattern; unfold it.

2. *Cutting:* For each flower, cut four petals.

3. *Assembling:* Bend a 3-inch length of the green-covered wire in half over the center of two of the petals, and twist the wire. Add the remaining two petals and twist the wire again to make a four-petal flower. Lay the twisted covered-wire ends along the top end of a length of 19-gauge stem wire, and secure the covered wire with a strip of floral tape. Wrap the entire stem wire with floral tape, adding the leaves as you wrap.

4. *Shaping and Coloring:* Shape the flower into four petals. Touch the centers and edges of the petals with the green chalk. Then touch the chalked areas with the watercolor brush dipped in the alcohol, to blend in the color. Let the petals dry.

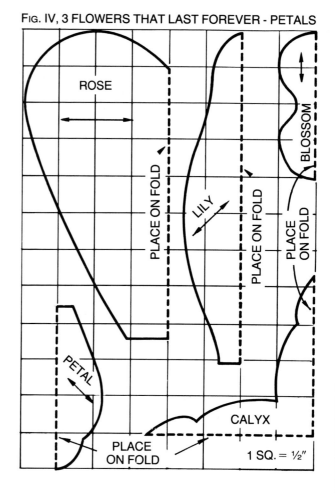

FIG. IV, 3 FLOWERS THAT LAST FOREVER - PETALS

ROSE

PLACE ON FOLD

LILY

PLACE ON FOLD

BLOSSOM

PLACE ON FOLD

PETAL

PLACE ON FOLD

CALYX

1 SQ. = ½"

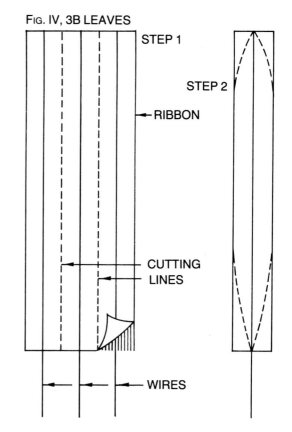

FIG. IV, 3B LEAVES

STEP 1

STEP 2

RIBBON

CUTTING LINES

WIRES

FIG. IV, 3A FLOWER CENTERS

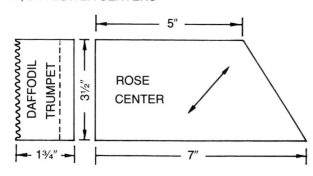

DAFFODIL TRUMPET

ROSE CENTER

5"

3½"

1¾"

7"

ROSES

Materials: Organdy dyed shades of red, yellow, pink and green, and sized *(see General Directions, Steps 2 and 3, page 136)*; 16-gauge stem wire; pencil; waxed dental floss; masking tape; white glue; green floral tape; rose leaves (available at most craft stores).

Directions:

1. Patterns: Enlarge the half-pattern pieces marked "Rose" and "Calyx" in Fig. IV, 3 *(page 137)*, on folded paper, following the directions on page 241, and folding the paper twice for the calyx. Cut out the patterns and unfold them. Draw the pattern marked "Rose Center" following the dimensions indicated in Fig. IV, 3A *(page 137)*.

2. Cutting: For each rose, cut seven to nine petals and a rose center from the red, yellow or pink fabric; cut a calyx from the green fabric.

3. Center: Bend one end of a length of stem wire to make a small hook. Without creasing the center strip, lightly fold it in half to a 1¾-inch width. With the 7-inch longer side facing you, hold the straight end of the folded center strip between your left thumb and forefinger. With your right hand, loosely wind the strip around your left thumb and forefinger. Pinch together the base of the rose center, insert the straight end of the hooked wire into the top of the center, and pull the wire through, catching the hook on the inside fabric. Pinch together the bottom edges of the center and fasten them to the stem wire with masking tape.

4. Petals: Using the pencil, roll one upper curved edge of a petal to the indentation. With the petal still on the pencil, push together the ends of the rolled part of the petal to crimp the fabric. Roll the other petal edge the same way. Repeat with the remaining petals.

5. Rose: Cut an arm's length of dental floss. Equally space three petals, cupped inward, around the rose center. Wind the floss around the petals about three times, pulling it very tight. Add three more petals, cupped outward, and wind the floss around them. Continue adding outward-cupped petals, one at a time, winding the floss around each to secure it. Finish winding the floss, and cover the entire floss-wrapped rose base with masking tape.

6. Calyx: Cut a small cross in the center of the calyx and push the rose stem through it, bringing the calyx up around the base of the rose. Spread glue on the inner surface of the calyx and fasten it to the base of the rose. Wrap the calyx base and the entire stem with floral tape, adding two sets of leaves as you wrap. Curl the calyx points by pulling them over a scissor blade.

7. Bud: Add one or two petals to a rose center and wrap the base of the bud with masking tape. Attach a calyx. Wrap the entire stem and the base of the calyx with floral tape, adding leaves as you wrap.

CROCUSES

Materials: Organdy dyed purple and sized *(see General Directions, Steps 2 and 3, page 136)*; 26-gauge covered wire dyed purple *(see General Directions, Step 4)*; small yellow peps (available at most craft stores); green floral tape; purple wide felt-tip marker; small watercolor brush; nail polish remover; 22-gauge wire; 19-gauge stem wire; 3-inch-wide green satin floral ribbon; white glue; masking tape.

Directions:

1. Pattern: Enlarge the half-pattern piece marked "Petal" in Fig. IV, 3 *(page 137)*, on folded paper, following the directions on page 241. Cut out the pattern and unfold it.

2. Cutting: For each crocus, cut six petals. Gently stretch the petal edges between your thumb and forefinger to shape the edges.

3. Petals: Cut six 3-inch lengths of the purple-covered wire. Glue one of the wires to the center back of each petal. Let the glue dry. Wrap together the stems of six to eight yellow peps with floral tape. Place the six petals around the peps, with the petals' wire backs facing inward. Twist all the petal and pep wires together. Using the purple marker, very lightly define the edge of each petal and make a heavier marking near the petal base around the peps. Touch the marked areas with the watercolor brush dipped in the nail polish remover, to soften the color. Let the petals dry completely.

4. Leaves: Cut four 11-inch lengths of the 22-gauge wire and two 9-inch lengths of the floral ribbon. Spread glue over the satin side of one length of ribbon. Continue as in Lilies, Step 5, *(page 141)*, but use four wires, spaced ¾ inch apart, to make four leaves *(see Fig. IV, 3B, page 137)*. Make two leaves for each crocus.

5. Assembling: Place the top end of a 7-inch length of 19-gauge stem wire against the twisted petal and pep wires, and wrap all the wires with masking tape. Wrap the entire stem wire with floral tape, adding the leaves near the bottom as you wrap. Shape the petals to curve upward and inward toward the peps.

Spring Fever

Delicate and distinctive, these blue-purple flowers would look beautiful on a kitchen counter or a window box to give a glimpse of spring all year long. Wire is glued to the backs of the petals so the petals can be formed easily into graceful shapes. Directions for the crocuses are on page 138.

I sing of brooks, of blossoms,
birds and bowers:
Of April, May, of June
and July flowers.
I sing of Maypoles, Hock-carts,
wassails, wakes,
Of bridegrooms, brides, and of their
wedding cakes.
— Robert Herrick

ANEMONES

Materials: Organdy dyed red, pink and purple, and sized *(see General Directions, Steps 2 and 3, page 136)*; 26-gauge covered wire dyed to match the fabric colors *(see General Directions, Step 4)*; white glue; black and red wide felt-tip markers; small watercolor brush; nail polish remover; black center stamens (available at most craft stores); 16-gauge stem wire; masking tape; green floral tape; leaves (available at most craft stores); cotton swabs; household bleach.

Directions:
1. *Pattern:* Enlarge the half-pattern piece marked "Petal" in FIG. IV, 3 *(page 137)* on folded paper, following the directions on page 241. Cut out the pattern and unfold it.
2. *Cutting:* For each anemone, cut twelve petals and six 4-inch lengths of covered wire the same color as the petals. Gently stretch the petal edges between your thumb and forefinger.

3. *Petals:* Coat 2 inches at one end of one matching wire with glue. Sandwich the glue-coated wire, centered, between two petals, letting the uncoated end of the wire extend beyond the bottom of the petals as a stem. Make five more petals the same way. When the petals are dry, lightly touch their edges with the black marker if the fabric is red, or the red marker if the fabric is pink or purple. Touch the marked areas with the watercolor brush dipped in the nail polish remover, to soften the color. Let the petals dry.
4. *Assembling:* Set the six petals around one of the stamens and twist all the wires together. Lay the top end of a length of 16-gauge stem wire against the petal and stamen wires, and wrap all the wires together with masking tape. Wrap the entire stem wire with floral tape, adding the leaves as you wrap.
5. *Bleaching:* Shape the flower heads *(see photo)*. Using a cotton swab dipped in undiluted bleach, dot the inside of each petal at the base to remove a patch of color. Let the petals dry.

LILIES

Materials: Sized white organdy *(see General Directions, Step 3, page 136)*; 3-inch-wide green satin floral ribbon; 28-gauge covered wire dyed green *(see General Directions, Step 4)*; white glue; apple green pastel chalk; small watercolor brush; nail polish remover; green fine-point fabric marker; slice of white bread; red nail polish; 19-gauge wire; 16-gauge stem wire; masking tape; green floral tape.

Directions:
1. Pattern: Enlarge the half-pattern piece marked "Lily" in FIG. IV, 3 *(page 137)* on folded paper, following the directions on page 241. Cut out the pattern and unfold it.
2. Cutting: For each lily, cut twelve petals and two 9-inch lengths of the floral ribbon. Gently stretch the petal edges between your thumb and forefinger to ripple the edges.
3. Petals: Cut six 6-inch lengths of the green-covered wire. Coat 4 inches at one end of one of the wires with glue. Sandwich the glue-coated wire, centered, between two petals, letting 2 inches of the wire extend beyond the bottom of the petals as a stem. Make five more petals the same way. When the petals are dry, run the apple green chalk along their edges. Then touch the chalked areas with the watercolor brush dipped in the nail polish remover, to soften the color. Using the green fabric marker, make closely spaced dots at the base of each petal. Continue making dots for about 2 inches up the petal, spacing them farther apart. Let the petals dry.
4. Stamens: Remove the crust from the white bread and crumble the bread to cornmeal consistency. Mix the crumbs with some glue and knead the mixture with your hands until it forms a smooth dough. Wrap the dough in plastic wrap and keep the unused portion covered while you work, to keep it from drying out. Cut six 5-inch lengths of the green-covered wire. Pinch off a pea-size piece of dough and push the end of one of the wires into it. Form the dough into a small hammer shape and let it dry. Color the shaped dough with the red nail polish. Make five more stamens.
5. Leaves: Spread glue over the satin side of one of the 9-inch lengths of floral ribbon. Cut three 11-inch lengths of the 19-gauge wire. Place the wires, 1 inch apart, on the glue-coated ribbon, letting them extend 2 inches beyond one end of the ribbon *(see FIG. IV, 3B, Step 1, page 137)*. Place the remaining 9-inch length of ribbon, satin side down, on top of the wires, and let the glue dry. Cut the ribbon between the wires into three pieces, and trim each piece into a leaf shape *(see FIG. IV, 3B, Step 2, page 137)*.
6. Assembling: Place the six petals around the six stamens and twist all the wires together. Lay the top end of a length of 16-gauge stem wire against the petal and stamen wires, and wrap all the wires together with masking tape. Wrap the entire stem wire with floral tape, adding two or three leaves and, if you wish, another lily as you wrap. Shape the petals into a lily.
7. Buds: Using only three petals and no stamens, shape the petals to be slightly curved and facing each other. Attach them to the top end of a length of stem wire. Trim a leaf to be shorter and narrower than a full-size leaf. Wrap the entire stem wire with floral tape, adding the shorter leaf as you wrap. Bend the bud at a right angle to the stem.

MEASURE FOR MEASURE

When making Flowers That Last Forever, it's a good idea to make one sample flower of each type, using less expensive muslin, if you wish. This will allow you to become familiar with the shaping techniques and help you to estimate yardage requirements. Decide how many flowers of each type you wish to make. Figure the yardage needed based on the width of the organdy and how much muslin was required to make one practice flower.

A morning-glory at my window satisfies me more than the metaphysics of books.
—Walt Whitman

C O U N T R Y
G·A·R·D·E·N·S

He that plants trees loves others besides himself.
—Scottish proverb

A country garden can help you to "get away from it all"—right in your own backyard. There's something wonderfully satisfying about working the earth and reaping its bounty, whether you're planting roses or rosemary.

If your dream is a backyard full of color, imagine a virtually care-free garden overflowing with brilliant wildflowers. Or a canopy of grapevines providing fresh green shade for your patio. Want to make the most of a split-rail fence? Cover it with sweet-smelling cascades of wisteria, planted about four feet apart *(see photo at left)*. We'll give you get-growing advice on annuals, perennials, climbers and twiners plus tips on keeping your garden healthy.

You can also bring a breath of country air indoors with our beautiful window gardens. In addition to lovely displays and arrangements, you'll find information on growing plants in virtually every window in your house.

Indoors or out, herbs are a fragrant addition to any garden. This chapter shows you how to plant, tend, collect and preserve fresh herbs—all those wonderful seasonings needed for authentic country cooking or richly scented potpourris.

If you're an avid gardener, you know how rewarding working with plants can be. If you're a novice, start with something small to try out your "green thumb". Love for the land is an American tradition—and this chapter celebrates that pioneer spirit in all of us.

Country Ease: Your country garden should look casual, not manicured, and might include some of these traditional favorites (from front to back): clarkia, marigold, zinnia and ammobium.

T·H·E G·O·O·D
E·A·R·T·H

In The Pink

A glorious mass of pink and white flowers cut fresh
from your garden can brighten any room in your
house—or add a special touch to your patio table.
Consider a "mixed bag" of posies, using color as the
unifying factor. The blooms used in our bouquet
are:"The Fairy" rose, zinnia, cockscomb, feverfew and
aster. Grapevine leaves are used as accents.

The world's favorite season is the
spring. All things seem possible
in May.
— Edwin Way Teale

Your country garden can be started as early as April, if you wish. Begin with a visit to your local nursery, garden center or home center for seeds and plants. You'll want to buy the *perennials* as plants, because it will take a year for them to bloom if they are started from seed. The *annuals* grow quickly and easily from seed sown right in the garden. You also can buy most of the annuals as small plants (seedlings) to get a head start on colorful blooming plants in the garden.

A Plan for Planting

All the flowers for the garden shown on pages 144-145 need at least six hours of sun daily, so choose a sunny spot — in the middle of the yard, along a fence or property line, bordering a driveway or walk.

Plan to put all the perennials at the edges or back of the garden, or at least grouped together, so you won't disturb their roots when you dig up the spent annuals at the end of the growing season.

Before you begin to plant, work well-rotted manure (about 25 pounds per 100 square feet of garden) or fertilizer (approximately 1 to 1½ quarts per 100 square feet) into the top 8 to 10 inches of soil to enrich the soil.

Plant the perennials and the roses first. Set them into the ground at the same level at which they were growing in their containers.

Plant the annual seedlings from the nursery next. Follow with the seeds of annuals that can be sown directly into the ground, such as zinnia, strawflower, marigold, clarkia and cockscomb.

Water the entire garden area well.

The rest is up to nature, and a little help from you. You'll find growing tips for specific flowers on pages 148-149.

THE GARDENER'S GRAPEVINE

Write or phone these gardening organizations for advice, referrals, publications and membership information.

Men's Garden Clubs of America
5560 Merle Hay Road
Johnston, Iowa 50131
(515) 278-0295

•

National Gardening Association
180 Flynn Avenue
Burlington, Vermont 05401
(802) 863-1308
Specializes in food gardening

•

National Pesticide Telecommunications Network
1-800-858-7378
A 24-hour service that answers questions about pesticide use and safety

•

Scott's Lawn Care Hotline
1-800-543-TURF
In Ohio, call: 1-800-762-4010
Hotline for questions about grass and lawn care
Open 8 A.M.-5 P.M. EST, Monday to Friday

To own a bit of ground, to scratch it with a hoe, to plant seeds, and watch their renewal of life — this is the commonest delight of the race, the most satisfactory thing a man can do.
—Charles Dudley Warner

TOOLS OF THE TRADE

Edger: *Square- or half-moon shaped tool that quickly cuts through grass and simplifies removing it along the edge of a garden.*

•

Spade: *Essential for taking off sod and for working the soil in a new garden.*

Garden fork: *Useful for breaking up and loosening the soil.*

•

Straight-edge rake: *For smoothing a bed before planting once the soil has been loosened.*

Trowel: *Used to dig holes for plants and to make furrows for seeds.*

•

Drip hose: *A water- and time-saver; laid out in the garden, the small holes in the hose deliver water where it's most needed — to the plants' roots.*

•

Mulch: *A soil covering that helps prevent weed growth, it can be sheets of black plastic (covered with decorative wood chips perhaps), or 2 to 3 inches of organic matter, such as straw, buckwheat hulls or wood chips.*

•

Handweeder: *For weeding close to plants without damaging the plants' roots.*

THE FALLING LEAVES . . .

Deciduous plants shed their foliage at the end of the growing season. Evergreen foliage stays green all year long. To find out how these plants fare in your regional area, visit a local nursery or landscaper.

Perennials

Artemesia, also known as "Silver King," spreads quickly by underground runners. Its silvery gray foliage and tiny flowers are perfect foils for vivid or pastel flowers, both in the garden and in flower arrangements.

◆ Artemesia is drought-tolerant, so it can be ignored once it's planted.

◆ Keep the plant in bounds by periodically cutting through the soil around it to sever the runners, or by letting the small plants develop, digging them up and transplanting them to other parts of the garden.

Black-eyed Susan brings cheerful spots of deep yellow to the garden, and **Queen Anne's lace** yields delicately-shaped blooms.

◆ These hardy flowers will grow under almost any condition, even poor soil or drought, but they should be planted in shade.

◆ The seed pod of Queen Anne's lace is very striking in arrangements, but if you want to keep the plant from spreading out of control, cut off the spent flower before it goes to seed.

Feverfew (*Chrysanthemum parthenium*), a bushy plant with fragrant flowers, will reseed itself anywhere, even in cracks in the pavement, year after year.

◆ Feverfew tolerates light shade.

"The Fairy" rose truly is a beginner's rose. It is very disease-resistant, so the usual spraying seldom is necessary. It's also a rapid grower, and will provide clusters of dainty pink flowers in the garden from spring to fall.

◆ To get the best bloom, feed "The Fairy" in the spring, when its leaves begin to show, again when the first flowers have faded, and one last time in the middle of summer. Lightly work about a cup of fertilizer into the soil around each bush.

> *Spring is wonderful. It makes you feel young enough to do all the things you're old enough to know you can't.*
>
> — Franklin P. Jones

nnuals

Ammobium and **strawflowers** are very easy to grow from seed.

As with most annuals, it's a good idea to wait until all danger of frost has passed and the soil is warm before sowing the seeds.

Asters can be grown from seedlings or seed for late summer color.

They will grow in light shade.

Clarkia unguiculata is a wonderfully bright pink California wildflower that is a perennial in warm climates, an annual in cooler areas.

Broadcast (scatter) the seed; don't sow it in rows.

Give the plants extra water during long periods of drought.

Cockscomb (*Celosia cristata*) produces large flowers in shades of orange, red and gold. The flowers are striking in the garden, as well as in dried and fresh flower arrangements.

Give the plants extra water to get larger flowers.

Larkspur, also known as annual delphinium, blooms early in shades of blue, lavender, pink and white.

Sow the seed as early in the year as the ground can be worked, because larkspur starts growing best in cool weather.

Marigold, salvia and **zinnia** will flourish in spite of neglect.

Salvia and marigold can be started indoors from seed about four weeks before the last spring frost, but they'll grow just as well, flowering a bit later, if they're sown directly into the ground.

◆ Marigold and zinnia will grow in any kind of soil, poor or enriched.

The more often zinnias are cut for indoor bouquets, the more flowers they'll produce.

All three annuals will reseed themselves; you'll find tiny seedlings under the mature plants, or popping out of the soil the following spring.

Statice is both an annual (*Limonium sinuata*) and a perennial (*L. tataraica* or *L. caspia*). All grow to about 2½ to 3 feet in height.

◆ Statice will grow in any kind of soil, poor or enriched, sandy or rocky.

◆ If statice is used in flower arrangements, the stems can be left to dry upright.

DON'T LET MOSQUITOES BUG YOU

You can't eliminate mosquitoes entirely but, according to Roger Grothaus, Ph.D., of the Johnson Wax Entomology Research Center, you can keep them from making you their main meal. Try these tactics during warm-weather months:

•

Make yourself "ugly" to mosquitoes. Avoid using cologne, scented cosmetics and hair spray when you go outdoors. Mosquito-repellents (especially those that contain N, N-diethylmetatoluamide, or "deet," and ethyl hexanediol) help mask your scent; reapply repellents after swimming or perspiring.

•

Wear light-colored, loose-fitting clothes. Dark clothes are more visible targets, and tight-fitting ones are easy to bite through.

•

Mosquito-proof your yard. Use chemical sprays to zap mosquitoes in their breeding sites: tall weeds and grasses, shrubbery and stagnant pools.

•

Set up a smoke screen. Barbecues, torches, repellent coils and citronella candles provide natural barriers.

•

Blow mosquitoes away. Wind or light breezes can help, so pick a camping or picnic spot where the air circulates freely.

•

Avoid peak pest times — at sunrise and sunset.

TRY A LITTLE TENDERNESS

Try this "tender" treatment for insect stings: Mix ¼ teaspoon of meat tenderizer with 2 teaspoons of water to make a paste. Apply the paste to a sting soon after the sting occurs. Papain, a papaya enzyme used to break down the muscle tissue in meats, will neutralize the insect venom.

ONCE BITTEN . . .

Some people say that vitamin B_{12}, or thiamine, is a natural bug repellent. Taken orally, 200 mg for adults and 100 mg for children daily can make insects think twice before they bite.

*The trees are in their autumn
beauty,
The woodland paths are dry,
Under the October twilight the water
Mirrors a still sky.*
— William Butler Yeats

A Twining Vine

Grapevine, which climbs on its own, is a beautiful cover for a trellis, arbor or chain-link fence. Set plants 3 feet apart. Grapevine requires yearly pruning to yield a healthy, luxuriant vine.

Climbing Plants

Flowering vines, leafy climbers, winding ivies—the best fences come from nature. They can camouflage brick beautifully, bring wood into bloom or create a privacy screen—with only a minimum of help from you. The guidelines below and the plant chart on pages 156-157 will get you off to a great start.

Choosing a Climbing Plant

Your living fence will do better if you match the plant to the kind of structure on which it grows best.

♦ **Hook-ons** Some climbers, such as climbing roses, hook their thorns onto a support. They grow best on open fences, such as chain-link, split-rail and picket, as well as on arbors and trellises.

♦ **Grabbers** Trumpet creeper and English ivy are among the climbers that anchor themselves with tiny rootlets or suction-cup graspers. They grow best on open fences. If you wish to grow them on a solid fence or wall, train them on coated wire strung between eye-hooks embedded in the surface, or on a lattice placed a few inches away from the fence or wall. This allows air to circulate between the plant and the surface, and prevents rootlets from damaging wood.

♦ **Winders** Some winding varieties, such as grapevines and ivies, twine themselves around wires and other easily grasped supports. Other varieties—clematis is an example—have coiling tendrils and don't need assistance. They grow best on open structures such as trellises, arbors and chain-link fences. Heavy, woody vines, such as wisteria and grape, can loosen boards and shingles. Grow these varieties on rugged frameworks with open cross-ties that can support the vines' weight.

Getting Plants Started

♦ Dig the planting hole twice as wide and 1½ times as deep as the root ball.

♦ Mix the soil removed from the hole with an equal amount of peat moss or compost and, unless the soil is very sandy, add a quart of sand to improve drainage.

♦ Sprinkle 3 tablespoons of a complete fertilizer in the bottom of the planting hole. Foliage plants need food that is high in nitrogen. The first number on a fertilizer label indicates the amount of nitrogen: 12-6-6 means 12% nitrogen, 6% phosphorous, 6% potassium. Flowering plants need a low-nitrogen, high-phosphorous food. The second number on the label is your cue for phosphorous; look for 5-10-10 or 5-10-5. Cover the fertilizer with 2 inches of loose soil before setting in the plant.

♦ In the fall, feed the plants again by scratching fertilizer into the topsoil around the plants, and watering it in.

Keeping Plants Healthy

♦ Water the plants every 7 to 10 days during their first season.

♦ To insure that moisture gets to the roots, form a "well" around each plant when you set it in the ground: Build up a ring of compacted soil that is 3 to 4 inches high and about 2 feet in diameter. Fill the well when you water; the ring will prevent the water from running off before it soaks in.

♦ Help the soil retain moisture in the summer by mulching the plants. Spread a 3- to 4-inch-thick layer of bark or pine needles over the soil.

Pruning and Shaping

♦ Cut off dead or broken branches with sharp pruning shears. Don't leave stubs; cut back each branch to the start of another branch.

♦ "Head back" vines that are starting to grow out of control by snipping off the growing tips. This also forces branching, which creates a bushier plant.

♦ For prettier, longer-lasting blooms, remove spent (dead or dying) blossoms during the flowering season.

Brilliant Blossoms

Bougainvillea, which does best in warm climates, flowers in masses of brilliant pink. Space plants 3 feet apart. Bougainvillea can cover a wall or fence in just one season. Make sure the structure can support the weight of the plants as they climb over the top.

A WATERFALL OF GREEN

Create a dramatic effect for your garden wall with fabulous foliage. Algerian ivy, for instance, produces a lush "waterfall" of green. Set plants 3 feet apart. To encourage branching, periodically snip off the growing tips of stems.

A Rose is a Rose

Red roses tumbling over a white picket fence lend a pretty, old-fashioned note to any garden. Set plants 3 feet apart and 18 inches from a fence. Attach the canes (stems) to the fence with plant ties. As they grow, gently guide the curving canes over the fence. If you arch the canes and tie them in a more or less horizontal position, you will get more even blooms, because a blooming stem will grow from every leaf axil. Here are some basic guidelines for growing roses.

♦ Roses need at least 5 to 6 hours of sun daily to perform well.

♦ Plant roses where they don't have to compete with tree and shrub roots, in a place where soil drains well and air circulates freely.

♦ Roses need plenty of water. Soak them thoroughly at planting time. In dry weather, water roses slowly to a soil depth of 8 to 10 inches once a week. Put the hose on the ground underneath the bushes and let water trickle out for several hours.

♦ Feed roses three times during the growing season: in the spring as soon as the first leaves appear, after the first wave of blooms has passed, and in mid-summer. Use an organic fertilizer, if possible. Don't feed roses at planting time.

♦ In climates where temperatures seldom go below 10° Farenheit, no winter protection is necessary. In colder regions, mound soil up around the canes to a height of 10 to 12 inches after the first frost.

A rose by any other name would smell as sweet.
— William Shakespeare

All that in this delightful garden grows,
Should happy be, and have immortal bliss.
— Edmund Spenser

A Delicate Balance

Lend a soft touch of color to a drab area in sun or partial shade with violet trumpet vine. Set plants 3 feet apart. To keep the plants from looking unruly, prune them often during the growing season. Trumpet vine needs a strong support, such as a thick trellis against a wall, or the links of a chain-link fence.

A Wall of Firethorn

Add warmth and color to a plain wall by espaliering firethorn. To create an espaliered firethorn (trained flat against a wall), attach wires in horizontal tiers to the wall. Set a young plant 1 foot from the wall. Remove all but the main stem, and two branches that get tied to the first wire tier. When the main stem grows to the second tier, train another two branches along the second tier. Continue training the firethorn in this manner up the wall.

QUICK GLOSSARY OF GARDENING TERMS

Acid soil: Soil without lime and with a pH factor below 7. Acid soils are not as fertile as alkaline soils.

•

Alkaline soil: Soil with a high lime content and a pH factor above 7.

•

Basal volunteer: A new plant that emerges at or near the base of a plant. Also called an off-set, volunteers often can be separated and potted up individually.

•

Broadcast: To scatter seeds, rather than sow them in rows.

•

Crown: The juncture at which the stem and roots meet, usually at the soil line.

•

Disbud: The removal of unwanted buds, usually to encourage larger, longer-lasting flowers from the remaining buds.

•

Forcing: Causing a plant to flower sooner and more prolifically, or to mature ahead of its normal season, by subjecting it to additional light, warmth and fertilizer.

•

Heading back: Cutting back the upper or terminal portions of a plant to stimulate denser growth.

•

Jumping: Moving a plant up to a pot several times larger than its original container. This encourages extensive root development, but not top growth.

•

Pinching out: Pinching or snipping off the growing tips of a plant to force side-branching and bushiness.

•

Sphagnum moss: A relatively sterile medium used to root cuttings or, when mixed with soil and other ingredients, to pot plants in. It holds 10 to 20 times its weight in water. **Unmilled sphagnum moss** is coarse; **milled sphagnum moss** is ground very finely and mixes easily with soil.

•

Tender plant: A plant that will not survive a heavy frost or freezing.

•

Xerophyte: A plant capable of surviving arid conditions.

Spring Has Sprung

Enjoy spring indoors weeks before the first sign of a leaf or bloom appears outside your window by forcing the branches of spring-flowering trees and shrubs into late-winter bloom. In the photo on page 159, forsythia blossoms herald the arrival of spring by adding a sunny yellow touch to an entryway. It's easy to force early blooming.

♦ On a sunny day, cut branches with flower buds on them (flower buds are plumper and rounder than leaf buds).

♦ Bring the branches indoors and place them in containers of warm water for about 30 minutes.

♦ Put the branches in cold water and set them in a cool, dimly lighted spot—the garage or basement.

♦ Mist the branches once or twice a day.

♦ When you see the buds beginning to swell, move the branches into a brightly lighted room and watch as they burst into bloom. No matter what the weather is like outdoors, you'll have spring inside your house.

Good choices for forcing: Alder, azalea, cherry, crab apple, dogwood, forsythia, early-blooming magnolia, pussy willow, redbud, rhododendron (only if you were planning to prune the shrub this year) and witch hazel.

PAINT YOUR WAGON

Once a child's small wheelbarrow or wagon has been outgrown, it can be turned into a handy yard-and-garden helper. To add new life to an old wagon, scrape off old, loose paint with a wire brush. Lightly sand the surface and paint it a high gloss, bright color. Use the wagon to carry garden tools around with you, or fill it with pots of summer flowers. If you drill a few drainage holes in the bottom, you can even plant right in the wagon.

W·I·N·D·O·W
G·A·R·D·E·N·S

Inside Splendor

Why relegate window boxes to outside the windows? You can add the color and warmth of your garden to any room in the house by bringing one or two boxes indoors and filling them with plants that love bright sunlight. In the photo above, geraniums and variegated ivy make a colorful accent in the dining area.

A Bedside Nosegay

For a sweetly old-fashioned note, set potted African violets and Cape primroses in a group of baskets. It's simple to achieve a nostalgic effect by using a picnic hamper or similar basket, or by lining a basket with paper doilies. Keep the plants in individual pots that are hidden with layers of sphagnum or Spanish moss. When the plants are not in bloom, you can remove them and replace them with other plants.

Keep three things in mind when you're selecting plants for various rooms in the house: the plants' light requirements, their moisture likes and dislikes and, if you wish to combine different plants in one container, their compatibility (you don't want to put a water-loving fern in the same pot with a drought-tolerant cactus, for example, because one of them will die).

Remember, too, that plants in a grouping should complement each other with differing forms (tree-like, shrubby, trailing), heights, colors (dark green, pale green, creamy, variegated), flowers (seasonal or ever-blooming) and leaf shapes (long and feathery, round, arrow-shaped). However, a grouping of the same kind of plant or plant family sometimes can be effective.

The chart on page 163 includes plant families, such as cactus and bromeliad, as well as individual plants, to get you started creating rooms filled with healthy, gorgeous greenery.

A Touch of the Southwest

Liven up a bare but sun-filled landing with drought-tolerant cacti and succulents in all shapes and sizes.

Into the Mist

The bathroom is a perfect place for humidity-loving plants: an orchid in an ivy-covered basket, Boston fern, baby's breath and a *Dryopteris*.

PLANTS FOR THE HOUSE

L·O·W L·I·G·H·T   (No direct sun needed)

Plant Names	Water	Feed	Flower Colors	Foliage Colors	Growth Habits
Bird's nest fern *Asplenium nidus*	EM	Monthly	—	2	Broad leaf rosette
Caladium	EM	Monthly	—	5,6,7,8	Heart-shaped leaf, upright
Chinese evergreen * *Aglaonema*	EM†	Quarterly	Insignificant	2,4	Oval leaf, upright
Dieffenbachia *	SD-EM	Monthly	Insignificant	2,6	Upright clumps
Gold-dust plant *Aucuba japonica*	SD	Every 2 weeks	Purple	6	Shrub
Norfolk island pine * *Araucaria excelsa*	EM	Monthly	—	2	Feathery tree to 4 feet
Peace Lily *Spathiphyllum*	EM	Every 2 weeks	White	1	Leaf clusters to 2 feet
Philodendron *	SD-EM†	Quarterly	—	2	Climber, trailer
Rabbit's foot fern *Davallia*	EM†	Monthly	—	3	Feathery, spreading
Rubber tree * *Ficus elastica*	SD-EM	Twice yearly	—	1	Broad leaf tree to 6 feet
Snake plant * *Sansevieria*	SD	Quarterly	Insignificant	1,6	Upright clumps
Spider plant *Chlorophytum*	EM†	Monthly	White	1,6	Trailing plantlets
Wandering jew *Tradescantia*	EM†	Monthly	White	2,6	Trailer

M·E·D·I·U·M L·I·G·H·T   (Some direct sun preferred in morning or afternoon)

Plant Names	Water	Feed	Flower Colors	Foliage Colors	Growth Habits
African violet *Saintpaulia*	EM	Every 2 weeks	Pink, blue, white, lavender, bicolor	1,6	Rosette, semitrailer
Baby's tears *Helxine soleirolii*	EM†	Monthly	—	2	Tiny leaf, spreader
Boston fern *Nephrolepis exaltata*	EM†	Every 2 weeks	—	3	Pendulous, feathery
Cape primrose *Streptocarpus*	EM	Every 2 weeks	Pink to purple	1	Rosette
Croton *Codiaeum*	EM	Monthly	—	7,8	Shrub
Crown of thorns * *Euphorbia milii*	SD	Monthly	Red, yellow	2	Shrub, thorny
Dracaena marginata *	EM†	Twice yearly	—	2,6,7,8	Slender leaf tree
Dryopteris **	EM†	Monthly	—	2	Feathery fern
Gloxinia *Sinningia*	EM	Every 2 weeks	Purple, red, lavender, bicolor	2	Rosette
Ivy *Hedera helix*	EM†	Every 2 weeks	—	1,6	Trailer
Maidenhair fern *Adiantum*	EM†	Twice yearly	—	3	Feathery
Orchids *	EM	Monthly	White, lavender, purple, bicolor	1,7	Depends on genus
Pigmy date palm *Phoenix roebelenii*	EM†	Quarterly	—	1	Feathery tree to 6 feet
Pothos **	SD-EM	Every 2 months	—	6	Climber, trailer
Schefflera **	SD†	Monthly	—	1	Shrub
Succulents *	SD	Monthly	—	1,3,4,6	Rosettes, trailers
Weeping fig *Ficus benjamina*	EM†	Monthly	—	2	Pendulous tree to 6 feet

H·I·G·H L·I·G·H·T   (As much direct sun as possible)

Plant Names	Water	Feed	Flower Colors	Foliage Colors	Growth Habits
Bromeliads **	EM	Monthly	Red, yellow, violet	1,2,6,7	Rosette
Cactuses	SD	Twice yearly	Red, yellow, white	1,2	All forms
Coffee tree ** *Coffea arabica*	EM	Monthly	White	1	Tree to 6 feet
Flowering maple ** *Abutilon*	EM†	Monthly	Red, yellow	2,6	Upright, trailer
Geranium *Pelargonium*	SD-EM	Monthly	All colors but blue	1,2,6	Upright, trailer
Herbs	EM	—	All colors	1,2,3,6	All forms
Miniature rose	EM†	Every 2 weeks	All colors but blue	1	Tiny shrub
Pencil cactus *Euphorbia tirucalli*	SD	Twice yearly	—	1	Tree to 6 feet

Notes: Name: * = can take brighter light or more sun; ** = can take lower light or less sun. *Caution:* Parts of the following plants may be harmful, especially to children or pets: *Caladium, Dieffenbachia,* gold-dust plant, peace lily, *Philodendron,* crown of thorns, pothos, ivy, pencil cactus. **Water:** SD = let soil dry out between waterings to a depth of 1 inch in small pots, 3 inches in large (10 inches +) pots and those containing cactuses and succulents; EM = keep soil evenly damp, but not soggy, and water when soil surface is dry; † = mist frequently. **Foliage Colors:** 1 = deep green; 2 = medium green; 3 = light green; 4 = blueish tinge; 5 = mostly cream; 6 = variegated green and cream or yellow; 7 = variegated green and red; 8 = variegated green, cream and red or pink.

A Country Welcome

Need inspiration for a delightfully different room divider? "Plant" one! Ours is a simple pine table overflowing with seasonal flowering plants that do well in indirect sun, and accented by some country offerings: a sheaf of wheat, a plate of nuts (with an old-fashioned nutcracker) and cinnamon sticks and a pretty piece of china. The plants shown on the table are, from left, bromeliads, croton and gloxinias. They're surrounded by a mini-forest on the floor (*from top left*): *Ficus, Dracaena,* Chinese evergreen, *Schefflera* and a pigmy date palm.

WINDOW GREENERY

Here's a brief rundown of different window exposures and the houseplants that grow successfully in them.

•

East (also southeast) — *where the sun lights up the window in the morning: Spider plant, begonia, geranium, asparagus fern, jade plant, umbrella plant, maidenhair fern.*

•

West (also northwest) — *where the sun arrives mid-afternoon: Creeping fig, ivy, African violet, snake plant, Christmas cactus, silver squill, coffee plant.*

•

South (also southwest) — *where direct sun may shine for as long as 6 to 8 hours daily: Column cactus, kalanchoe, aloe (also known as medicine plant), portulaca, club foot.*

•

North (also northeast) — *where the only sun is indirect, bouncing through a neighboring building or filtered through low-branching trees: Small-leaf wandering Jew, Swedish ivy, spider plant, rubber tree, split-leaf philodendron, coleus, Chinese evergreen.*

*There is no season such delight
can bring,
As summer, autumn, winter, and
the spring.*
—William Browne

Plants From Produce

You can grow houseplants easily from produce you buy at the supermarket. The following are growing guidelines from The Rare Pit & Plant Council.

Preparation

♦ Check all produce before you buy it. Don't purchase produce that has been chemically treated to retard spoilage.

♦ Select fresh, slightly overripe fruits.

♦ After eating the produce, wash the seeds or pits in warm water to get rid of any remaining pulp, and let the seeds dry.

Planting

♦ Plant the seeds or pits right away; they're viable only for a short time.

♦ Sow small seeds, pits and nuts in a sterile seed-starting mix in 2½-inch pots, or in compressed peat pellets that swell to 2½ inches when placed in water.

♦ Sow large pits and tubers in dampened peat moss placed in self-sealing plastic bags.

♦ Put the pots or bags on top of the refrigerator or in some other consistently warm spot; direct sunlight isn't necessary at this stage.

♦ Check daily to be sure the planting medium hasn't dried out; it should be kept damp, but not soggy.

♦ When the roots of the bagged large pits are approximately 4 inches long, transplant the seedlings to pots that are about 1 inch larger in diameter than the pits themselves.

♦ Once the seedlings grow a second set of leaves (the first leaves that appear when the seeds sprout are not true leaves), transplant the seedlings to 3- or 4-inch pots.

Growing

♦ Place young seedlings in indirect light; full sunlight will scorch them.

♦ Water seedlings sparingly; they should be moist but not soggy.

♦ Feed seedlings weekly with a balanced water-soluble fertilizer, such as 20-20-20, diluted to one quarter of the strength recommended on the label.

♦ Give each plant regular care to insure a long, healthy life.

Avocado (Persea americana)

♦ Avocado is available all year in supermarkets.

♦ The avocado pit is one of the easiest to grow, but do the following to raise an attractive plant: When the stem is 6 inches tall, cut it back to 4 inches, cutting directly above the spot where a tiny leaf is forming. The stem will branch at that spot. As the branches grow, periodically pinch off their growing tips to promote fullness.

♦ Avocado pits can be started and grown in soil or water. To start an avocado pit in soil, leave the top 1 to 1½ inches of the pit exposed above the soil. To start a pit in water, partially insert three toothpicks into the pit, spacing them evenly around the middle. "Hang" the pit in a glass of water by resting the toothpicks on the rim of the glass, immersing the bottom half of the pit in the water.

Light: A sunny east window, or 2 feet back from a south or west window.

Water: Keep the soil evenly moist; the leaves will turn brown if the soil dries out.

Chinese Star Apple (Averrbou carambola)

♦ The fruit is available in most food stores from fall to spring; it is a yellow, waxy, 3- to 4-inch-long oblong that has brown ridges when it is ripe.

♦ The Chinese star apple is a graceful, slow-growing, conical tree. Its leaves close at night.

♦ The seeds sprout in 10 to 14 days.

Light: A sunny east or south window.

Water: Keep the soil evenly moist; never let it dry out completely.

Citrus Fruits:
Grapefruit (Citrus paradisi)
Kumquat (Fortunella margarita)
Lemon (C. limon)
Orange (C. mitis and other species, hybrids)

♦ Citrus fruits are available all year, except for kumquat, which is available only in winter.

♦ Citrus plants are attractive windowsill plants when they are young, and striking accent trees when they mature.

♦ Citrus seeds sprout in about two weeks if they are given a warm spot (75° to 80°) in which to grow. The plants grow slowly, and should be repotted every year until they are in 8- to 10-inch containers.

Light: A sunny east or south window.

Water: Allow the soil of most citrus plants to dry an inch or two below the surface between waterings, but keep a kumquat plant's soil evenly moist. Mist leaves occasionally, especially if the plants are surrounded by hot, dry air.

Coffee Tree (*Coffea arabica*)

Green coffee beans are available all year in gourmet food stores; do not plant roasted coffee beans. If possible, get a fresh, bright-red "cherry" from a growing coffee tree. Plant the entire bean that is inside the "cherry"—don't split the bean.

The coffee tree, with its fragrant flowers, is easy to grow and can reach 6 to 7 feet in height indoors. Repot the plant each year in a container that is 1 to 2 inches larger than the old container until the plant is in an 8- to 10-inch pot. Thereafter, top-dress the plant yearly by removing the top 1 to 2 inches of soil and replacing it with fresh soil.

Planted green coffee beans sprout in approximately 10 to 14 days.
Light: A sunny east window, or a few feet back from a south window.
Water: Keep the soil evenly moist; the tips and edges of the leaves will turn brown if the soil dries out.

Mango (*Mangifera indica*)

The fruit is available all year in Oriental and Hispanic specialty food stores and in supermarket gourmet sections.

♦ A beautiful plant, mango has leaves that turn from red to deep green as they mature. The plant flowers easily and is a fast grower when it is young.

Pry open each husk to get to the large seed inside. The seeds sprout in two to three weeks.
Light: A sunny east, south or west window.
Water: Keep the soil evenly moist.

Passion Flower (*Passiflora edulis*)

The fruit is available all year in some grocery stores and in supermarket gourmet sections.

A fast-growing vining plant, the passion flower will climb on a trellis or around a circular wire frame. Its flowers are exquisitely beautiful.

The seeds are small; a single fruit contains hundreds. Wash and plant the seeds immediately, and they will sprout in two to three weeks.
Light: Not particular; a sunny or a shady window is fine.
Water: Keep the soil evenly moist.

Peanut (*Arachis hypogaae*)

Raw peanuts are available all year in health food stores and in Oriental specialty food stores.

The peanut vine is small, growing only about 1½ feet tall. Its flowers, which form at the tips of the stems, grow into the soil where the peanuts will form. Plant the vine in a clear container to observe this process.

Planted peanuts sprout in 7 to 10 days.
Light: A sunny east or west window.
Water: Allow the soil to dry an inch or two below the surface between waterings.

Pomegranate (*Punica granatum*)

♦ The fruit is available in late fall in supermarkets.

♦ The standard pomegranate is very difficult to bring into bloom indoors. The dwarf variety will flower in one to two years from seed (seeds for the dwarf can be obtained from Park Seed Company, Greenwood, SC 29647-0001).

♦ The seeds take up to two months to germinate, so be patient. Don't let the soil dry out while the seeds are germinating. To keep the soil moist longer, slip the pot into a plastic bag and tie the bag closed.
Light: A sunny east or south window.
Water: Keep soil evenly moist, but don't mist the plant.

Sweet Potato (*Ipomoea batatas*)

♦ The tubers are available all year in supermarkets.

♦ The sweet potato vine is very easy and quick to grow. It will climb on a trellis or around a window frame, or it can be allowed to hang down from a container.

♦ Start the tuber the same way you would an avocado—suspended in a glass of water.
Light: A sunny east or south window; diffuse sunlight in a window shaded by trees or buildings.
Water: If you keep the sweet potato vine growing in water, be sure the water level just covers the bottom of the tuber.

H·E·R·B
G·A·R·D·E·N·S

The Great Indoors

Bring the country charm of an herb garden indoors. Plant a variety of herbs together in several different types of containers (baskets, terra cotta pots, pottery, and so on) and place the containers in a casual arrangement on your kitchen windowsill. The herbs will lend an "outdoorsy" air to your kitchen, and also will be handy for cooking purposes.

Potted Plots

If you live in the city, or if you like to have fresh herbs close at hand, you can plant herbs in a strawberry planter or in several large pots grouped together on the terrace or patio. Try planting a variety of herbs in one pot—the hodge-podge look of several different plants in one container will heighten the "country" quality of your herb mini-garden.

re you tired of regularly watering, spraying and fertilizing your garden? If you long for a garden that can flourish on its own, plant an herb garden—this type of garden thrives on neglect.

Herb gardens require very little maintenance. Rainfall provides all the water herbs need, except during a long summer drought. Their aromatic oils repel most insects, eliminating the need for pesticides (which shouldn't be sprayed on edible herbs). Unlike vegetable gardens, herbs don't require periodic applications of fertilizer. In fact, too much fertilizer produces lush foliage—lovely to look at, but those lush green leaves have less aromatic oils and flavor.

A successful herb garden must have plenty of sun, good soil and good drainage. Herbs need at least five hours of sun daily, so select the sunniest patch in your yard. If possible, plant the garden close to your kitchen door; it makes quick dashes for fresh herbs a lot easier. An 8 x 4-foot plot is an easy size to care for.

Contrary to popular belief, herbs don't grow well in poor soil. They do better in moderately rich soil, so work about two inches of compost or rotted cow or horse manure into the top layer of soil. (Some gardeners advise adding 5-10-5 fertilizer to the initial bed; this is necessary only if you add peat moss to the soil instead of compost or manure.) Be sure the soil pH falls in the 6.0 to 7.5 range (your county extension service will test the soil for you).

Poorly drained soil is the main cause of herb garden failure. To test how well the soil drains, dig a hole a foot wide and a foot deep, fill it with water and let the water set for an hour. If any water remains in the hole, you'll need to mix some sand with the soil to improve its porosity.

You now are ready to plant your herb garden. Basil, chervil, coriander, dill, fennel and sweet marjoram are easy annual herbs to cultivate (fennel and sweet marjoram technically are perennials, but they are so tender they're treated as annuals). Check the height the mature plants will have. Plant the short herbs in the front and the tall herbs in the back of the garden. Sow the seeds of annual herbs directly into the soil after all danger of frost has passed. Wait to sow basil seed until the soil has warmed up thoroughly; basil is very susceptible to damage from cold. Press the seeds into the soil, forming saucer-like depressions to catch water. Keep the seeds moist until they germinate. Thin the seedlings after they're 2 inches tall.

Plant perennials and biennials (a plant that lives for two years; parsley is a biennial) where they won't be disturbed during the winter. Many perennials have long germination times and slow growth, so it's best to buy young seedlings at a local garden center. Sage, rosemary, mint, oregano, tarragon, thyme, lavender and chives are perennial herbs. With the exception of rosemary, which is very tender, perennials can be planted outside after the last spring frost.

To plant herbs in containers, use a good commerically packaged potting soil or a soilless medium, which is lighter in weight.

Annual Herbs

These herbs are planted yearly.

Basil Available in many varieties and colors, basil can be grown from seed or nursery-grown plants. To increase the size and fullness of the plant, pinch off the growing tips of the stems often. When the plant begins to flower, harvest the leaves by cutting each branch just above its first pair of leaves. The basil plant will grow full-size again and be ready for another harvest in 3 to 4 weeks. Use the harvested leaves fresh, or freeze or dry them.
Site: Full sun.
Height: 2 to 2½ feet.
Flowers: Midsummer.

Cilantro Also known as coriander or Chinese parsley, cilantro can be grown from seed. Sow seeds every few weeks for a supply of fresh leaves throughout the summer.
Site: Full sun or partial shade.
Height: 2 to 2½ feet.
Flowers: Midsummer.

Dill Dill can be grown from seed. Sow dill seeds often until hot weather sets in. Pick the leaves before the plant starts branching.
Site: Full sun.
Height: 2 to 3 feet in flower.
Flowers: Midsummer.

Parsley A biennial (producing leaves the first year, flowers the second), parsley is difficult to grow from seed. It can be grown from nursery-grown plants as an annual and used for its leaves.
Site: Partial shade.
Height: 6 to 12 inches.
Flowers: Early summer the second year.

Perennial Herbs

These herb plants last for years, dying to the ground in winter and growing again from the roots in spring.

Chives Chives can be grown from seed or nursery-grown plants. Use the outer leaves, clipped at the base; they are the more mature growth.
Site: Full sun or partial shade.
Height: 1 to 2 feet.
Flowers: Early summer.

Mint Another tough herb, mint can be grown from divisions or nursery-grown plants. To prevent mint from taking over the garden, encircle the plant with metal stripping sunk into the soil, or periodically cut off runners with a spade.
Site: Full sun or partial shade.
Height: 2 to 3 feet.
Flowers: Mid- to late summer.

Oregano Virtually indestructible, oregano can be grown from cuttings, divisions or nursery-grown plants.
Site: Full sun.
Height: 1 to 3 feet.
Flowers: Midsummer.

Sage Available in many varieties and colors, sage can be grown from seed.
Site: Full sun.
Height: 2 to 2½ feet.
Flowers: Summer.

Thyme "Common" thyme is grown most often for culinary use. Plant seeds, cuttings or divisions.
Site: Full sun.
Height: 6 to 12 inches.
Flowers: Early summer.

Tender Perennial Herbs

These herb plants need special care in winter in areas where temperatures fall below freezing.

French Tarragon This herb cannot be grown from seed, so plant cuttings or nursery-grown plants. Space the plants 2 feet apart, because they spread. Protect the roots in winter with a thick mulch.
Site: Full sun or partial shade.
Height: 1 to 2 feet.
Flowers: Early summer.

Rosemary A beautiful evergreen herb with upright and creeping forms, rosemary can be grown from cuttings or nursery-grown plants. Rosemary should be wintered indoors in a cool spot, and the soil never should be allowed to dry out completely. Outdoors in summer, rosemary can withstand periods of drought.
Site: Full sun.
Height: 2 to 4 feet.
Flowers: Late spring.

Sweet Marjoram Usually raised as an annual, sweet marjoram can be grown from cuttings, divisions or nursery-grown plants. Protect the roots in winter by covering the soil with a 3- to 4-inch-thick layer of organic mulch (dried leaves, pine needles, and so on).
Site: Full sun.
Height: 2 feet.
Flowers: Midsummer.

TINY TROWELS

Regular-size garden trowels may be too large to use in small flowerpots. When repotting small plants, use an ordinary shoehorn instead; it makes an excellent pint-size trowel.

ollect fresh herbs on sunny mornings, just after the dew has evaporated. Don't be shy about pinching off leaves to flavor food; pinching stimulates plant growth. Just leave at least one third of each plant intact.

To preserve herbs, collect their leaves just before they flower. (Mints are an exception—harvest them while they're in full bloom.) Here are some methods for preserving herbs.

♦ *Air drying* Tie small bunches of stalks with string and hang them upside down in a warm, dry, dark place, such as a closet or an attic. When the herbs are dry and crisp, in about 10 days, strip the leaves from the stalks by placing the herbs on a clean piece of paper and rubbing the stalks between your palms until all the leaves fall off. With thyme, rosemary and oregano, strip the leaves by running your thumb and forefinger down the stalks. Discard the stalks. Rub the leaves through a fine mesh strainer to remove any stem bits. Store the herbs in air-tight containers. Be sure the herbs are dried completely before storing them, or they will collect mold.

♦ *Oven drying* Place the leaves on a baking sheet in a 100° oven, with the door slightly open, for about 90 minutes; be sure not to burn the leaves. Or place the leaves between pieces of paper toweling and heat them in a microwave oven for about one minute; this method retains color best.

♦ *Freezing* This method works wonderfully with basil, marjoram, tarragon, mint, dill and chives. Blanch the herbs in boiling water. Submerge them in cold water and drain them well. Wrap the herbs in plastic wrap or aluminum foil and freeze them. Be sure to label all the packages, because frozen herbs often are difficult to identify. When needed, chop off the desired amounts. Frozen herbs retain their flavor for about 2 months, but they can become limp when thawed, so they're best used in cooking.

Cooking with Herbs

Basil has a hint of mint and anise flavor that is just right for chicken, fish and pasta dishes, or in a tomato-mozzarella combination. Add it raw, as a garnish, or at the very last moment of cooking.

Chives offer a delicate oniony taste that jazzes up eggs, burgers, vegetables, cottage cheese, cocktail dips and more. Sprinkle it fresh on food just before serving.

Cilantro, also known as coriander, has an exotic lemon and lavender-laced flavor that nicely balances hot, spicy foods, such as salsa and chili. It's most potent uncooked.

Dill, light and lemony, enhances soups, sauces, fish, poultry and salad dressings. The fresh leaves are good raw in dressings, or added at the end of cooking.

Marjoram, a mellower version of oregano, goes wonderfully with tomato dishes and with summer vegetables such as zucchini or eggplant. Add it fresh, toward the end of cooking.

Mint is marvelous, and potent, so use it sparingly. It lends a cool, refreshing edge to fruit salads, vegetables, and, of course, roast leg of lamb. Use it cooked or raw.

Oregano gives a zesty accent to Greek, Italian and Mexican cooking. Strong and aromatic, it wakes up pizza, eggs, vegetables, pork and poultry. It also can be served raw in salads.

Parsley, either the curly variety, or the more flavorful flat-leaf Italian variety *(shown in photo, page 173)*, has a pleasantly mild taste. Serve it raw as a garnish, and in salads or salad dressings. Serve it cooked in soups or in meat, vegetable and fish dishes.

Rosemary has a pinelike taste that stands up well to hours of cooking. It adds a special touch to roasted poultry or beef, as well as to stuffings and vegetables, and is especially good with mushrooms.

Sage has a minty flavor that complements meats such as veal or pork, as well as duck. It's also a hit in poultry stuffings and sausages, panfried with calf's liver or cooked in other dishes.

Tarragon, a favorite of French chefs, has a subtle but distinctive anise flavor that goes well with fish, poultry, eggs and sauces. It also livens up tartar sauce. Use it cooked or raw.

Thyme, with its pungent flavor and gentle aroma of mint and lemon peel, is delicious on roasted meats or added to stews, casseroles, soups and sauces. It also works well with other herbs. Cook it briefly.

Marjoram
Thyme
Chives
Parsley
Cilantro
Rosemary
Basil
Mint
Dill
Tarragon
Oregano
Sage

Herb Power

Fresh or dry, herbs add a wonderful flavor to many dishes. To get the most from cooking with herbs, follow these tips.

♦ Rinse fresh herbs in cold water before using them, and remove any discolored leaves.

♦ One herb can perk up food, two can be twice as nice. However, be cautious when trying out new herbs; it's easy to overwhelm the flavor of food with strong herbs such as sage and rosemary.

♦ Fresh herbs generally don't stand up to long cooking; add them right before the dish is done.

♦ To keep herbs fresh for a day or two after picking, place them in an airtight glass jar or plastic container and refrigerate them.

♦ When substituting frozen herbs for fresh herbs in cooking, use the same amounts.

♦ Dried herbs are stronger than fresh herbs, so use 1 teaspoon of dried herbs in place of 1 *tablespoon* of fresh herbs.

♦ Store dried herbs away from heat in a cool, dimly lit place. Dried herbs will keep for up to a year; after that, they should be replaced.

COUNTRY
C·O·O·K·I·N·G

'Tis an ill cook that cannot lick his own fingers.
—William Shakespeare

What would country living be without home cooking? Fragrant apple pie baking in the oven . . . steamy homemade soup dished up on a wintery night . . . crunchy sweet corn at a family picnic . . . tastes that don't need to be dressed up with exotic vegetables and hard-to-find spices.

Country living means hospitality—nothing fancy, just a relaxing good time. In this chapter we give you recipes for a chill-chasing family supper and a casual picnic for a crowd. Some of the dishes take a little work, but nothing good comes easy.

We also give you recipes for delicious breads and sweets like Grandma used to bake. Old-Fashioned Wheat Bread, Applesauce Cake, Walnut Raisin Carrot Loaf . . . the kids will love 'em and so will the adults! Make extra to send to your camper or to your collegian far from home.

You'll find fresh ideas for using farmstand produce. Our "pick of the crop" recipes feature healthy salads and side dishes, as well as an array of remarkable desserts, such as Blueberry Buttermilk Cake, Cheese Apple Cobbler and Plum Chiffon Pie.

We stayed away from fancy techniques and names you can't pronounce to bring you the kind of good food your family loves, the kind of cooking that lets you know you're home.

The kitchen really is the heart of a country home. Displaying all your ingredients can be terrific inspiration for whipping up something delicious—and it's a beautiful country look as well.

HOT AND HEARTY SUPPER

(for 8)

*Sweet Pepper Tomato Soup**

*Belgian Endive and Boston Lettuce
with Cumin Vinaigrette**

*Shepherd's Pie**

*Honey-Glazed Peas**

*Creamy Corn Casserole**

*Apple Walnut Tart**

*Lemon Butter Cake**

*English Stilton Cheese with Fresh Fruit
and Crackers*

*Spicy Citrus Mulled Wine**

Coffee, Tea

*Recipe follows

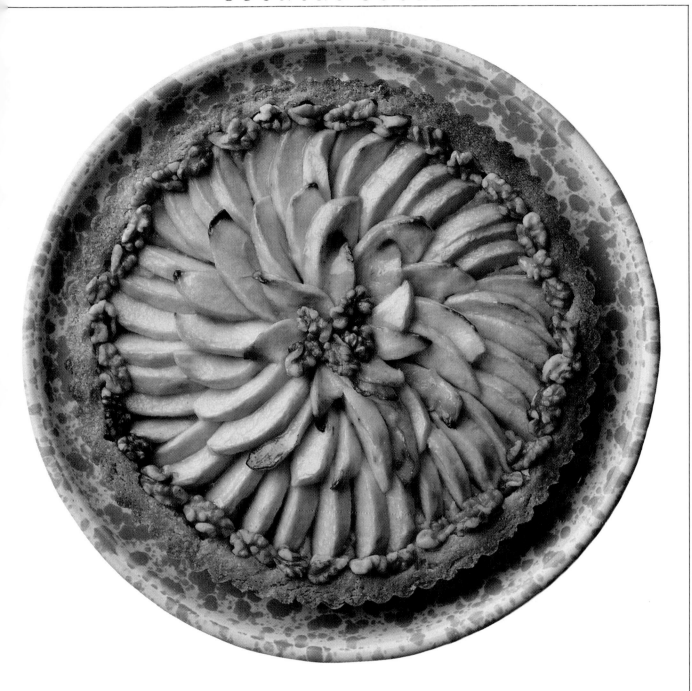

Apple Walnut Tart (recipe, page 182)

The friendly cow all red and white,
I love with all my heart;
She gives me cream with all
her might,
To eat with apple tart.
— Robert Louis Stevenson

SWEET PEPPER TOMATO SOUP

Makes 8 servings.

Nutrient Value Per Serving: 192 calories, 3 g protein, 14 g fat, 15 g carbohydrate, 43 mg sodium, 29 mg cholesterol.

5	tablespoons unsalted butter
1	teaspoon olive oil
1	large onion, peeled, quartered and thinly sliced
4	tomatoes (6 ounces each), peeled, seeded and chopped (3 cups)
2	sweet red peppers (6 ounces each), cored, seeded and diced (2½ cups)
1	tablespoon fresh thyme OR: 1½ teaspoons leaf thyme, crumbled
2	teaspoons sweet paprika
⅛	teaspoon sugar
6	cups Chicken Stock (recipe, page 185) OR: chicken broth
	Salt and pepper, to taste
1½	tablespoons all-purpose flour
¾	cup dairy sour cream OR: heavy cream*

Garnish:
1	cup finely diced ripe tomatoes
1	cup finely diced sweet green pepper
2	to 3 tablespoons snipped fresh chives

1. Prepare the Soup: Melt 3 tablespoons of the butter with the oil in a large casserole dish over medium heat. Add the onion and cook until it is soft, but not browned, for about 5 minutes. Stir in the tomatoes, red peppers, thyme, paprika and sugar. Cook over medium-low heat until all the tomato juices have evaporated, for about 25 minutes.

2. Stir in the Chicken Stock or broth and the salt and pepper. Bring to boiling. Lower the heat and simmer, partially covered, for 25 minutes, or until the vegetables are tender.

3. Strain the soup, reserving the broth and the solids separately. Place the solids in the container of a food processor or an electric blender, working in batches, if necessary. Cover and whirl until the purée is smooth. Whisk the purée into the reserved broth.

4. Melt the remaining butter in the casserole dish over medium heat. Stir in the flour. Cook, stirring, for 1 minute; do not let the flour brown. Slowly whisk in the soup and bring it to boiling. Lower the heat and simmer, partially covered, for 10 minutes. (The soup may be made ahead to this point and frozen.)

5. Whisk in the sour cream or heavy cream and just heat the soup through; do not let it boil. Season the soup with the salt and pepper. Serve the soup hot in individual soup bowls. Garnish with the diced tomato and green pepper and the chives.

Note: *For a lighter soup, omit the cream.*

BELGIAN ENDIVE AND BOSTON LETTUCE WITH CUMIN VINAIGRETTE

Makes 8 servings.

Nutrient Value Per Serving: 222 calories, 1 g protein, 24 g fat, 4 g carbohydrate, 145 mg sodium, 0 mg cholesterol.

2	heads Boston lettuce
4	heads Belgian endive OR: 2 large bunches watercress
8	radishes
2	small avocados
2	tablespoons lime juice

Cumin Vinaigrette:
12	tablespoons lime juice
2	teaspoons ground cumin
1	teaspoon salt
½	teaspoon ground white pepper
1	cup olive oil
½	cup vegetable oil
1	teaspoon grated lime zest (green part of rind only)

1. Remove and discard discolored or bruised leaves from the Boston lettuce. Remove the remaining leaves and wash them in several changes of cold water. Dry the leaves in a salad spinner or blot them dry with paper toweling; you should have about 16 cups. Set aside the Boston lettuce.

2. Cut the core end from the Belgian endive and remove the leaves. Or remove and discard any blemished watercress leaves and tough stems. Rinse the watercress leaves in cold water. Dry them in a salad spinner or blot them dry with paper toweling. Set aside the endive or watercress.

3. Cut the radishes into thin slices and set them aside.

4. Halve the avocados and remove the pits. Cut each half lengthwise into quarters. Remove the skin. Cut each piece diagonally into small slivers. Toss the avocado with the 2 tablespoons of lime juice in a small bowl and set aside.

5. Prepare the Cumin Vinaigrette: Combine the lime juice, cumin, salt, white pepper, olive and vegetable oils and lime rind in a small screw-top jar. Shake until the ingredients are well blended.

6. On each of 8 individual salad plates, arrange the Belgian endive spears, if you are using endive, in a star pattern, with the core ends meeting in the center of the plate. Arrange Boston lettuce leaves in a circular pattern on top of the endive. Top with watercress, if you are using it in place of Belgian endive. Arrange the radish slices and avocado pieces on top. Drizzle each salad with a little of the vinaigrette.

SHEPHERD'S PIE

A classic dish from the British Isles — hot, hearty and full of flavor.

Bake at 350° for 30 to 35 minutes.
Makes 8 servings.

Nutrient Value Per Serving: 462 calories, 24 g protein, 29 g fat, 24 g carbohydrate, 651 mg sodium, 86 mg cholesterol.

- 3 pounds lean ground beef
- 1½ tablespoons vegetable oil
- 3 medium-size onions, peeled and chopped moderately fine (about 2¼ cups)
- 3 medium-size carrots, peeled and chopped moderately fine (about 1½ cups)
- 1½ tablespoons tomato paste*
- 3 tablespoons all-purpose flour
- 1½ cups beef broth
- 1½ cups fresh vegetables (peas, carrots, beans and corn) OR: frozen mixed vegetables
- 1½ teaspoons salt
- ¼ teaspoon freshly ground white pepper

Topping:
- 7 medium-size potatoes (about 2.8 pounds), boiled until tender, peeled and mashed
- 3 tablespoons butter or margarine
- 4 to 5 tablespoons milk OR: heavy cream
- ¾ teaspoon salt
- ⅛ teaspoon freshly ground white pepper

1. Preheat the oven to moderate (350°).

2. Brown the ground beef in the oil in a very large, heavy skillet over medium-high heat for 3 to 4 minutes on each side. Break up the meat well.

3. Add the onion and the carrots. Cover the skillet and cook over medium heat for 5 minutes. Blend in the tomato paste, flour and broth. Cook, stirring constantly, for 3 to 5 minutes.

4. Stir in the mixed vegetables, the 1½ teaspoons of salt and the ¼ teaspoon of white pepper. Cover the skillet and cook over medium-low heat for 10 minutes. Transfer the skillet mixture to an ungreased, shallow 2-quart casserole dish.

5. Prepare the Topping: Mix the mashed potatoes with 1 tablespoon of the butter or margarine and just enough of the milk or heavy cream to make the potatoes fluffy. Season with the salt and white pepper.

6. Spread the mashed potato mixture over the top of the meat mixture in the casserole dish. Run the tines of a fork diagonally over the potatoes. Give the casserole dish a quarter turn and repeat with the fork tines. Dot the top of the casserole with the remaining two tablespoons of butter.

7. Bake, uncovered, in the preheated moderate oven (350°) for 30 to 35 minutes, or until the Shepherd's Pie is bubbly and lightly browned. Serve the Shepherd's Pie at once.

Note: *Leftover tomato paste can be frozen by the tablespoon in small plastic bags to use another time.*

HONEY-GLAZED PEAS

Makes 8 servings.

Nutrient Value Per Serving: 48 calories, 2 g protein, 2 g fat, 7 g carbohydrate, 55 mg sodium, 4 mg cholesterol.

- 2 packages (10 ounces) frozen green peas
- 2 tablespoons honey
- 2 tablespoons butter
    Salt and pepper, to taste

Prepare the frozen peas following the package directions. Drain the peas and place them in a bowl. Stir in the honey, butter and salt and pepper.

CREAMY CORN CASSEROLE

Bake at 350° for 35 to 40 minutes.
Makes 8 servings.

Nutrient Value Per Serving: 291 calories, 13 g protein, 22 g fat, 12 g carbohydrate, 623 mg sodium, 120 mg cholesterol.

- 2   eggs
- 1½ cups dairy sour cream
- 2   cups fresh corn kernels (from 3 or 4 ears)
  OR: 1 package (10 ounces) frozen corn kernels, thawed
- ½ cup fresh white bread crumbs
- 1   can (4 ounces) chopped green chili peppers
- 1   teaspoon finely chopped canned or pickled jalapeño peppers
- 1   teaspoon salt
- ¼ teaspoon freshly ground pepper
- 8   ounces Monterey Jack cheese, cut into ¾-inch cubes
- ½ cup (2 ounces) shredded Cheddar cheese

1. Preheat the oven to moderate (350°). Grease a 10-inch quiche dish or 6-cup shallow baking dish.
2. Combine the eggs with the sour cream in a large bowl. Mix in the corn, bread crumbs, chili peppers, jalapeño peppers, salt and pepper. Stir in the Monterey Jack cheese. Pour the corn mixture into the dish.
3. Bake in the preheated moderate oven (350°) for 35 to 40 minutes, or until a knife inserted in the center of the baked corn comes out clean. Sprinkle the top of the baked corn with the Cheddar cheese for the last 5 minutes of baking.
4. Let the dish stand on a wire rack for 10 minutes. Cut the baked corn into wedges to serve.

APPLE WALNUT TART

Bake at 350° for 45 minutes.
Makes 8 servings.

Nutrient Value Per Serving: 511 calories, 5 g protein, 28 g fat, 64 g carbohydrate, 197 mg sodium, 81 mg cholesterol.

- 1¼ cups all-purpose flour
- ¾ cup plus ½ cup firmly packed light brown sugar
- ½ cup (1 stick) butter
- 1   egg, slightly beaten
- 1   cup walnuts
- ¼ cup golden raisins
- 5   cups ¼-inch-thick, peeled, cored apple slices (2 pounds), Rome Beauty or Cortland
- ¼ cup (½ stick) butter, melted
- ½ cup walnut halves, for garnish (optional)
  Vanilla ice cream OR: whipped cream (optional)

1. Combine the flour with ¾ cup of the brown sugar in a medium-size bowl. Cut in the ½ cup of butter and the egg with a pastry blender until the mixture is crumbly. Shape the dough into a disk, wrap it in plastic wrap and refrigerate it for 1 hour.
2. Preheat the oven to moderate (350°).
3. Flatten the dough with a rolling pin on a lightly floured board to a 12½-inch circle; sprinkle with a little flour if the dough becomes too sticky. Transfer the dough to a 10x1-inch fluted tart pan with a removable bottom. Press and pull up the dough, making sure it is level with the top of the pan (like all sweet crusts, this one is difficult to work with). Press the dough firmly into the fluted side, keeping the dough a full ¼ inch thick; if the crust is thinner, it may slip down during baking. Place the tart shell in the freezer until it is very firm, for 20 to 25 minutes.
4. Grind the 1 cup of walnuts in a food processor for 2 seconds until it is coarsely ground. Sprinkle the ground walnuts and the raisins onto the tart shell.
5. Toss the apple slices with the remaining ½ cup of brown sugar in a bowl. Arrange the slices in a circular pattern on top of the raisins and walnuts in the tart shell. Drizzle the melted butter over the apple slices.
6. Bake in the preheated moderate oven (350°) for 45 minutes, or until the apples are soft. Cool the tart on a wire rack. Remove the side of the pan. If you wish, arrange walnut halves around the edge of the tart and serve the tart with vanilla ice cream or whipped cream.

LEMON BUTTER CAKE

Double your pleasure — two delectable cakes from one batter.

Bake at 325° for 1 hour and 20 to 25 minutes.
Makes 2 loaves (15 slices each).

Nutrient Value Per Serving: 524 calories, 7 g protein, 18 g fat, 86 g carbohydrate, 259 mg sodium, 117 mg cholesterol.

4²/₃ cups sifted all-purpose flour
2¹/₂ cups dried currants
2¹/₂ teaspoons baking powder
1¹/₄ cups (2¹/₂ sticks) butter, softened
2¹/₂ cups granulated sugar
3 tablespoons fresh lemon juice
1¹/₂ teaspoons vanilla
4 eggs
1¹/₄ cups lowfat milk

Glaze:
1 cup sifted 10X (confectioners' powdered) sugar
1 tablespoon lemon juice mixed with 2 teaspoons
    water OR: 4 to 5 teaspoons water

1. Preheat the oven to slow (325°). Grease two 9 x 5 x 3-inch loaf pans well.
2. Place ²/₃ cup of the flour in a medium-size bowl. Add the currants and toss well to coat them. Set aside the currants.
3. Sift the remaining flour with the baking powder onto wax paper.
4. Beat together the butter, granulated sugar, the 3 tablespoons of lemon juice and the vanilla until light and fluffy in a large bowl with an electric mixer. Beat in the eggs, one at a time.
5. Add the flour mixture alternately with the milk in 3 or 4 additions, beginning and ending with the flour mixture, and mixing after each addition just enough to combine the ingredients. Fold in the currants and the flour used to coat them. Spoon the batter into the prepared pans, dividing it evenly between the pans. Smooth the top of the batter.
6. Bake in the preheated slow oven (325°) for 1 hour and 20 to 25, minutes or until the cakes are lightly browned, springy to the touch and begin to pull away from the sides of the pans. Cool the cakes in the pans on wire racks for 15 minutes. Carefully loosen the cakes around the edges with a thin-bladed spatula. Turn out the cakes onto the wire racks and cool them, right side up, for 1 hour.

7. Prepare the Glaze: Whisk the 10X (confectioners' powdered) sugar with enough of the lemon juice mixture to make the mixture thick but pourable. Place wax paper under the wire racks. Drizzle the cakes evenly with the glaze. Before it hardens, smooth the glaze evenly over the tops of the cakes with a spatula. Let the glaze harden before cutting the cakes.

Note: *These cakes freeze well; wrap one tightly in plastic wrap and store it in the freezer to enjoy later.*

SPICY CITRUS MULLED WINE

Makes eight 6-ounce drinks.

Nutrient Value Per Serving: 347 calories, 0 g protein, 0 g fat, 49 g carbohydrate, 19 mg sodium, 0 mg cholesterol.

2 bottles (750 ml/each) dry red wine
1 cup light brown sugar
8 sticks cinnamon, 3 inches long
32 allspice, whole
32 cloves, whole
2 strips orange zest (orange part of rind only),
    each 1 x 4 inches long
2 cups orange-flavored liqueur OR: brandy
    Cinnamon sticks, for garnish
    Strips of orange zest, for garnish

Combine the wine with the cup of light brown sugar in a large enamel or stainless steel saucepan. Cut two 6-inch squares of cheesecloth and place 4 of the cinnamon sticks, 16 whole allspice, 16 whole cloves and a strip of orange zest on each square. Tie the pieces of cheesecloth into bags. Add the spice bags to the wine mixture. Bring the mixture just to boiling, reduce the heat to low and simmer for 15 minutes. Remove the spice bags with tongs and discard them. Stir in the 2 cups of orange-flavored liqueur or brandy. Pour the mulled wine into heatproof glass mugs. Garnish each mug with the cinnamon sticks and strips of orange zest.

H·O·M·E·M·A·D·E
S·O·U·P·S

Hearty Tomato and Rice Soup (recipe, page 186)

Soup of the evening, beautiful soup!
—Lewis Carroll

CHICKEN STOCK

Make stock the day before you plan to use it and refrigerate it overnight; the fat will solidify on top and can easily be removed. For stock-on-hand, freeze stock in ice cube trays, transfer the cubes to a freezer bag and store the cubes in the freezer for up to 8 weeks.

Makes 3 quarts.

Nutrient Value Per Cup: 41 calories, 0 g protein, 2 g fat, 5 g carbohydrate, 26 mg sodium, 0 mg cholesterol.

1   *3-pound chicken, quartered*
2   *pounds chicken wings OR: chicken necks and gizzards*
2   *large carrots, scraped and halved*
2   *large stalks celery with tops, halved*
1   *parsley root, scraped OR: 1 small bunch parsley*
1   *bay leaf*
1   *large leek, well cleaned, with 3 inches of greens OR: 1 large onion, peeled and studded with 1 clove*
⅛ *teaspoon salt**
6   *to 8 black peppercorns*

1. Combine the chicken, chicken parts, carrots, celery, parsley root or parsley, bay leaf, leek or onion, salt and peppercorns in a large casserole dish. Add 12 to 14 cups of cold water, or enough to cover the ingredients by 2 inches. Slowly bring the mixture to boiling, skimming off any scum that rises to the surface.
2. Partially cover the casserole dish and simmer the stock for 2 hours. Strain and cool the stock, uncovered, at room temperature. When it is completely cool, refrigerate the stock, uncovered, until the next day.**
3. Remove the fat from the surface of the stock and discard it. Transfer the stock to a casserole dish. Bring the stock to boiling. Pour it into 1-quart containers or ice cube trays. Cool the stock, uncovered. When it is completely cool, refrigerate or freeze the stock.

Notes: **You may wish to add more salt, to taste, to the stock if you will be using it to make soups.*
**Stocks must be cooled, uncovered, to prevent them from turning sour. If the stock has been refrigerated for 2 to 3 days, bring the stock to boiling and simmer it for 4 minutes before using it.

SAVORY LEEK SOUP

Makes about 16 servings.

Nutrient Value Per Serving: 78 calories, 2 g protein, 6 g fat, 6 g carbohydrate, 508 mg sodium, 8 mg cholesterol.

¼ *cup (½ stick) unsalted butter*
2   *tablespoons vegetable oil*
2   *pounds leeks OR: green onions, trimmed, well rinsed and thinly sliced*
2   *cloves garlic, finely chopped*
3   *tablespoons all-purpose flour*
2   *quarts Chicken Stock (recipe at left) OR: chicken broth, heated*
    Ground white pepper, to taste
    Salt, to taste

1. Heat together the butter and the oil in a large casserole dish or Dutch oven. Add the leeks or green onion and stir to coat them. Cover the casserole dish and cook over low heat for 15 minutes; the leeks should be very soft.
2. Add the garlic and cook over medium heat, uncovered, stirring frequently, until the leeks are lightly browned, for about 15 to 20 minutes.
3. Sprinkle the flour over the leeks and stir to combine the ingredients. Cook, stirring, for 2 to 3 minutes.
4. Slowly stir in the hot Chicken Stock. Simmer, partially covered, for about 30 minutes or until the flavor develops.
5. Season the soup with the white pepper and the salt. Serve the soup in mugs with your favorite crackers.

CREAMY CHEESE AND BROCCOLI SOUP

Makes 12 servings.

Nutrient Value Per Serving: 240 calories, 5 g protein, 21 g fat, 9 g carbohydrate, 237 mg sodium, 63 mg cholesterol.

Creamy Cheese and Broccoli Soup:
- 8 ounces Stilton cheese
- 7 tablespoons unsalted butter
- 1 bunch broccoli (about 12 ounces), trimmed, peeled and cut into 1-inch pieces (about 4 cups)
- ⅓ cup diced celery
- 1 cup finely chopped onion
- ¼ teaspoon white pepper
- 7 cups Chicken Stock (recipe, page 185) OR: chicken broth
- 2½ tablespoons all-purpose flour
- 1¼ cups half-and-half OR: heavy cream*

Vegetable Garnish:
- 1 medium-size leek, trimmed of all but 1 inch of greens, well washed and cut lengthwise into fine julienne sticks
- 1 celery stalk, cut into fine julienne sticks
- 1 cup tiny broccoli flowerets

1. Prepare the Soup: Trim the Stilton cheese of its outer yellow-brown crust and use only the center. You should have about 6 ounces. Crumble the cheese and set it aside.
2. Melt 4 tablespoons of the butter in a large, heavy casserole dish over medium heat. Add the broccoli, celery, onion and white pepper. Partially cover the dish and simmer just until tender, for about 5 minutes.
3. Stir in the Chicken Stock or broth. Bring the mixture to boiling. Lower the heat and simmer, covered, for 30 to 35 minutes, or until the vegetables are very tender.
4. Strain the soup, reserving the solids and liquid separately. Place the solids, with ½ cup of the reserved liquid, in the container of a food processor. Cover and whirl until the purée is very smooth. Whisk the purée into the remaining reserved liquid and set aside.
5. Melt the remaining butter in the casserole dish over medium heat. Whisk in the flour and cook, whisking constantly, until the mixture is hazelnut brown, for

about 2 minutes; be very careful not to scorch the flour. Add the purée and whisk until the ingredients are blended. Bring mixture to boiling. Lower the heat and simmer, whisking occasionally, for 15 minutes.
6. Combine the half-and-half or heavy cream with the Stilton cheese in the container of a food processor. Cover and whirl until the cheese mixture is smooth. Whisk the cheese mixture into the casserole dish until all the ingredients are well blended. Heat the soup just until it is heated through; do not boil the soup.
7. Stir the leek and celery sticks and the broccoli flowerets into the soup. Cook just until the vegetable garnishes are tender. Serve the soup hot.

Note: For a lighter soup, omit the half-and-half. Reserve 1 cup of the liquid broth after straining the soup and purée the Stilton cheese with the reserved liquid rather than with the half-and-half.

HEARTY TOMATO AND RICE SOUP

Makes 8 servings.

Nutrient Value Per Serving: 213 calories, 21 g protein, 5 g fat, 22 g carbohydrate, 665 mg sodium, 56 mg cholesterol.

- 1½ pounds top round, cut into 1-inch cubes
- 2 quarts water
- 1 can (35 ounces) tomatoes, undrained
- 3 beef bouillon cubes
- ½ teaspoon freshly ground pepper
- ½ teaspoon leaf thyme, crumbled
- ¼ teaspoon leaf marjoram, crumbled
- 5 carrots, peeled and sliced ½ inch thick
- 5 stalks celery, sliced ½ inch thick
- 1 onion, coarsely chopped
- ½ cup uncooked white rice

1. Brown the beef in a large saucepan. Add the water and bring to boiling. Lower the heat and simmer for 20 minutes, or until the meat is almost tender.
2. Stir in the tomatoes with their liquid, breaking up the chunks with a spoon. Add the bouillon, pepper, thyme and marjoram. Simmer the mixture for 1 hour. Add the carrots, celery, onion and rice for the last 30 minutes of cooking.

WILD MUSHROOM SOUP

This soup is bursting with the wonderfully rich, earthy flavor of wild mushrooms.

Makes 6 servings.

Nutrient Value Per Serving: 276 calories, 5 g protein, 23 g fat, 15 g carbohydrate, 545 mg sodium, 75 mg cholesterol.

2   ounces dry Chilean mushrooms OR: shiitake, porcini or Polish mushrooms

2   cups warm water

4   cups beef bouillon

¼   cup (½ stick) unsalted butter

3   bunches green onions, trimmed of 2 inches of greens, thinly sliced (3 cups)

2   cloves garlic, peeled and smashed

⅛   teaspoon freshly ground black pepper

3   tablespoons all-purpose flour

1   cup heavy cream

3   to 4 tablespoons finely chopped parsley, for garnish

6   fresh white button mushrooms, stemmed and thinly sliced, for garnish

1. Combine the Chilean mushrooms with the warm water in a medium-size bowl. Set the mushrooms aside to soak for 30 minutes, or until they are softened. Carefully lift the mushrooms out of the water and set them aside. Strain the water through a fine-meshed sieve lined with paper toweling or cheesecloth, and set aside. Run the mushrooms under cold water to remove any remaining grit.

2. Combine the soaked mushrooms, and soaking liquid with the bouillon in a medium-size saucepan. Bring the mixture to boiling over medium heat. Lower the heat and simmer, covered, for 30 minutes, or until the mushrooms are tender. Drain the mushrooms, reserving the cooking liquid. Finely chop the mushrooms. Strain the cooking liquid through a fine-meshed sieve lined with paper toweling or cheesecloth to make certain no grit remains. Reserve the cooking liquid and the mushrooms separately.

3. Melt the butter in a heavy-bottomed casserole dish over low heat. Add the green onion, garlic, black pepper and 2 to 3 tablespoons of the reserved cooking liquid. Cover the casserole dish and cook until the green onion is soft, for about 3 minutes.

4. Whisk in the flour until it is well blended. Add the remaining reserved cooking liquid. Bring the mixture to boiling. Lower the heat and add the reserved mushrooms. Cover and simmer for 20 minutes. (The soup may be made ahead to this point and frozen.)

5. Stir in the heavy cream and cook just until the soup is heated through. Serve the soup at once, garnished with the parsley and the button mushrooms.

MARVELOUS MUSHROOMS

Select fresh mushrooms with caps that are tightly closed so the gills on the underside are not visible. Mushrooms contain a lot of water, so as they age, the water evaporates and the underside opens up and the top shrivels. Store mushrooms, unwashed, in a ventilated container or a brown paper bag in the refrigerator. Rich in vitamin D, mushrooms are practically without calories. To clean, wipe the caps with damp paper toweling. If a lot of dirt clings to the underside, swish in a bowl of cold water; drain and pat dry. Wash only the mushrooms you're going to use immediately.

FAMILY REUNION PICNIC

(for 12)

*Sensational Spinach Soup**

*Spicy Pickled Shrimp**

*Corn with Lemon Lime Butter**

*Marinated Chicken and Vegetable Brochettes**

*Country Ham with Honey Mustard**

*Tangy Vegetable Salad**

*Confetti Salad with Fresh Basil Dressing**

*Mixed Fruit with Lemon Juice and Port**

*Hush Puppies**

*Strawberry Rhubarb Cobbler**

*Fudge Brownies With Amaretto Cream
Frosting**

Mint Iced Tea

*Old-Fashioned Lemonade**

Recipe follows

Country Ham with Honey Mustard (recipe, page 192);
Corn with Lemon Lime Butter (recipe, page 191)

A Jug of Wine, a Loaf of Bread
—and Thou
Beside me singing in the Wilderness—
— Edward FitzGerald

SENSATIONAL SPINACH SOUP

Hot or cold, this soup is beautiful to look at and a delight to eat.

Makes 12 servings.

Nutrient Value Per Serving: 71 calories, 3 g protein, 5 g fat, 5 g carbohydrate, 365 mg sodium, 7 mg cholesterol.

2   large cloves garlic, finely chopped
2   tablespoons chopped fresh tarragon
      OR: 2 teaspoons leaf tarragon, crumbled
2   tablespoons olive oil
2   quarts Chicken Stock (recipe, page 185)
      OR: chicken broth
1   pound boiling potatoes, peeled and cut into
      ½-inch-thick slices
2   pounds fresh spinach, well washed and
      stems removed
1½ cups dairy sour cream
2   teaspoons grated lemon zest
      (yellow part of rind only)
2   tablespoons fresh lemon juice
      Additional dairy sour cream, for garnish
      (optional)
      Additional grated lemon zest, for garnish
      (optional)

1. Sauté the garlic and the tarragon in the oil in a 2-quart saucepan for 20 seconds. Add the Chicken Stock or broth; bring to boiling. Add the potatoes and cook until they are tender, for about 10 minutes. Transfer the potatoes and 2 cups of the cooking liquid to the container of a food processor or an electric blender. Whirl until the purée is smooth. Transfer the purée to a serving bowl.
2. Add the spinach to the remaining broth mixture in the saucepan. Simmer for about 2 minutes, or just until the spinach is wilted. Purée the spinach mixture in the food processor or electric blender until it is smooth. Add the sour cream, lemon zest and lemon juice. Cover and whirl until all the ingredients are blended. Add the spinach mixture to the puréed potatoes.
3. Serve the soup hot or chilled. If you wish, garnish it with additional sour cream and grated lemon zest.

SPICY PICKLED SHRIMP

Along the coast of North Carolina, shrimp are considered the prized catch-of-the-day.

Makes 16 appetizer servings, or 8 entrée or salad servings.

Nutrient Value Per Appetizer Serving: 120 calories, 20 g protein, 2 g fat, 9 g carbohydrate, 262 mg sodium, 131 mg cholesterol.

4   pounds large shrimp in the shell
6   quarts boiling water mixed with 1 tablespoon salt
6   large silverskin onions OR: small yellow onions,
      thinly sliced
24 whole allspice
24 peppercorns
30 whole cloves
6   whole bay leaves
1   small lemon, thinly sliced
6   blades mace (optional)
6   cups cider vinegar mixed with 2 cups cold water

1. Cook the shrimp in the boiling salted water in a large kettle for 3 minutes. Drain. Shell and devein the shrimp.
2. Layer the shrimp and the onions in a 1-gallon glass jar, sprinkling them with the allspice, peppercorns and cloves as you go and tucking in, here and there, the bay leaves, lemon slices and, if you wish, blades of mace.
3. Pour in the vinegar mixture. Cover and refrigerate the shrimp for at least 3 to 4 hours.
4. Drain the shrimp well and serve.

Note: *After the pickling liquid is drained from the shrimp, they keep well in the refrigerator for 2 to 3 days.*

SWAP MEET

Plan some entertainment for your family reunion. Tell everyone to bring something that still is usable but that he or she wants to discard. You'll wind up with an array of items, from books, pictures and casserole dishes to radios, jewelry and clothing. Give each person a turn choosing a "treasure."

GRILLING SKILLS

To Grill Chicken Breasts, *skinned and on the bone: Spray the grill rack and both sides of the chicken breasts with nonstick vegetable cooking spray. For a 7-ounce chicken breast half, grill over medium coals, bone side down, for 30 minutes. Turn the chicken and grill for 5 to 10 minutes more, or until the meat no longer is pink near the bone.*

•

To Grill a Whole Fish: *Spray a grill basket with nonstick vegetable cooking spray. Preheat the grill basket on the grill or in a fireplace. Place the fish in the basket. Set the basket on top of the grill or in the fireplace. Grill the fish for 10 minutes per inch of thickness, measured at its thickest part. Turn the fish halfway through the cooking time.*

CORN WITH LEMON LIME BUTTER

Makes 12 servings.

Nutrient Value Per Serving: 147 calories, 3 g protein, 9 g fat, 18 g carbohydrate, 15 mg sodium, 21 mg cholesterol.

12   ears tender young corn, husked
½   cup (1 stick) unsalted butter or margarine
    Juice of 1 lemon
    Juice of 1 lime
    Large pinch ground white pepper

1. Place about 1 inch of water in a large pot and bring the water to boiling. Place the corn in the boiling water in the pot and cook it for 2 for 6 minutes, or until the corn is tender.
2. Melt the butter or margarine in a small saucepan over low heat. Stir in the lemon and lime juices and the ground white pepper.
3. Place the corn on a serving platter and brush the lemon-lime mixture over the corn. Serve immediately.

MARINATED CHICKEN AND VEGETABLE BROCHETTES

Broil or grill for 10 to 12 minutes.
Makes 12 servings.

Nutrient Value Per Serving: 73 calories, 10 g protein, 2 g fat, 4 g carbohydrate, 258 mg sodium, 22 mg cholesterol.

Soy Marinade:
    4   tablespoons fresh lemon juice
    4   tablespoons soy sauce
    2   tablespoons vegetable oil
    2   teaspoons finely chopped, peeled fresh gingerroot
    2   cloves garlic, finely chopped

    4   whole boned, skinless chicken breasts (about
        2 pounds), cut into 1½-inch cubes
    2   packages (10 ounces) frozen artichoke hearts,
        thawed and drained
   12   large mushrooms, trimmed and quartered
    4   sweet red or green peppers, halved, cored and cut
        into 1-inch pieces
    2   medium-size red onions, cut into
        1-inch pieces
        Hot cooked rice

1. Prepare the Soy Marinade: Combine the lemon juice, soy sauce, oil, ginger and garlic in a medium-size mixing bowl.
2. Add the chicken and stir to coat. Cover the bowl and refrigerate the chicken and marinade for several hours, or overnight.
3. Thread the chicken, artichoke hearts, mushrooms, red or green peppers and the onion in an attractive order on 12 metal skewers.
4. Broil or grill the brochettes 4 inches from the source of the heat, turning and basting with the marinade, for 10 to 12 minutes. Serve the brochettes with hot cooked rice.

COUNTRY HAM WITH HONEY MUSTARD

This classic of down-home cooking is a guaranteed crowd pleaser. Use leftovers to make fabulous sandwiches with the Honey Mustard.

Bake at 325° for about 4 hours, then at 375° for 20 minutes.

Makes sixteen 3-ounce servings, with ample leftovers.

Nutrient Value Per 3-Ounce Serving: 177 calories, 19 g protein, 8 g fat, 7 g carbohydrate, 1,278 mg sodium, 50 mg cholesterol.

16 pounds fully cooked, smoked, bone-in whole ham
1   cup firmly packed light brown sugar
⅓   cup Burgundy OR: other full-bodied red wine
½   cup chopped fresh herbs, such as parsley, sage, rosemary and thyme
    Honey Mustard (recipe follows)

1. Preheat the oven to slow (325°). Trim the rind, if any, from the ham. Cut off the fat covering to about a ¼-inch thickness. Place the ham, fat side up, on a rack in a roasting pan.

2. Bake the ham in the preheated slow oven (325°) for about 4 hours, or until a thermometer inserted in the center of the ham, without touching the bone, registers 150°.

3. Remove the ham from the oven. Raise the oven temperature to moderate (375°). Using a sharp knife, score the ham fat in a diamond pattern. Stir together the brown sugar and the Burgundy or other red wine in a small bowl until the mixture is smooth. Brush the wine mixture over the ham.

4. Bake the ham in the preheated moderate oven (375°) for 20 minutes, basting with the wine mixture once or twice.

5. Remove the ham from the oven. Sprinkle the herbs into the surface cuts in the ham. Let the ham stand for at least 15 minutes before carving. Serve the ham with the Honey Mustard.

Honey Mustard: Combine 2 cups of Dijon-style mustard or grainy mustard and 6 tablespoons of honey in a small bowl. Mix to blend the ingredients well. *Makes about 2½ cups.*

Nutrient Value Per Tablespoon: 27 calories, 1 g protein, 1 g fat, 4 g carbohydrate, 151 mg sodium, 0 mg cholesterol.

HERBAL ESSENCE

When using fresh herbs, such as parsley, thyme, rosemary or chives, hold the sprigs closely together and snip them with sharp kitchen scissors. You'll find the herbs will be light and fluffy, not bruised and wet as they often are when you chop them with a knife.

TANGY VEGETABLE SALAD

Try this remedy for the dog days of summer: an ice-cold salad with a tangy lemon dressing.

Makes 12 servings.

Nutrient Value Per Serving: 42 calories, 2 g protein, 2 g fat, 5 g carbohydrate, 43 mg sodium, 0 mg cholesterol.

3   large cucumbers (8 ounces each), peeled and sliced ¼ inch thick
18 medium-size radishes, sliced ⅛ inch thick
3   medium-size tomatoes (4 ounces each), thinly sliced
3   tablespoons chopped parsley
9   tablespoons lemon juice OR: your favorite bottled dressing
    Pinch salt
6   tablespoons finely chopped unsalted peanuts

Combine the cucumbers, radishes, tomatoes and parsley in a medium-size bowl. Add the lemon juice or bottled dressing and the salt. Toss to coat the vegetables. Divide the salad among 12 individual salad plates. Top each portion with ½ tablespoon of the unsalted peanuts.

CONFETTI SALAD WITH FRESH BASIL DRESSING

Bake beets at 425° for 1 hour.
Makes 12 servings.

Nutrient Value Per Serving: 194 calories, 2 g protein, 15 g fat, 15 g carbohydrate, 165 mg sodium, 0 mg cholesterol.

Fresh Basil Dressing:

- 6   tablespoons balsamic vinegar
- 1   teaspoon salt
- 1   cup olive oil
- 6   tablespoons chopped fresh basil

Confetti Salad:

- 8   beets (5 ounces each), tops removed
- 4   small zucchini (4 ounces each), cut into ¼-inch-thick rounds
- 10   tablespoons olive oil
- ½   teaspoon salt
- 2   cloves garlic, peeled and smashed
- 2   tablespoons balsamic vinegar
- 4   tablespoons chopped fresh basil
- 2   pounds green beans, stemmed
- 2   sweet red peppers, cored, seeded and cut into 1-inch cubes
- 2   sweet yellow peppers, cored, seeded and cut into 1-inch cubes
- 2   sweet orange peppers, cored, seeded and cut into 1-inch cubes
- 2   pounds red new potatoes
    Sprigs of watercress, for garnish

1. Prepare the Fresh Basil Dressing: Combine the vinegar with the salt in a bowl. Whisk in the oil. Add the basil.

2. Prepare the Confetti Salad: Preheat the oven to hot (425°). Wrap each beet in aluminum foil. Bake in the preheated hot oven (425°) oven for 1 hour, or until the beets are pierced easily with a knife. When they are cool enough to handle, unwrap the beets. Slip off the skins, using paper toweling or a paring knife and rubber gloves. Cut each beet into 8 wedges and place the wedges in a bowl. Drizzle with 4 tablespoons of the dressing.

3. Sauté the zucchini in 6 tablespoons of the oil in a large skillet until they are golden brown. Drain the zucchini on paper toweling. Toss it in a clean bowl with the salt, garlic, vinegar and basil.

4. Blanch the green beans in boiling salted water until they are crisply tender. Drain the green beans, run

them under cold water and drain them again. Transfer the green beans to a clean bowl and toss them with the remaining oil.

5. Blanch the red, yellow and orange peppers in boiling salted water until they are crisply tender. Drain the peppers, run them under cold water and drain them again. Toss the peppers in a clean bowl with 6 tablespoons of the dressing.

6. Boil the potatoes in their skins until they are tender. Drain. When they are cool enough to handle, peel the potatoes. Slice them into ¼-inch-thick rounds. Transfer the potatoes to a clean bowl and toss them with half the remaining dressing.

7. To serve, toss the beans with the remaining dressing. Distribute the vegetables among 12 individual salad plates. Garnish with the watercress.

HAVE FLATWARE, WILL TRAVEL

The next time you have a picnic at the beach, carry your utensils in the silverware basket from the dishwasher. Return the soiled flatware to the basket; you can put the basket right into the dishwasher when you get home for a fast and easy cleanup.

MIXED FRUIT WITH LEMON JUICE AND PORT

Makes 12 servings.

Nutrient Value Per Serving: 183 calories, 1 g protein, 0 g fat, 42 g carbohydrate, 6 mg sodium, 0 mg cholesterol.

- 18   tablespoons super-fine sugar
- 1   cup fresh lemon juice (from about 3 lemons)
- 1   cup ruby port
- ⅜   teaspoon white ground pepper
- 3   cups cubed ripe mango
- 3   cups cubed ripe papaya
- 3   cups blueberries
- 3   cups raspberries

1. Combine the sugar, lemon juice, port and pepper in a medium-size bowl. Whisk to blend well.

2. Add the mango, papaya, blueberries and raspberries. Stir gently to combine the ingredients. Serve the salad at room temperature, or chilled.

HUSH PUPPIES

Tasty morsels of fried corn bread—so named because, in the old days, they were fed to hunting dogs to keep them quiet while their masters ate.

Makes about forty 3-inch hush puppies.

Nutrient Value Per Hush Puppy: 32 calories, 1 g protein, 0 g fat, 6 g carbohydrate, 91 mg sodium, 7 mg cholesterol.

    Vegetable oil for deep-frying
2⅓ cups sifted stone-ground cornmeal,
        preferably white*
  4 teaspoons sugar
  1 teaspoon salt
  1 teaspoon baking soda
  ½ teaspoon baking powder
  ¼ cup very finely chopped onion
  1 large egg
1¼ cups buttermilk

1. Heat 1½ inches of oil in a deep skillet over medium heat until the oil registers 375° on a deep-fat frying thermometer.

2. Meanwhile, combine the cornmeal, sugar, salt, baking soda and baking powder in a large bowl, pressing out all the lumps. Whisk together the onion, egg and buttermilk in a small bowl.

3. Make a well in the center of the cornmeal mixture. Pour in the buttermilk mixture all at once and stir briskly just to mix the ingredients.

4. Scrape the batter into a pastry bag fitted with a large plain tip. Pipe the batter into a 3-inch-long cylinder onto an oiled pancake turner. Carefully slide the batter off the turner into the hot oil. Repeat, frying up to 6 or 8 hush puppies at a time. Fry the hush puppies, turning them as needed, for 2 to 2½ minutes, or until they are richly browned on all sides. Adjust the burner heat as necessary to keep the temperature of the oil at 375°. Skim any browned bits from the surface of the oil.

5. As the hush puppies brown, lift them with a slotted spoon and set them on a baking sheet lined with paper toweling to drain. Set the baking sheet, uncovered, in a warm oven (250°) until all the hush puppies are ready.

6. Serve the hush puppies hot with shellfish or with fried, barbecued or broiled fish or chicken.

Note: *Be sure to use stone-ground cornmeal; hush puppies made with granular meal come apart when they are fried in hot oil.*

STRAWBERRY RHUBARB COBBLER

A deliciously different version of the classic cobbler.

Bake at 400° for 25 minutes.
Makes 8 servings.

Nutrient Value Per Serving: 336 calories, 4 g protein, 5 g fat, 71 g carbohydrate, 427 mg sodium, 2 mg cholesterol.

  1 pound fresh rhubarb, washed and cut into 1-inch
        pieces, OR: 1 package (1 pound) frozen
        unsweetened cut rhubarb, thawed
        (about 4 cups)
1¼ cups plus ⅓ cup sugar
  ½ cup water
2½ tablespoons cornstarch
  2 pints fresh strawberries, washed, dried and hulled,
        OR: 1 package (1 pound) frozen unsweetened
        strawberries, thawed (about 4 cups)
  ½ cup milk
  2 cups buttermilk baking mix
  1 tablespoon grated orange zest
        (orange part of rind only)

1. Combine the rhubarb, ¾ cup of the sugar and ¼ cup of the water in a large saucepan. Cook over low heat, stirring occasionally, just until the rhubarb is tender; do not overcook.

2. Combine the remaining ¼ cup of water with the cornstarch and ½ cup of the remaining sugar in a bowl. Stir until the mixture is smooth. Stir the cornstarch mixture into the rhubarb. Cook, stirring constantly, until the rhubarb mixture thickens and bubbles. Remove the saucepan from the heat. Stir in the strawberries. Pour the strawberry-rhubarb mixture into a 2-quart shallow 11¾ x 7½ x 1¾-inch baking dish.

3. Preheat the oven to hot (400°). As it preheats, place the baking dish in the oven to heat the strawberry mixture, for about 15 minutes. Place a baking sheet on the oven rack below the baking dish to catch drips.

4. Stir the milk into the buttermilk baking mix in a medium-size bowl until a soft dough forms. Turn out dough onto a lightly floured surface. Knead dough 8 to 10 times. Roll out dough to a 13 x 12-inch rectangle.

5. Combine the orange zest with the remaining ⅓ cup of sugar. Sprinkle the mixture over the surface of the dough. Roll up the dough, jelly-roll style, starting with a long side. Cut the roll crosswise into 18 slices, each about ¾ inch thick.

6. Remove the baking dish from the oven. Arrange the slices on the top. Bake for 25 minutes more, or until the biscuits are golden brown.

FUDGE BROWNIES WITH AMARETTO CREAM FROSTING

A chocolate-lover's dream, made even richer by the addition of semisweet chocolate chunks and nuts.

Bake at 350° for 25 to 30 minutes.
Makes 4 dozen brownies.

Nutrient Value Per Brownie With Frosting: 197 calories, 2 g protein, 11 g fat, 25 g carbohydrate, 48 mg sodium, 28 mg cholesterol.

1	cup butter or margarine
¾	cup baking cocoa
2	cups sugar
4	eggs
2	teaspoons vanilla
1	cup unsifted all-purpose flour
½	teaspoon salt
1	package (12 ounces) semisweet chocolate chunks
1	cup broken pecans
	Amaretto Cream Frosting (recipe follows)

1. Preheat the oven to moderate (350°). Grease a 13 x 9 x 2-inch baking pan.
2. Melt the butter or margarine in a medium-size saucepan over low heat. Remove the melted butter from the heat.
3. Add the cocoa to the butter and stir until the ingredients are well blended. Add the sugar and mix well. Add the eggs, one at a time, beating well after each addition. Stir in the vanilla, flour and salt. Do not overbeat the batter. Stir in the chocolate chunks and pecans. Spread the batter evenly in the prepared pan.
4. Bake in the preheated moderate oven (350°) for 25 to 30 minutes, or until a wooden pick inserted in the center of the brownies comes out clean. Let the brownies cool in the pan on a wire rack. Frost the brownies with the Amaretto Cream Frosting.

Amaretto Cream Frosting: Beat ½ cup (1 stick) of softened butter until it is fluffy in a medium-size bowl with an electric mixer. Beat in 1 package (1 pound) of 10X (confectioners' powdered) sugar alternately with 2 tablespoons of amaretto and 2 tablespoons of milk until the frosting is smooth and a good spreading consistency.

OLD-FASHIONED LEMONADE

Make a batch of the lemon syrup and keep it handy in the refrigerator. Then, when you're ready for a cold glass of tangy lemonade, simply combine the water and ice with a little of the syrup.

Makes 12 servings.

Nutrient Value Per Serving: 127 calories, 0 g protein, 0 g fat, 35 g carbohydrate, 1 mg sodium, 0 mg cholesterol.

Lemon Syrup:

2	teaspoons grated lemon zest (yellow part of rind only)
2	cups lemon juice (from 8 to 10 lemons)
1½	to 2 cups sugar
9	cups water
2	lemons, sliced
	Ice cubes
	Fresh mint leaves OR: lemon slices, for garnish (optional)

1. Prepare the Lemon Syrup: Combine the lemon zest, lemon juice and sugar in a 4-cup glass measure. Stir to dissolve the sugar. Chill the syrup, covered, until you are ready to use it.
2. To make lemonade by the pitcher, combine the lemon syrup with the water and the sliced lemons in a large pitcher. Stir to mix the ingredients. Add ice cubes just before serving. Garnish with mint leaves or lemon slices, if you wish.
3. To make lemonade by the glass, measure 3 tablespoons of the lemon syrup, or to taste, into a tall 10- or 12-ounce glass. Add ice cubes and water, and stir to mix. Garnish with the mint leaves, or the lemon slices, if you wish.

Lemon Spritzer: Measure 2 to 3 tablespoons of the lemon syrup into a 10-ounce stemmed glass. Add chilled club soda, and garnish with a lemon wedge.

G·R·A·N·D·M·A'S
B·A·K·E·D G·O·O·D·I·E·S

Spicy Fruit and Nut Cake (recipe, page 197)

Bread is the staff of life,
but pudding makes a good crutch.
— Scottish proverb

SPICY FRUIT AND NUT CAKE

A cake that's so moist and tender, it practically melts in your mouth!

Bake at 350° for 45 to 50 minutes.
Makes 16 servings.

Nutrient Value Per Serving: 417 calories, 5 g protein, 23 g fat, 51 g carbohydrate, 150 mg sodium, 60 mg cholesterol.

1   cup pitted prunes, cut into small pieces
1   cup coarsely chopped walnuts
2   cups sifted all-purpose flour
1   teaspoon baking soda
1½ teaspoons ground cinnamon
1½ teaspoons ground nutmeg
1   teaspoon ground allspice
¼   teaspoon salt
2   cups sugar
1   cup vegetable oil
1   cup buttermilk
2   teaspoons vanilla
3   eggs
    Sweet Butter Glaze (recipe follows)
    Unsweetened whipped cream, for garnish
    (optional)

1. Preheat the oven to moderate (350°). Generously grease and flour a 9-inch (12-cup) Bundt® pan.
2. Combine the prunes with the walnuts and ½ cup of the flour in a bowl.
3. Sift together the remaining 1½ cups of flour with the baking soda, cinnamon, nutmeg, allspice and salt into a large bowl. Add the sugar, oil, buttermilk, vanilla and eggs. Beat with an electric mixer at medium-high speed for about 1 minute, or until the flour mixture is creamy smooth. Add the prune mixture and fold it in lightly but thoroughly. Pour the batter into the prepared pan.
4. Bake in the preheated moderate oven (350°) for 45 to 50 minutes, or until the cake pulls away from the sides of the pan and is springy to the touch. Cool the cake upright in the pan on a wire rack for 15 minutes.
5. Prepare the Sweet Butter Glaze.
6. Loosen the cake around the edges with a thin-bladed spatula and invert the cake onto the wire rack. Pierce the cake all over with a wooden pick. Set the wire rack, with the cake on it, over a large, round platter. Slowly ladle the glaze evenly over the cake.

If any glaze runs off, spoon it back on the cake until most of the glaze has been absorbed and the cake surface is slightly shiny. Cool the cake thoroughly.
7. Transfer the cake to a serving platter. Cut the cake into wedges and, if you wish, garnish each wedge with a dollop of unsweetened whipped cream.

Sweet Butter Glaze: Combine ½ cup of granulated sugar, ½ cup of buttermilk, ½ teaspoon of baking soda and ¼ cup (½ stick) of unsalted butter in a saucepan. Cook over medium heat, stirring occasionally, until the butter melts and the mixture boils. Remove the topping from heat.

COCONUT PECAN BLONDIES

Bake at 350° for 35 minutes.
Makes 2 dozen bars.

Nutrient Value Per Blondie: 231 calories, 2 g protein, 12 g fat, 29 g carbohydrate, 138 mg sodium, 44 mg cholesterol.

2¼ cups unsifted all-purpose flour
1   teaspoon baking powder
¼   teaspoon salt
1   cup (2 sticks) butter or margarine, softened
2   cups firmly packed light brown sugar
2   eggs
2   teaspoons vanilla
1   cup pecans, chopped
1   cup flaked coconut

1. Preheat the oven to moderate (350°). Grease a 13 x 9 x 2-inch baking pan.
2. Stir together the flour, baking powder and salt in a small bowl until the ingredients are well mixed.
3. Beat together the butter or margarine and the brown sugar in a large bowl until they are light and fluffy. Beat in the eggs, one at a time, until they are well blended. Mix in the vanilla. Stir in the flour mixture until all the ingredients are well blended. Fold in the pecans and the coconut until they are well mixed. Spread the batter evenly with a rubber spatula in the prepared pan.
4. Bake the blondies in the preheated moderate oven (350°) for 35 minutes, or until the top springs back when lightly touched with your fingertips. Cool in the pan on a wire rack. Cut into 24 bars.

APPLESAUCE CAKE

A delicious, old-fashioned cake flecked with raisins and walnuts.

Bake at 350° for 1 hour and 10 minutes.
Makes 16 servings.

Nutrient Value Per Serving: 418 calories, 5 g protein, 14 g fat, 71 g carbohydrate, 298 mg sodium, 58 mg cholesterol.

3	cups unsifted all-purpose flour
2	teaspoons baking soda
1	teaspoon baking powder
3	teaspoons ground cinnamon
1½	teaspoons ground nutmeg
1	teaspoon ground cloves
½	teaspoon salt
¾	cup (1½ sticks) butter or margarine, at room temperature
2	cups sugar
2	eggs
2	cups unsweetened applesauce
1	cup walnuts, chopped
1	cup raisins
	Apple Glaze (recipe follows)

1. Preheat the oven to moderate (350°). Grease and flour the bottom and sides of a 10-inch tube pan.
2. Stir together the flour, baking soda, baking powder, cinnamon, nutmeg, cloves and salt in a medium-size mixing bowl.
3. Beat the butter or margarine with the sugar and the eggs in a large bowl until they are light and fluffy. Stir in the flour mixture alternately with the applesauce, beginning and ending with the flour mixture. Fold in the walnuts and the raisins. Turn the batter evenly into the prepared pan, smoothing the top of the batter with a rubber spatula to make it level.
4. Bake in the preheated moderate oven (350°) for 1 hour and 10 minutes, or until a cake tester inserted in the center of the cake comes out clean. Cool the cake in the pan on a wire rack for 10 minutes. Remove the cake from the pan and cool the cake on the wire rack to room temperature.
5. Spoon the Apple Glaze over the top of the cake so it drizzles down the sides.

Apple Glaze: Place 2 cups of unsifted 10X (confectioners' powdered) sugar in a small bowl. Gradually stir in 3 to 4 tablespoons of apple juice until the glaze is smooth and a good spreading consistency.

OLD SALEM GINGERBREAD

This unique gingerbread is made with fresh gingerroot. The recipe comes from the collection of Louisa Senseman (1822-1854) and is served in the Salem Tavern in Old Salem, North Carolina.

Bake at 375° for 55 to 60 minutes.
Makes 16 servings.

Nutrient Value Per Serving: 378 calories, 4 g protein, 15 g fat, 58 g carbohydrate, 78 mg sodium, 89 mg cholesterol.

1	cup plus 2 tablespoons (2¼ sticks) unsalted butter, softened
2	cups sugar
3	eggs
1	cup molasses
⅓	cup finely chopped, peeled fresh gingerroot
	Finely grated zest of 2 oranges (orange part of rind only)
1	teaspoon ground cinnamon
⅛	teaspoon ground cloves
1	teaspoon baking soda
1	tablespoon cider vinegar
3⅓	cups sifted all-purpose flour
1	cup milk
	Whipped cream, for garnish (optional)

1. Preheat the oven to moderate (375°). Generously grease and flour a 13 x 9 x 2-inch baking pan.
2. Beat the butter in a large bowl until it is light and fluffy. Gradually beat in the sugar until it is well mixed. Beat in the eggs, one at a time, beating well after each addition. Mix in, one at a time and in the following order, the molasses, ginger, orange zest, cinnamon and cloves. Stir together the baking soda and the vinegar in a small bowl. Blend the baking soda mixture into the butter mixture.
3. Stir in the flour alternately with the milk, beginning and ending with the flour, and stirring after each addition only enough to combine the ingredients. Spread the batter evenly in the prepared pan.
4. Bake in the preheated moderate oven (375°) for 55 to 60 minutes, or until a cake tester inserted in the center of the cake comes out clean and the cake pulls away from the sides of the pan. Cool the cake in the pan on a wire rack.
5. Cut the cake into squares to serve. Garnish the squares with dollops of whipped cream, if you wish.

MORAVIAN SUGAR CAKE

A coffee cake that is uncommonly spongy and rich, thanks to its high proportion of yeast, butter and sugar.

Bake at 375° for 18 to 20 minutes.
Makes 2 large flat cakes (12 servings each).

Nutrient Value Per Serving: 214 calories, 4 g protein, 9 g fat, 31 g carbohydrate, 109 mg sodium, 44 mg cholesterol.

2	envelopes active dry yeast
½	cup granulated sugar
1	cup warm water (105° to 115°)*
½	cup firmly packed unseasoned mashed potatoes
2	tablespoons nonfat dry milk powder
1	teaspoon salt
1	cup (2 sticks) unsalted butter or margarine, melted
2	eggs
4½	to 5 cups unsifted all-purpose flour
¾	cup firmly packed light brown sugar
1	teaspoon ground cinnamon

1. Combine the yeast with ½ teaspoon of the granulated sugar in ½ cup of the warm water in a large bowl. Stir to dissolve the yeast. Let the yeast mixture stand for 5 minutes.

2. Add the remaining granulated sugar and warm water, the mashed potatoes, dry milk powder, salt, half the melted butter, the eggs and 1 cup of the flour to the yeast mixture. Beat the potato-yeast mixture with an electric mixer at low speed until all the ingredients are blended. Raise the mixer speed to high and beat until the potato-yeast mixture is very smooth, for about 2 minutes. Beat in 3 cups of the remaining flour, 1 cup at a time.

3. Turn out the dough onto a lightly floured surface. Knead the dough for about 2 minutes, using ½ to 1 cup of the remaining flour, to make a soft dough that looks smooth.

4. Generously grease two 15 x 10 x 1-inch jelly-roll pans. Divide the dough in half. Place each half into a prepared pan. With well-buttered hands, flatten the dough over the bottom of each pan, pushing it well into the corners. Brush about 2 tablespoons of the remaining melted butter over each top; the butter will keep the dough from drying out. Let the dough rise, uncovered, in a warm place, away from drafts, until it is doubled in bulk, for 25 to 35 minutes.

5. While the dough rises, combine the brown sugar with the cinnamon in a small bowl.

6. With your fingers, poke deep holes over the surfaces of both pans of dough. Sprinkle the tops as evenly as possible with the cinnamon sugar. Drizzle with the remaining melted butter. Let the dough rise in a warm place, away from drafts, until it approaches the rims of the pans, for 10 to 15 minutes.

7. Preheat the oven to moderate (375°).

8. Bake in the preheated moderate oven (375°) for 18 to 20 minutes, or until the tops are browned and the cakes feel spongy-firm.

9. Cool the cakes in the pans on a wire rack for 15 to 20 minutes. Cut the cakes into large squares to serve.

Note: *Warm water should feel tepid when dropped on your wrist.*

Moravian Lovefeast Buns: *These are served at Moravian Lovefeasts, which are special musical services usually held during the Christmas and Easter holidays.*

Follow the directions in Steps 1 and 2 above, adding ½ teaspoon of ground nutmeg and ½ teaspoon of ground mace with the first cup of flour. Continue with Steps 2 and 3, working in enough of the remaining flour to make a soft and sticky dough. Scrape the dough into a well-buttered bowl and butter the top of the dough. Cover the bowl and let the dough rise in a warm place, away from drafts, until it is doubled in bulk, for about 1 hour. Punch down the dough and divide it in half. Roll out each half to a ½-inch thickness on a well-floured pastry cloth with a well-floured, stockinette-covered rolling pin. Cut the dough into 2½- to 2¾-inch rounds with a floured cookie cutter. Place the rounds, 3 inches apart, on greased baking sheets. Cover the baking sheets and let the rounds rise in a warm place, away from drafts, until they are doubled in bulk, for about 45 minutes. Bake in a preheated moderate oven (350°) for 15 minutes, or until the buns are golden brown. Transfer the buns to wire racks. Brush them generously with ¼ cup (½ stick) of melted unsalted butter. Serve the buns warm or at room temperature as dinner rolls, or use them as hamburger buns.
Makes 24 buns.
Nutrient Value Per Bun: 226 calories, 3 g protein, 10 g fat, 30 g carbohydrate, 116 mg sodium, 49 mg cholesterol.

God's mill grinds slow, but sure.
— George Herbert

CANDY IN THE SNOW

Here's a special winter treat to satisfy the sweetest tooth. You only need one ingredient, and a generous snowfall. Gently boil ½ cup of maple syrup until it has thickened, for about 5 minutes. Fill a bowl with clean snow and drizzle the hot syrup over it. The syrup will harden into "candy" you can eat with your fingers.

HOMEMADE GRANOLA CRUNCH

This granola is full of natural goodness. Try it with milk for breakfast, by the handful as a snack, or use it as an ingredient in other recipes.

Bake at 300° for 1 hour.
Makes 9 cups.

Nutrient Value Per ½ Cup: 288 calories, 6 g protein, 15 g fat, 37 g carbohydrate, 134 mg sodium, 0 mg cholesterol.

4	cups old-fashioned oats (11 ounces)
1	cup flaked coconut (about 2 ounces)
1	cup coarsely chopped pecans (4 ounces)
½	cup unsalted sunflower seeds (2½ ounces)
½	cup wheat germ (about 2 ounces)
½	cup firmly packed light brown sugar
1	teaspoon ground cinnamon
1	teaspoon salt
½	cup vegetable oil
½	cup water
2	tablespoons honey
1	teaspoon vanilla
1	cup raisins
1	cup coarsely chopped dates (about 5 ounces)

1. Preheat the oven to slow (300°). Lightly grease a 15½ x 10½ x 1-inch jelly-roll pan.
2. Combine the oats, coconut, pecans, sunflower seeds, wheat germ, brown sugar, cinnamon and salt in a large bowl.
3. Stir together the oil, water, honey and vanilla in a small bowl. Pour the honey mixture over the oat mixture. Mix well to combine the ingredients. Spread the mixture evenly in the prepared jelly-roll pan.
4. Bake in the preheated slow oven (300°), stirring every 15 minutes, for 1 hour, or until the mixture is golden brown and slightly crunchy. Cool in the pan on a wire rack. Stir in the raisins and the dates. Store the granola in an airtight container.

OLD-FASHIONED SUGAR COOKIES

A mouth-watering taste of days gone by. The dough for these delicious cookies must "season" overnight, so begin the recipe a day ahead.

Bake at 325° for 15 minutes.
Makes about 5 dozen cookies.

Nutrient Value Per Cookie: 55 calories, 1 g protein, 3 g fat, 7 g carbohydrate, 28 mg sodium, 20 mg cholesterol.

2	cups plus 2 tablespoons sifted all-purpose flour
½	teaspoon baking soda
½	teaspoon cream of tartar
½	teaspoon salt
½	teaspoon ground nutmeg
¾	cup (1½ sticks) unsalted butter, at room temperature
1¼	cups sugar
¾	teaspoon vanilla
½	teaspoon lemon extract
¼	teaspoon almond extract
2	eggs
1	egg yolk

1. Sift together the flour, baking soda, cream of tartar, salt and nutmeg onto wax paper. Set aside the mixture.
2. Beat the butter in a medium-size bowl until it is light and fluffy. Gradually beat in the sugar until it is well mixed. Mix in the vanilla, lemon extract and almond extract. Beat in the eggs and the egg yolk. Stir in the flour mixture to make a soft, sticky dough. Wrap the dough in aluminum foil and let it "season" overnight in the refrigerator.
3. Next day, preheat the oven to slow (325°). Lightly grease baking sheets.
4. Work with about one quarter of the dough at a time, and keep the rest refrigerated. Roll out the dough on a well-floured pastry cloth with a well-floured, stockinette-covered rolling pin to about a ⅛-inch thickness. Cut the dough into 2¾- to 3-inch rounds with a floured cookie cutter. Place the cookies, 2 inches apart, on the prepared baking sheets.
5. Bake in the preheated slow oven (325°) for 15 minutes, or until the cookies are lightly browned around the edges. Remove the cookies at once to wire racks to cool. To keep the cookies crisp, store them in airtight containers.

CHOCOLATE CHIP OATMEAL COOKIES

Bake at 350° for 10 to 12 minutes.
Makes about 5 dozen cookies.

Nutrient Value Per Cookie: 70 calories, 1 g protein, 4 g fat, 8 g carbohydrate, 36 mg sodium, 11 mg cholesterol.

1	cup plus 2 tablespoons unsifted all-purpose flour
1	cup quick-cooking oatmeal
2	tablespoons Dutch-process unsweetened cocoa
¾	teaspoon baking soda
¾	cup (1½ sticks) salted butter or margarine, softened
½	cup granulated sugar
½	cup firmly packed light brown sugar
1	egg
1	teaspoon vanilla
1	package (6 ounces) semisweet chocolate pieces
½	cup walnuts, chopped

1. Preheat the oven to moderate (350°). Grease two baking sheets.
2. Stir together the flour, oatmeal, cocoa and baking soda in a bowl.
3. Beat the butter or margarine with the granulated sugar and the brown sugar in a large bowl until light and fluffy. Beat in the egg and the vanilla. Stir in the flour mixture until it is well blended. Fold in the chocolate pieces and the walnuts. Drop the cookie batter by teaspoonfuls, 2 inches apart, onto the prepared baking sheets.
4. Bake in the preheated moderate oven (350°) for 10 to 12 minutes, or until the cookies are lightly browned on top. Let them stand on the baking sheets for 3 minutes. Remove the cookies to wire racks to cool.

B·R·E·A·D·S
A·N·D S·P·R·E·A·D·S

Cream Cheese Loaf (recipe, page 203);
Mincemeat Braid (recipe, page 205)

Better is half a loaf than no bread.
—John Heywood

CREAM CHEESE LOAF

Bake at 325° for 40 minutes.
Makes 2 loaves (15 slices each).

Nutrient Value Per Slice: 122 calories, 3 g protein, 3 g fat,
21 g carbohydrate, 98 mg sodium, 14 mg cholesterol.

6   *cups unsifted all-purpose flour*
2   *tablespoons sugar*
1   *teaspoon salt*
1   *envelope fast-rising dry yeast*
1   *cup water*
1   *cup milk*
2   *tablespoons margarine*
4   *ounces (half an 8-ounce package) cream cheese,*
      at room temperature
1   *egg yolk mixed with 1 tablespoon water*
4   *teaspoons instant onion flakes*

1. Combine 3½ cups of the flour with the sugar, salt
and yeast in a large bowl. Stir to mix all the
ingredients.
2. Combine the water, milk and margarine in a small
saucepan. Heat the milk mixture to 130°; the mixture
should feel comfortably hot to the touch. Add the milk
mixture to the flour mixture. Add the cream cheese.
Beat the milk cream cheese mixture with an electric
mixer at low speed until all the ingredients are
blended. Raise the mixer speed to medium and beat
the mixture for 3 minutes. Mix in 1½ cups of the
remaining flour, ½ cup at a time, scraping down the
sides of the bowl with a spatula.
3. Turn out the dough onto a lightly floured surface.
Using up to 1 cup of the remaining flour, knead the
dough until it is smooth and elastic, for about 5
minutes.
4. Shape the dough into a ball. Place the dough in a
large greased bowl and turn the greased side up.
Cover the bowl and let the dough rise in a warm place,
away from drafts, until it is doubled in bulk, for about
30 minutes (you'll know the dough has doubled when
you press your finger into the dough and the
indentation remains).

5. Preheat the oven to slow (325°). Grease two
8½ x 4½ x 2½-inch loaf pans.
6. Punch down the dough and knead it briefly. Divide
the dough in half. Roll out each half to a rectangle
about 12 x 8½ inches. Roll up each rectangle from a
short end and pinch together the edges. Place each
rectangle in a prepared pan. Cover the pans and let the
dough rise in a warm place, away from drafts, until it is
doubled in bulk, for about 30 minutes.
7. Bake the loaves in the preheated slow oven (325°)
for 30 minutes. Brush the loaves with the egg yolk
mixture and sprinkle them with the onion flakes. Bake
for 10 minutes more, or until the loaves are golden
brown and sound hollow when tapped with your
fingertips. Remove the loaves from the pans to wire
racks to cool.

WALNUT RAISIN CARROT LOAF

Carrots, walnuts and raisins spiced with cinnamon, nutmeg and cloves: A slice of this loaf is especially scrumptious when spread with cream cheese.

Bake at 350° for 45 minutes.
Makes 1 loaf (12 slices).

Nutrient Value Per Slice: 217 calories, 4 g protein, 11 g fat, 27 g carbohydrate, 215 mg sodium, 46 mg cholesterol.

1½ cups unsifted all-purpose flour
½ cup sugar
1 teaspoon baking powder
1 teaspoon baking soda
1 teaspoon ground cinnamon
½ teaspoon salt
¼ teaspoon ground nutmeg
¼ teaspoon ground cloves
2 eggs
6 tablespoons vegetable oil
1 teaspoon vanilla
1¼ cups grated carrots (about 8 ounces)
½ cup walnuts, chopped
⅓ cup raisins
   Pecan halves (optional)

1. Preheat the oven to moderate (350°). Grease an 8½ x 4½ x 2⅝-inch loaf pan.
2. Stir together the flour, sugar, baking powder, baking soda, cinnamon, salt, nutmeg and cloves in a small bowl until all the ingredients are well blended.
3. Beat the eggs in a large bowl until they are well blended. Add the oil, vanilla and carrots. Beat the egg mixture until all the ingredients are blended. Stir in the flour mixture until it is well blended. Fold in the walnuts and the raisins. Turn the dough into the prepared pan. Place a row of pecan halves down the top center, if you wish.
4. Bake in the preheated moderate oven (350°) for 45 minutes, or until a wooden pick inserted in the center of the loaf comes out clean. Cool the loaf in the pan for 10 minutes. Turn out the loaf onto a wire rack to cool to room temperature.

Note: *The loaf slices better if it is stored overnight.*

OLD-FASHIONED WHEAT BREAD

Chock-full of oats, bran, wheat germ and whole wheat flour, this tasty bread has a lovely, light texture.

Bake at 400° for 30 minutes.
Makes 3 loaves (14 slices each).

Nutrient Value Per Slice: 142 calories, 5 g protein, 2 g fat, 25 g carbohydrate, 340 mg sodium, 7 mg cholesterol.

2 tablespoons active dry yeast (about three ¼-ounce packages)
1 cup warm water (105° to 115°)*
1 quart milk
5 tablespoons butter
5 tablespoons sugar
2 tablespoons salt
3 cups whole wheat flour
1 cup uncooked old-fashioned oats
1 cup wheat bran
½ cup wheat germ
5½ cups bread flour
2 tablespoons melted butter (optional)

1. Sprinkle the yeast over the warm water in a small bowl and stir to dissolve the yeast. Set aside the yeast mixture.
2. Heat together the milk, butter, sugar and salt in a small saucepan over low heat just until the butter is melted. Cool the milk mixture to lukewarm and transfer it to a very large bowl.
3. Stir in the yeast mixture, whole wheat flour, oats, bran and wheat germ. Beat the milk-flour mixture with an electric mixer until all the ingredients are well blended. Gradually add the bread flour, 1 cup at a time, until a soft dough is formed. If the dough becomes too stiff, use a wooden spoon to mix it.
4. Turn out the dough onto a floured board and knead it until it is smooth, for about 10 minutes. Transfer the dough to a greased bowl and turn the greased side up. Cover the bowl with plastic wrap and let the dough rise in a warm place, away from drafts, until it is doubled in bulk, for about 45 minutes.
5. Punch down the dough and let it rise again in a warm place, away from drafts, until it is doubled in bulk, for about 30 minutes.
6. Preheat the oven to hot (400°). Grease three 9 x 5-inch loaf pans.

7. Turn out the dough onto a floured work surface and cut it into thirds. Knead each third to shape it, and place it in a prepared pan. Cover the pans with plastic wrap and let the loaves rise in a warm place, away from drafts, until they are nearly doubled in bulk, for about 30 minutes.

8. Bake in the preheated hot oven (400°) for 30 minutes, or until the loaves sound hollow when tapped with your fingertips. Turn out the loaves onto wire racks to cool. If you wish to have a softer crust, brush the loaves with melted butter when they come out of the oven.

Note: *Warm water should feel tepid when dropped on your wrist.*

MINCEMEAT BRAIDS

Bake at 350° for 45 minutes.
Makes 2 braids (16 slices each).

Nutrient Value Per Slice: 121 calories, 2 g protein, 2 g fat, 24 g carbohydrate, 121 mg sodium, 12 mg cholesterol.

4   cups unsifted all-purpose flour
¼   cup firmly packed brown sugar
1   teaspoon salt
1   envelope fast-rising dry yeast
1   cup milk
¼   cup water
2   tablespoons butter or margarine
1   egg
1½   cups bottled mincemeat
    Sugar Glaze (recipe follows)

1. Combine 2 cups of the flour with the brown sugar, salt and yeast in a large bowl. Stir to mix all the ingredients.

2. Combine the milk, water and butter or margarine in a small saucepan. Heat the milk mixture to 130°; the mixture should feel comfortably hot to the touch. Add the milk mixture to the flour mixture. Add the egg. Beat the milk-egg mixture with an electric mixer at low speed until all the ingredients are blended. Raise the mixer speed to medium and beat for 3 minutes. Mix in 1 cup of the remaining flour, ½ cup at a time, scraping down the sides of the bowl with a spatula.

3. Turn out the dough onto a lightly floured surface. Using up to 1 cup of the remaining flour, knead the dough until it is smooth and elastic, for about 5 minutes.

4. Shape the dough into a ball. Place the dough in a greased large bowl and turn the dough greased side up. Cover the bowl and let the dough rise in a warm place, away from drafts, until it is doubled in bulk, for about 30 minutes.

5. Preheat the oven to moderate (350°). Grease 2 baking sheets.

6. Punch down the dough and divide it into 6 equal pieces. Roll each piece between your palms into a "sausage" about 10 inches long. Flatten each "sausage" with a rolling pin until it is 3 inches wide. Spoon ¼ cup of the mincemeat lengthwise down the center of each piece.

7. Bring the long sides of each piece up over the filling and pinch the edges closed to seal. Braid together 3 mincemeat "sausages" to make 1 loaf and pinch together the ends to seal. Place the braid on a prepared baking sheet. Repeat to make the second mincemeat braid.

8. Cover the baking sheets and let the braids rise in a warm place, away from drafts, until they are doubled in bulk, for about 30 minutes.

9. Bake in the preheated moderate oven (350°) for 45 minutes, or until the braids are browned and sound hollow when tapped with your fingertips. Cool the braids on wire racks.

10. Drizzle the Sugar Glaze over the braids.

Sugar Glaze: Place 1 cup of sifted 10X (confectioners' powdered) sugar in a small bowl. Gradually stir in 1 to 2 tablespoons of milk until the glaze is thin enough to drizzle over the braids.

GLAZED WHOLE WHEAT RAISIN BREAD

For ease in serving, slice the finished loaf, freeze it, and pop the slices into the toaster oven whenever you wish. The glaze will become soft and translucent when the bread is toasted.

Bake at 325° for 50 minutes.
Makes 1 loaf (16 slices).

Nutrient Value Per Slice: 187 calories, 5 g protein, 2 g fat, 38 g carbohydrate, 156 mg sodium, 18 mg cholesterol.

1½ cups water
1½ cups raisins
 1 tablespoon granulated sugar
 1 package active dry yeast
 2 cups whole wheat flour
1½ to 2 cups unsifted all-purpose flour
 ½ cup dry nonfat milk powder
 1 teaspoon salt
 1 egg
1½ tablespoons vegetable oil

Glaze:
 ¾ cup sifted 10X (confectioners' powdered) sugar
 ⅛ teaspoon vanilla
 2 to 3 teaspoons water

1. Combine the 1½ cups of water with the raisins and the granulated sugar in a saucepan. Bring the mixture to boiling to plump the raisins. Strain the liquid into a large bowl and reserve the raisins. Cool the liquid to 110° (it should feel tepid to the touch).
2. Stir the yeast into the liquid to dissolve it. Let the yeast mixture stand until it is bubbly, for about 10 minutes.
3. Stir together the whole wheat flour, 1½ cups of the all-purpose flour, the milk powder and salt in a medium-size bowl.
4. Mix the egg and the oil into the yeast mixture. Stir in the flour mixture and enough of the remaining all-purpose flour to make a soft dough.
5. Turn out the dough onto a lightly floured surface. Knead the dough until it is smooth and elastic, for about 10 minutes, adding only enough of the remaining all-purpose flour to prevent the dough from sticking to the surface.

6. Place the dough in a greased bowl and turn the greased side up. Cover the bowl with a damp towel and let the dough rise in a warm place, away from drafts, until it is doubled in bulk, for 1½ hours.
7. Punch down the dough and roll it out to a ¾-inch thickness. Sprinkle the dough with the reserved raisins. Roll up the dough and shape it into a loaf. Place the loaf in a lightly greased 9 x 5 x 3-inch loaf pan. Cover the pan and let the loaf rise in a warm place, away from drafts, until it is doubled in bulk, for 1 hour.
8. Preheat the oven to slow (325°).
9. Bake in the preheated slow oven (325°) for 50 minutes, or until the loaf is browned and sounds hollow when tapped with your fingertips. Remove the loaf from the pan to a wire rack to cool for 10 minutes.
10. Meanwhile, prepare the Glaze: Place the 10X (confectioners' powdered) sugar in a small bowl. Stir in the vanilla and the water until the glaze is smooth and a good spreading consistency.
11. Spread the cooled bread with the glaze. Let the bread cool to room temperature.

SPIRALED HERB BREAD

Bake at 375° for 30 to 35 minutes.
Makes 2 loaves (12 slices each).

Nutrient Value Per Slice: 146 calories, 4 g protein, 4 g fat,
22 g carbohydrate, 232 mg sodium, 20 mg cholesterol.

³/₄	cup chopped fresh basil
¹/₄	cup grated Parmesan cheese
2	tablespoons finely chopped pine nuts
1	tablespoon chopped fresh marjoram
5	to 5¹/₂ cups unsifted all-purpose flour
1	tablespoon sugar
2	teaspoons salt
1	envelope fast-rising dry yeast
1	cup milk
5	tablespoons butter
1¹/₄	cups water
1	egg mixed with 1 tablespoon water
2	tablespoons sesame seeds

1. Combine the basil, Parmesan cheese, pine nuts and
marjoram in a small bowl. Set aside the basil mixture.
2. Combine 4 cups of the flour with the sugar, salt and
yeast in a large bowl. Stir to mix the ingredients well.
3. Heat the milk and the butter in a small saucepan
over medium heat until the butter is melted. Remove
the saucepan from the heat. Add the water. Cool the
mixture to 130°; the liquid should feel comfortably hot
to the touch. Add the milk mixture to the flour
mixture. Beat the milk-flour mixture with a wooden
spoon until it is smooth. Gradually stir in enough of
the remaining flour to make a soft dough.
4. Turn out the dough onto a lightly floured surface.
Knead the dough until it is smooth and elastic, for 5 to
6 minutes, adding more of the remaining flour as
needed to prevent the dough from sticking. Form the
dough into a ball. Place the dough in a greased bowl
and turn the dough greased side up. Cover the bowl
with a clean towel and let the dough rise in a warm
place, away from drafts, until it is almost doubled in
bulk, for 30 minutes.
5. Grease two 8¹/₂ x 4¹/₂-inch loaf pans.
6. Turn out the dough onto a lightly floured surface.
Divide the dough into 2 equal pieces. Roll out 1 piece
to a 10 x 7-inch rectangle; do not knead the dough at
this point or it will become too dense and elastic.
Sprinkle the dough with half of the basil mixture.

Press the mixture into the dough with a spatula. Tightly
roll up the dough from a short end and place the roll,
seam side down, in one of the prepared loaf pans.
Repeat with the remaining dough and basil mixture.
Cover the pans and let the loaves rise in a warm place,
away from drafts, until the loaves almost reach the tops
of the pans, for about 30 minutes.
7. Preheat the oven to moderate (375°). Make 3
shallow diagonal cuts in the top of each loaf. Brush the
tops with the egg mixture and sprinkle with the
sesame seeds.
8. Bake in the preheated moderate oven (375°) for
30 to 35 minutes, or until the loaves are golden brown
and sound hollow when tapped with your fingertips.
Remove the loaves from the pans to wire racks to cool.
Cool the loaves completely before slicing them.

SPICY APPLE GRANOLA MUFFINS

Bake at 400° for 15 to 20 minutes.
Makes 12 muffins.

Nutrient Value Per Muffin: 213 calories, 4 g protein, 11 g fat, 26 g carbohydrate, 232 mg sodium, 24 mg cholesterol.

2	cups Homemade Granola Crunch (recipe, page 200)
1	cup sifted all-purpose flour
1/4	cup firmly packed light brown sugar
2	teaspoons baking powder
1/2	teaspoon ground cinnamon
1/4	teaspoon ground nutmeg
1/4	teaspoon salt
1	cup finely chopped peeled cooking apples, such as Granny Smith (1 medium-size apple)
1/2	cup milk
1/3	cup margarine, melted and cooled to room temperature
1	egg, slightly beaten
1	teaspoon vanilla

1. Preheat the oven to hot (400°). Grease twelve 2½-inch muffin-pan cups.
2. Combine the Homemade Granola Crunch, flour, brown sugar, baking powder, cinnamon, nutmeg and salt in a large bowl. Mix all the ingredients well. Stir in the apples. Make a well in the center of the mixture.
3. Combine the milk, margarine, egg and vanilla in a small bowl. Pour the milk mixture into the well in the granola mixture. Stir just to combine the ingredients. Spoon the batter into the prepared muffin-pan cups.
4. Bake the muffins in the preheated hot oven (400°) for 15 to 20 minutes, or until a wooden pick inserted in the centers comes out clean. Cool the muffins in the pan on a wire rack for 5 minutes. Turn out the muffins. Serve the muffins warm, or cool them completely on the wire rack.

BANANA MOCHA MUFFINS

Bake at 400° for 25 to 30 minutes.
Makes 24 muffins.

Nutrient Value Per Muffin: 208 calories, 2 g protein, 11 g fat, 28 g carbohydrate, 162 mg sodium, 32 mg cholesterol.

2½	cups unsifted all-purpose flour
1	teaspoon baking powder
1/2	teaspoon baking soda
1/2	teaspoon salt
1	tablespoon instant coffee granules
1	tablespoon hot water (125° to 130°)*
1 1/3	cups mashed fully-ripe banana (about 3 bananas)
1	cup (2 sticks) butter or margarine, softened
1 1/4	cups sugar
1	egg
1	cup semisweet chocolate pieces

1. Preheat the oven to hot (400°). Grease twenty-four 2½-inch muffin-pan cups.
2. Stir together the flour, baking powder, baking soda and salt in a small bowl. Set aside the flour mixture.
3. Dissolve the instant coffee in the hot water. Stir the liquid into the bananas. Set aside the banana mixture.
4. Beat together the butter or margarine and the sugar in a large bowl until light and fluffy. Beat in the egg. Mix in the banana mixture. Stir in the flour mixture until it is well blended. Fold in the chocolate pieces. Spoon the batter into the prepared muffin-pan cups, dividing it evenly among the cups.
5. Bake the muffins in the preheated hot oven (400°) for 25 to 30 minutes, or until a wooden pick inserted in the centers comes out clean. Turn out the muffins onto a wire rack to cool.

***Note:** Hot water should feel comfortably hot when dropped on your wrist.*

BETTER THAN BUTTER: SWEET SPREADS

Honey Butter: *½ cup (1 stick) unsalted butter, softened, blended together with 1 tablespoon of honey and, if you wish, ⅓ cup of raisins*

•

Fruit Butter: *½ cup (1 stick) unsalted butter, softened, whipped together with 4 tablespoons of jam or preserves (try raspberry, strawberry or apricot)*

•

Spiced Butter: *1 cup (2 sticks) unsalted butter, softened, blended with ¼ cup of honey and ½ teaspoon of freshly grated nutmeg or 2 tablespoons of cinnamon*

STRAWBERRY CORN MUFFINS

Bake at 400° for 15 minutes.
Makes 12 muffins.

Nutrient Value Per Muffin: 160 calories, 3 g protein, 4 g fat, 26 g carbohydrate, 193 mg sodium, 27 mg cholesterol.

½   cup chopped fresh strawberries
¼   cup plus 1 tablespoon sugar
1   cup yellow cornmeal (preferably stone ground)
1   cup unbleached all-purpose flour
1   tablespoon baking powder
1   container (8 ounces) strawberry lowfat yogurt
1   extra-large egg
3   tablespoons safflower oil
1   teaspoon baking soda
1   teaspoon vanilla

1. Preheat the oven to hot (400°). Place paper liners in 12 muffin-pan cups.
2. Toss together the strawberries and 1 tablespoon of the sugar in a small bowl.
3. Stir together the cornmeal, flour, baking powder and remaining ¼ cup of sugar in a medium-size bowl.
4. Beat together the yogurt, egg, oil, baking soda and vanilla in a small bowl. Add the strawberries with their juice. Pour the liquid ingredients over the dry ingredients and stir with a large spoon just until blended; do not overmix. Spoon the batter into the prepared muffin-pan cups.
5. Bake the muffins in the preheated hot oven (400°) for 15 minutes, or until the tops are golden and spring back when lightly pressed with your fingertip.

PINEAPPLE OATMEAL MUFFINS

Pineapple juice adds a tangy sweetness to the recipe. For sweeter muffins, add 2 tablespoons of sugar to the oat and flour mixture.

Bake at 400° for 25 minutes.
Makes 12 muffins.

Nutrient Value Per Muffin: 157 calories, 4 g protein, 5 g fat, 24 g carbohydrate, 251 mg sodium, 0 mg cholesterol.

1   cup old-fashioned rolled oats OR: oat bran
¾   cup whole wheat flour
¾   cup all-purpose flour
1   tablespoon baking powder
1½   teaspoons ground ginger
½   teaspoon baking soda
½   teaspoon salt
3   egg whites
1   can (8 ounces) crushed pineapple in juice
½   cup skim milk
2   tablespoons corn oil
½   cup dried currants OR: raisins

1. Preheat the oven to hot (400°). Place paper liners in 12 muffin-pan cups.
2. Stir together the oats or oat bran, the whole wheat and all-purpose flours, the baking powder, ginger, baking soda and salt in a medium-size bowl.
3. Combine the egg whites, pineapple with its juice, milk, oil and currants or raisins in a small bowl until well blended. Pour the liquid ingredients over the dry ingredients and stir just until the dry ingredients are moistened. Do not overmix. Spoon the batter into the prepared muffin-pan cups.
4. Bake the muffins in the preheated hot oven (400°) for 25 minutes, or until the tops are golden and spring back when lightly pressed with your fingertip.

P·I·C·K O·F
T·H·E C·R·O·P

Cheese Apple Cobbler (recipe, page 213)

APPLE RAISIN PIE

Bake at 425° for 55 minutes.
Makes 8 servings.

Nutrient Value Per Serving: 432 calories, 3 g protein, 20 g fat, 60 g carbohydrate, 291 mg sodium, 17 mg cholesterol.

1   package (11 ounces) pie crust mix

Filling:
1¼   pounds Golden Delicious apples
         (about 3 medium-size apples)
1¼   pounds Granny Smith apples
         (about 3 medium-size apples)
⅓   cup sugar
2½   tablespoons cornstarch
¾   teaspoon ground cinnamon
¼   teaspoon ground ginger
½   cup golden raisins
2   tablespoons frozen orange juice concentrate
2½   teaspoons lemon juice
1½   tablespoons unsalted butter

Glaze:
2   tablespoons heavy cream
1   teaspoon sugar
½   teaspoon cider vinegar

1   tablespoon sugar
     Crème fraîche or whipped cream (optional)

1. Preheat the oven to hot (425°).
2. Prepare the pie crust mix, following the package directions for a 9-inch double-crust pie. Roll out all the dough to a 12-inch-diameter single crust. Fit the crust into a 9-inch pie plate. Turn the edges under and make a high, free-form edge.
3. Prepare the Filling: Peel, quarter and core the apples. Cut them into ¼-inch-thick slices and place them in a large bowl. Combine the sugar, cornstarch, cinnamon and ginger in a small bowl. Sprinkle the mixture over the apples and toss gently to mix the ingredients. Let the apple-spice mixture stand for 10 minutes.
4. Combine the raisins, orange juice concentrate and lemon juice in a bowl. Add the raisin mixture to the apple mixture. Pile the filling into the crust. Dot the filling with the butter.

5. Prepare the Glaze: Combine the heavy cream, sugar and vinegar in a small bowl. Brush the glaze on the pie crust rim. Place the pie on a baking sheet. Cover only the apple filling with a piece of lightly buttered aluminum foil, buttered side down.
6. Bake on the middle rack in the preheated hot oven (425°) for 10 minutes. Cover the whole pie, including the crust, with a piece of buttered aluminum foil. Bake for 40 minutes more. Remove the aluminum foil. Sprinkle the top of the pie with the 1 tablespoon of sugar. Bake for 5 minutes more. Serve the pie with crème fraîche or whipped cream, if you wish.

"A" IS FOR APPLE

These are the most widely available varieties. Your region may have its own specialties.

•

Cortland: Mild flavor; excellent raw or in pies and all cooking.

•

Crispin/Mutsu: Very crisp, sweet eating apple; known by either name.

•

Golden Delicious: Sweeter flavor than Red Delicious; an all-purpose apple.

•

Granny Smith: Moderately tart flavor, bright green color; prized for snacks, salads and cooking.

•

McIntosh: Very juicy, slightly tart flavor; great uncooked, baked or in sauces.

•

Red Delicious: Sweetish flavor, crunchy; best raw in salads, fruit cups or as snacks.

•

Rome: Slightly tart flavor; the best for baking and cooking.

•

Winesap: Moderately tart flavor; superb raw, cooked or baked.

Comfort me with apples: for
I am sick of love.

— The Song of Solomon

CRANBERRY AND SAUSAGE STUFFED APPLES

Bake at 375° for 30 minutes.
Makes 8 servings.

Nutrient Value Per Serving: 438 calories, 15 g protein, 22 g fat, 48 g carbohydrate, 555 mg sodium, 97 mg cholesterol.

1   pound sweet Italian sausage
2   medium-size onions, chopped (1½ cups)
2   tablespoons butter
¼   cup white wine
3   cups cranberries (12 ounces), coarsely chopped
1   egg, slightly beaten
2   tablespoons chopped parsley
2   tablespoons brown sugar
1½ cups shredded white Vermont Cheddar cheese
      (6 ounces)
8   large baking apples, such as Rome Beauty
      or Granny Smith (8 to 10 ounces each)
1   tablespoon lemon juice
¼   cup bourbon
¼   cup water
16 whole cranberries, for garnish

1. Remove and discard the casing from the sausage. Crumble the sausage into a large skillet. Cook the sausage over medium heat until it no longer is pink, stirring occasionally. Remove the sausage with a slotted spoon to paper toweling to drain.

2. Wipe out the skillet. Sauté the onion in the butter in the skillet until it is softened, for 3 to 4 minutes. Add the wine and cook, scraping up any browned bits with a wooden spoon, until the wine is slightly reduced. Pour the wine mixture into a medium-size bowl.

3. Add the sausage, chopped cranberries, egg, parsley, brown sugar and 1 cup of the Vermont Cheddar cheese to the bowl. Mix all the ingredients well.

4. Slice off 1 inch from the top of each apple and core the apple with a melon baller. Scoop out the remaining flesh, leaving a ¼-inch shell. Place the apple flesh in a heavy, medium-size saucepan. Add the lemon juice, bourbon and water to the saucepan. Simmer the apple mixture, partially covered, until it is a thick applesauce, for about 30 minutes.

5. Preheat the oven to moderate (375°).

6. Spoon about ¾ cup of the sausage filling into each apple. Sprinkle the tops with the remaining ½ cup of Vermont Cheddar cheese, dividing it equally among the apples. Place 2 whole cranberries on the top of each apple for garnish. Place the apples in a large baking dish.

7. Bake the apples in the preheated moderate oven (375°) for 30 minutes. Let the apples stand for 10 minutes. Serve them with the applesauce on the side.

THE APPLE STORE

To keep apples tasty, store them in a crisper or plastic bag in the coldest part of the refrigerator. To freeze apples, peel, core and slice them. Dip the slices in lemon juice. Pack the apple slices closely in freezer containers and freeze them.

APPLES: NOW YOU'RE COOKIN'!

There are all sorts of ways to use uncooked apples to make dishes more interesting and appealing. Just a few suggestions:

•

Grate raw apples into coleslaw for a snappy new taste.

•

Scoop out uncooked apples, dice the scooped-out pulp and mix it with tuna, chicken, salmon or fruit salad. Fill the apple shells with the salad. Or serve ice cream or berries in the apple shells.

•

Combine equal parts of uncooked apple slices and steamed carrot slices, snow pea pods and green beans. Toss the salad with French dressing and chill it.

•

Slice uncooked apples, top them with cheese, pâté or cooked sausage and serve them as hors d'oeuvres.

•

Chop uncooked apples and mix them with granola and lemon yogurt for a great snack.

CHEESE APPLE COBBLER

This cobbler is the perfect choice for an end-of-supper delight or a hearty Sunday brunch.

Bake at 400° for 30 to 35 minutes.
Makes 8 servings.

Nutrient Value Per Serving: 372 calories, 8 g protein, 15 g fat, 53 g carbohydrate, 293 mg sodium, 44 mg cholesterol.

<table>
<tr><td>2</td><td>pounds apples, peeled, cored and thinly sliced (6 cups)</td></tr>
<tr><td>1</td><td>cup sugar</td></tr>
<tr><td>1¼</td><td>cups all-purpose flour</td></tr>
<tr><td>¼</td><td>teaspoon ground cinnamon</td></tr>
<tr><td>1½</td><td>teaspoons baking powder</td></tr>
<tr><td>1½</td><td>cups shredded Vermont Cheddar cheese (6 ounces)</td></tr>
<tr><td>⅓</td><td>cup (5⅓ tablespoons) melted butter</td></tr>
<tr><td>¼</td><td>cup milk</td></tr>
</table>

1. Preheat the oven to hot (400°). Lightly grease an 8 x 8 x 2-inch baking pan.
2. Combine the apples, ¾ cup of the sugar, ¼ cup of the flour and the cinnamon in a large bowl. Toss the ingredients together. Spread the mixture evenly in the prepared pan.
3. Combine the remaining 1 cup of flour and ¼ cup of sugar with the baking powder and the Vermont Cheddar cheese in a large bowl. Toss the ingredients to combine them. Add the melted butter and the milk, stirring just until the ingredients are combined. Spoon the cheese mixture over the apple mixture in the pan.
4. Bake in the preheated hot oven (400°) for 30 to 35 minutes, or until the topping is crisp and golden, and the apples are tender. Serve the cobbler warm.

The best of all physicians is apple pie and cheese!
— Eugene Field

ORANGES WITH RASPBERRIES AND RUBY PORT

A veritable treasure trove of golden oranges, brilliant raspberries and ruby port.

Makes 8 servings.

Nutrient Value Per Serving: 395 calories, 2 g protein, 0 g fat, 97 g carbohydrate, 5 mg sodium, 0 mg cholesterol.

<table>
<tr><td>8</td><td>large navel oranges</td></tr>
<tr><td>4</td><td>cups boiling water</td></tr>
<tr><td>1½</td><td>cups sugar</td></tr>
<tr><td>1</td><td>cup cold water</td></tr>
<tr><td>1</td><td>package (10 ounces) frozen raspberries, partially thawed</td></tr>
<tr><td>½</td><td>cup red currant jelly OR: black currant jelly</td></tr>
<tr><td>¼</td><td>cup ruby port wine OR: vintage port wine</td></tr>
<tr><td>2</td><td>tablespoons cassis</td></tr>
</table>

1. Thinly peel the zest (orange part of the rind only) lengthwise from 3 of the oranges with a swivel-bladed vegetable peeler. Cut the zest lengthwise into ⅛-inch-wide strips. Blanch the strips in the boiling water for 10 minutes. Drain the strips well.
2. Combine the sugar with the cold water in a medium-size, heavy saucepan. Bring to boiling, stirring to dissolve the sugar. Boil, uncovered and without stirring, for 5 minutes. Add the zest strips. Lower the heat and simmer, uncovered, for 15 minutes. Drain.
3. Combine the raspberries, red or black currant jelly, ruby or vintage port and the cassis in the container of an electric blender or a food processor. Cover and whirl until the mixture is puréed. Strain the purée to remove the seeds.
4. Peel the remaining rind and pith from all 8 oranges. Slice the oranges crosswise into ¼-inch-thick circles. Layer the oranges and the raspberry mixture into a 2-quart serving bowl. Drizzle any remaining raspberry mixture over the top. Cover and refrigerate for 2 to 3 hours before serving.
5. To serve, pile the candied zest over the top.

PLUM PRIMER

Casselman: Tangy-sweet flavor, red color.

•

Friar: Sweet-tart flavor, deep black color.

•

Kelsey: Sweet-tart flavor, green ripening to yellow-red color.

•

Laroda: Sweet-tangy flavor, red over yellow color.

•

Roysum: Sweet flavor, reddish blue color.

PLUM WONDERFUL

One pound of fresh plums equals 6 medium-size (2-inch-diameter) plums, 2½ cups of sliced plums, 2 cups of diced plums or 1¾ cups of puréed plums.

For the best plums, choose plump fruit with the mature color for its variety. To test for ripeness, press the plum gently with your palm; it should yield slightly, but not feel mushy.

•

Avoid plums with breaks in the skin, immature fruit (comparatively hard, not fully colored) and overripe fruit (very soft, leaking juice).

•

If you do buy firm, unripe plums, they can be softened and ripened in a loosely closed paper bag. Keep the bag at room temperature for 3 to 4 days and check the progress of the plums daily. Refrigerate the plums when they are ripe.

•

Puréed plums are great for making sauces. They also can be frozen in ice cube trays to use in fruit drinks or with club soda.

•

To freeze plums, halve or quarter them, spread them on a baking sheet and freeze them until they are firm. Place the frozen plums in covered freezer containers or plastic bags and return them to the freezer.

PLUMS 'N NUTS OATMEAL BREAD

Bake at 350° for 45 minutes.
Makes 12 servings.

Nutrient Value Per Serving: 203 calories, 5 g protein, 7 g fat, 30 g carbohydrate, 203 mg sodium, 26 mg cholesterol.

2	teaspoons distilled white vinegar
	Milk
2	cups all-purpose flour
⅓	cup firmly packed light brown sugar
2½	teaspoons baking powder
¾	teaspoon baking soda
¼	teaspoon salt
1	cup quick-cooking oats (not instant)
1	cup chopped firmly ripe plums
½	cup walnuts, chopped
1	egg
2	tablespoons vegetable oil

1. Preheat the oven to moderate (350°). Grease and flour an 8½ x 4½-inch loaf pan.
2. Pour the vinegar into a 1-cup measure. Add enough milk to make 1 cup of liquid. Let the milk mixture stand for 10 minutes to sour.
3. Combine the flour, brown sugar, baking powder, baking soda and salt in a bowl. Stir in the oats, plums and walnuts.
4. Beat the egg in a bowl. Add the soured milk and the oil. Pour the egg mixture all at once into the dry ingredients and stir to moisten the dry ingredients. Turn the batter into the prepared pan.
5. Bake in the preheated moderate oven (350°) for 45 minutes, or until a wooden pick inserted in the center of the bread comes out clean. Remove the bread from the pan to a wire rack to cool. Store the bread overnight for easier slicing.

PLUM CHIFFON PIE

Look for plums that are a deep ruby color to make this mouth-watering, creamy treat.

Makes 8 servings.

Nutrient Value Per Serving: 281 calories, 5 g protein, 15 g fat, 33 g carbohydrate, 177 mg sodium, 123 mg cholesterol.

1¼ pounds ripe plums, halved, pitted and
     cut into wedges
½ cup water
⅓ cup plus ¼ cup sugar
1 envelope unflavored gelatin
3 eggs, separated
1 teaspoon lemon juice
1¼ teaspoons grated lemon zest
     (yellow part of rind only)
     Pinch salt
½ cup heavy cream
     Baked 9-inch pie shell
     Additional whipped cream, for garnish (optional)
     Fresh plum wedges, for garnish (optional)

1. Combine the plums, ¼ cup of the water and ⅓ cup of the sugar in a small saucepan. Bring the mixture to boiling. Lower the heat and simmer, covered, until the plums are soft, for about 10 minutes. Remove the saucepan from the heat and cool the plum mixture slightly. Pour the undrained plum mixture into the container of an electric blender or a food processor. Cover and whirl until the plum mixture is puréed; you should have about 2 cups of purée.
2. Sprinkle the gelatin into the remaining ¼ cup of water and set aside to soften the gelatin.
3. Slightly beat the egg yolks in the small saucepan. Stir in the puréed plums and the lemon juice. Cook over low heat, stirring constantly, just to boiling. Remove the saucepan from the heat. Stir in the gelatin until it is dissolved. Stir in the lemon zest. Pour the egg-plum mixture into a bowl. Refrigerate, stirring often, until the mixture mounds slightly.

Life's a pudding full of plums . . .
Let us take it as it comes!
—W.S. Gilbert

4. Beat the egg whites with the salt in a bowl until soft peaks form. Gradually beat in the remaining ¼ cup of sugar until stiff peaks form.
5. Beat the heavy cream in a small bowl until it is stiff. Fold the egg whites and the whipped cream into the egg-plum mixture until the ingredients are well-blended. Turn the filling into the baked pie shell.
6. Refrigerate the pie for at least 3 hours. Garnish with additional whipped cream and fresh plum wedges, if you wish.

RASPBERRIES IN CREAM

Makes 8 servings.

Nutrient Value Per Serving: 272 calories, 2 g protein, 18 g fat, 28 g carbohydrate, 22 mg sodium, 64 mg cholesterol.

4	cups raspberries
2	tablespoons red currant jelly
¼	cup 10X (confectioners' powdered) sugar
3	tablespoons orange juice
1½	cups heavy cream
¼	cup dairy sour cream
⅓	cup light-flavored honey

1. Combine the raspberries, red currant jelly, 10X (confectioners' powdered) sugar and orange juice in the container of a food processor or an electric blender. Whirl until the mixture is puréed. Strain the raspberry purée and discard the seeds. Refrigerate the raspberry purée until it is chilled, for 2 hours.

2. Combine the heavy cream with the sour cream in a small bowl. Beat with an electric mixer until soft peaks begin to form. Gradually beat in the honey until stiff peaks form. Gently fold the raspberry purée into the whipped cream. Transfer the mixture to a decorative serving bowl and serve immediately.

BLUEBERRY BUTTERMILK CAKE

Bake at 350° for 60 minutes.
Makes 12 servings.

Nutrient Value Per Serving: 350 calories, 5 g protein, 18 g fat, 44 g carbohydrate, 172 mg sodium, 83 mg cholesterol.

½	cup slivered almonds
2	tablespoons plus ¾ cup granulated sugar
2	cups plus 1 tablespoon unsifted all-purpose flour
1½	teaspoons baking powder
½	teaspoon baking soda
¼	teaspoon salt
¼	teaspoon ground ginger
14	tablespoons (1¾ sticks) unsalted butter, at room temperature
½	cup firmly packed light brown sugar
2	eggs
1	teaspoon grated lemon zest (yellow part of rind only)
¾	teaspoon vanilla
¼	teaspoon almond extract
1	cup buttermilk
1	cup blueberries
½	teaspoon lemon juice

1. Preheat the oven to moderate (350°). Generously grease a 10 x 4-inch (16-cup) kugelhof pan. Sprinkle the pan with the almonds and 1 tablespoon of the granulated sugar.

2. Sift 2 cups of the flour with the baking powder, baking soda, salt and ginger onto wax paper.

3. Beat together the butter, ¾ cup of the remaining granulated sugar and the brown sugar until light and fluffy in a large bowl with an electric mixer. Beat in the eggs, one at a time, beating well after each addition. Mix in the lemon zest, vanilla and almond extract.

4. Alternately fold the flour mixture and the buttermilk into the batter, beginning and ending with the flour mixture.

5. Toss the remaining 1 tablespoon of flour and 1 tablespoon of granulated sugar with the blueberries and the lemon juice in a small bowl.

6. Pour the batter into the prepared pan and smooth the top. Scatter the blueberry mixture over the top and gently push the blueberries into the batter until they are just covered.

7. Bake in the preheated moderate oven (350°) for 60 minutes, or until a cake tester inserted near the center of the cake comes out clean. Cool the cake in the pan on a wire rack. Run a thin knife around the edges to loosen it, and invert the cake onto a serving plate.

STRAWBERRY KROPSUA

This Finnish dessert pancake will collapse as soon as it emerges from the oven, so don't be alarmed. After standing for a few minutes, the custard-like interior becomes even tastier.

Bake at 425° for 20 minutes.
Makes 6 servings.

Nutrient Value Per Serving: 254 calories, 8 g protein, 7 g fat, 39 g carbohydrate, 165 mg sodium, 148 mg cholesterol.

Strawberry Topping:
 1   pint strawberries, rinsed and hulled
 2   to 3 tablespoons granulated sugar
 1   tablespoon brandy OR: red wine
 ½   teaspoon vanilla

Kropsua (Pancake):
 3   eggs
 ¼   cup granulated sugar
 ¼   teaspoon salt
 2   cups milk
 1   teaspoon vanilla
 1   cup unsifted all-purpose flour
 1   teaspoon vegetable oil
 1   tablespoon 10X (confectioners' powdered) sugar
     Thin curls of lemon peel, for garnish (optional)

1. Prepare the Strawberry Topping: Cut the strawberries in half and place them in a bowl. Add the granulated sugar, brandy or red wine and the vanilla. Stir until the sugar dissolves. Cover the bowl and set aside the topping.

2. Preheat the oven to hot (425°).
3. Place a well-seasoned 9- or 10-inch cast-iron skillet in the preheated hot oven (425°) for 10 minutes.
4. Meanwhile, prepare the Kropsua: Beat together the eggs, granulated sugar and salt in a large bowl with an electric mixer. Beat in the milk and the vanilla. Gradually whisk in the flour until the batter is smooth and well blended.
5. Using a potholder, remove the heated skillet from the oven and brush it with the oil. Pour in the batter.
6. Bake in the preheated hot oven (425°) for 20 minutes, or until the Kropsua is puffed and golden. Remove the skillet to a wire rack and let it stand for 10 minutes. Dust the pancake with the 10X (confectioners' powdered) sugar, sprinkling it through a sieve. Serve hot with the Strawberry Topping. Garnish with thin curls of lemon peel, if you wish.

CAST IRON CARE

If the pan or skillet is new, wash it with soap and water, rinse it well and wipe dry. Thoroughly dry the pan in a preheated slow oven (200°) for 5 minutes. Pour 1 to 2 inches of cooking oil into the pan and place the pan over very low heat until the oil shimmers and is very hot. Turn off the heat and allow the oil to cool to room temperature. Repeat the heating and cooling two more times. Discard the oil and wipe the pan clean with paper toweling. After each use, wash the pan, if necessary, but do not use abrasives. To remove stubborn dirt, sprinkle the pan with salt and rub it with a sponge or soft cloth. Dry the pan thoroughly, wipe it with lightly oiled paper toweling and store it in an airy, dry place. An oven with a pilot light is an ideal storage place, or a pot rack in an airy kitchen. If a pan or skillet has become rusty, season it as for a new pan.

PEACHES AND CREAM TART

Bake at 400° for 40 minutes.
Makes 10 servings.

Nutrient Value Per Serving: 343 calories, 5 g protein, 20 g fat, 38 g carbohydrate, 195 mg sodium, 140 mg cholesterol.

1½	cups unsifted all-purpose flour
½	cup plus 2 tablespoons sugar
1	teaspoon baking powder
⅛	teaspoon salt
½	cup (1 stick) butter
3	eggs
½	teaspoon grated lemon zest (yellow part of rind only)
4	large peaches (2¼ to 2½ pounds)
1	tablespoon cornstarch
1	tablespoon lemon juice
1	cup heavy cream
¼	teaspoon ground nutmeg

1. Preheat the oven to hot (400°).

2. Stir together the flour, 2 tablespoons of the sugar, the baking powder and salt in a bowl. Cut in the butter with a pastry blender or two knives until the mixture resembles bread crumbs.

3. Combine 1 of the eggs with the lemon zest in a small bowl. Sprinkle the egg mixture over the flour mixture. Toss with a fork just until the flour mixture is moist. Work the pastry with your fingertips until it holds together.

4. Press the pastry evenly over the bottom and 2 inches up the sides of a 9-inch springform pan.

5. Dip the peaches in a saucepan of boiling water for 30 seconds, then into ice water for 1 minute. Peel, halve, pit and cut the peaches into slices; you should have about 5 cups. Combine the peaches, the remaining ½ cup of sugar, the cornstarch and lemon juice in a medium-size bowl. Toss to mix the ingredients well. Arrange the peach slices, overlapping, in the bottom of the pastry-lined pan.

6. Bake the tart in the preheated hot oven (400°) for 20 minutes.

7. Meanwhile, beat the remaining 2 eggs with the heavy cream and the nutmeg in a small bowl. Pour the cream mixture over the partially baked peaches.

8. Bake the tart for 20 minutes more, or until the cream is firm around the edges, the center is soft-set and the top is golden. Remove the tart to a wire rack to cool for at least 2 hours. Remove the side of the pan. Cool the tart completely. The tart tastes even better if it is refrigerated overnight before serving.

CRANBERRY NUT BREAD

Bake at 325° for 1 hour.
Makes 1 loaf (12 slices).

Nutrient Value Per Slice: 240 calories, 5 g protein, 9 g fat, 36 g carbohydrate, 192 mg sodium, 46 mg cholesterol.

2	cups sifted all-purpose flour
½	teaspoon salt
1½	teaspoons baking powder
½	teaspoon baking soda
1	large navel orange
	Boiling water
2	tablespoons vegetable shortening
2	eggs
1	cup sugar
1	cup fresh or thawed frozen cranberries, coarsely chopped
1	cup chopped walnuts

1. Preheat the oven to slow (325°). Grease a 9 x 5 x 3-inch loaf pan.

2. Sift together the flour, salt, baking powder and baking soda onto wax paper.

3. Grate the zest (orange part of the rind only) from the orange. Measure and reserve 1 tablespoon of zest. Squeeze the juice from the orange into a 2-cup measure. Add enough boiling water to make ¾ cup of liquid. Stir in the reserved orange zest and the shortening until the shortening is melted.

4. Beat the eggs in a large bowl until foamy. Gradually beat in the sugar and continue to beat until the egg mixture is thick and light.

5. Stir the flour mixture into the egg mixture alternately with the orange mixture, blending well after each addition. Stir in the cranberries and the walnuts. Spoon the batter into the prepared pan.

6. Bake in the preheated slow oven (325°) for 1 hour, or until the center springs back when lightly pressed with your fingertip. Cool the bread in the pan on a wire rack for 10 minutes. Turn out the bread from the pan and cool it completely. Store the bread overnight for easier slicing.

FARMER'S CHOICE: SELECTING FRESH VEGETABLES

Beets: Select small, round beets with smooth, firm flesh and fresh green tops; cut 1 inch off the tops of the beets; refrigerate the beets in a plastic bag for up to two weeks.

•

Corn: Select worm- and decay-free ears (if your market will allow it, peel back the tip of each husk and test a kernel with your fingernail; it should be firm and spurt a milky fluid); use the ears immediately, or refrigerate them with their husks intact for up to three days.

•

Eggplant: Select firm, smooth, glossy eggplants that feel heavy for their size; use them as soon as possible, or store them for up to two days in the refrigerator vegetable drawer, or in a cool, dark, humid place.

Green Beans: Select smooth, blemish-free, crisp pods that "snap" easily; refrigerate them, unwashed, in a plastic bag for up to three days.

•

Spinach: Select fresh, crisp, dark green leaves; refrigerate them unwashed, in a plastic bag, and use them as soon as possible.

•

Sweet Peppers: Select firm, well-shaped, thick-fleshed peppers with glossy surfaces; refrigerate them, unwashed, in the crisper for up to one week.

•

Tomatoes: Select firm, smooth-skinned, even-colored, blemish-free tomatoes; do not refrigerate them or they will become mushy; store them in a cool place, away from sunlight, until they are ripe.

•

Yellow Squash and Zucchini: Select young, small, fresh, firm, blemish-free squash; refrigerate them, unwashed, in a plastic bag for up to four days.

STIR-FRIED EGGPLANT WITH ORIENTAL DRESSING

Makes 6 servings.

Nutrient Value Per Serving: 139 calories, 2 g protein, 11 g fat, 9 g carbohydrate, 898 mg sodium, 0 mg cholesterol.

2   medium-size eggplants (¾ pound each), cut into 1 x ¼ x ¼-inch sticks
1   tablespoon salt

Oriental Dressing:
2   tablespoons soy sauce
1   tablespoon Oriental sesame oil
1   tablespoon white wine OR: rice vinegar
1   teaspoon sugar
2   tablespoons finely chopped green onion
1   tablespoon finely chopped garlic
1   teaspoon chili paste (optional)
½   teaspoon finely chopped gingerroot
½   cup finely chopped fresh cilantro

¼   cup peanut oil

1. Place the eggplant sticks in a colander and toss them with the salt. Let them drain for 1 hour.
2. Meanwhile, prepare the Oriental Dressing: Whisk together the soy sauce, Oriental sesame oil, wine or vinegar and the sugar in a medium-size serving bowl. Stir in the green onion, garlic, chili paste if you wish, ginger and cilantro.
3. Pat the eggplant dry with paper toweling. Heat the peanut oil in a wok or skillet over medium-high heat. Add the eggplant and stir-fry for 5 minutes, or until the eggplant is tender. Remove the wok from the heat. Stir in the dressing. Serve the mixture warm or cold.

O farmers, pray that your summers
be wet
and your winters clear.
—Virgil

SAUTÉED PEPPER SALAD

This colorful salad is a wonderful accompaniment to grilled chicken, steaks, chops or burgers. It tastes even better if you refrigerate it overnight.

Makes 8 servings.

Nutrient Value Per Serving: 97 calories, 2 g protein, 6 g fat, 11 g carbohydrate, 75 mg sodium, 0 mg cholesterol.

10	large sweet yellow peppers (about 3 pounds), cored, seeded and cut lengthwise into ¼-inch-wide strips
1	cup green beans, stemmed
3	tablespoons vegetable oil
3	medium-size firm, ripe tomatoes, cored, seeded and coarsely chopped
3	medium-size cloves garlic, crushed
3	tablespoons catsup
1	teaspoon freshly ground white pepper
½	teaspoon salt
2	tablespoons chopped parsley (preferably flat-leaf Italian), for garnish

1. Sauté the yellow peppers and the green beans in the oil in a large, heavy skillet over medium heat for 6 to 8 minutes, or until the peppers are crisply tender.
2. Meanwhile, place the tomatoes, garlic, catsup, white pepper and salt in a large, heatproof bowl. As soon as the yellow peppers are cooked, add the beans and peppers to the bowl and toss them with the tomato mixture. Let the salad stand at room temperature for at least 30 minutes before serving. Garnish with parsley.

A writer is like a bean plant — he has his little day, and then gets stringy.
— E.B. White

SAUTÉED TOMATOES WITH BLUE CHEESE SAUCE

This side dish makes a good accompaniment to grilled chops or baked chicken.

Makes 6 servings.

Nutrient Value Per Serving: 210 calories, 8 g protein, 17 g fat, 8 g carbohydrate, 673 mg sodium, 46 mg cholesterol.

6	medium-size tomatoes (about 2 pounds)
¼	cup (½ stick) butter
6	ounces blue cheese, crumbled (about 1½ cups)
¼	cup half-and-half
2	tablespoons finely chopped parsley
½	teaspoon salt
¼	teaspoon freshly ground pepper

1. Preheat the oven to slow (250°). Halve the tomatoes crosswise.
2. Melt the butter in a 10-inch skillet over medium-high heat. Add the tomatoes, cut side down, and cook for 3 minutes. Turn over the tomatoes and cook for 2 to 3 minutes more. Remove the tomatoes to a serving platter and keep them warm in the preheated slow oven (250°).
3. Stir the blue cheese, half-and-half, parsley, salt and pepper into the skillet. Cook over medium heat, whisking constantly, until the sauce is smooth and bubbling slightly. Pour the sauce over the tomatoes and serve the tomatoes hot.

MARINATED CORN SALAD

Makes 12 servings.

Nutrient Value Per Serving: 153 calories, 1 g protein, 14 g fat, 8 g carbohydrate, 190 mg sodium, 0 mg cholesterol.

1	cup water
2	cups fresh corn kernels (3 ears)
2	cups cooked, cut green beans
1	cup chopped sweet red pepper
1	small onion, sliced
¾	cup vegetable oil
6	tablespoons red wine vinegar
1	teaspoon salt
½	teaspoon dried dillweed
⅛	teaspoon sugar
	Lettuce leaves (optional)

1. Bring the water to boiling in a medium-size saucepan. Add the corn. Cover and cook for 3 minutes, or just until the corn is tender. Drain the corn and place it in a large, nonmetal bowl.

2. Add the green beans, red pepper and onion to the corn and toss to combine the ingredients.

3. Combine the oil, vinegar, salt, dillweed and sugar in a screw-top jar. Shake well to blend the ingredients. Pour the dressing over the corn mixture. Toss lightly until all the ingredients are well mixed. Cover the bowl and refrigerate the salad overnight. Serve the salad in a lettuce-lined salad bowl, if you wish.

HERB SAUTÉED SUMMER SQUASH

Makes 4 servings.

Nutrient Value Per Serving: 92 calories, 2 g protein, 7 g fat, 8 g carbohydrate, 446 mg sodium, 8 mg cholesterol.

1½	pounds yellow ("summer") squash
2	cloves garlic, finely chopped
½	teaspoon leaf rosemary, crumbled
1	tablespoon olive oil
1	tablespoon butter
2	tablespoons chopped parsley
1	tablespoon lemon juice
¾	teaspoon salt
¼	teaspoon freshly ground pepper

1. Cut the squash lengthwise into ¼-inch slices. Cut the slices crosswise into ¼-inch strips.

2. Sauté the garlic and the rosemary in the oil and the butter in a large skillet for 5 seconds. Add the squash and cook, stirring constantly, until the squash is crisply tender, for about 4 minutes.

3. Add the parsley, lemon juice, salt and pepper. Toss to combine the ingredients. Transfer the squash to a serving platter.

MINT AND GARLIC MARINATED ZUCCHINI

Makes 6 servings.

Nutrient Value Per Serving: 30 calories, 2 g protein, 0 g fat, 6 g carbohydrate, 372 mg sodium, 0 mg cholesterol.

2	pounds green or yellow zucchini, cut into 1-inch pieces
½	cup olive oil
½	cup red wine vinegar
1½	teaspoons sugar
1	teaspoon salt
¼	teaspoon freshly ground pepper
2	tablespoons finely chopped fresh mint OR: 1 tablespoon leaf mint, crumbled
2	cloves garlic, finely chopped

1. Lightly brown the zucchini in the oil in a 12-inch skillet for about 5 minutes. Remove the zucchini with a slotted spoon to a shallow serving dish.

2. Add the vinegar, sugar, salt and pepper to the skillet. Bring to boiling and simmer, uncovered, stirring, for 3 minutes. Pour the vinegar mixture over the zucchini. Add the mint and the garlic.

3. Cover the serving dish and refrigerate the zucchini for several hours, or overnight, turning the zucchini several times. Serve the zucchini at room temperature.

CUCUMBER BEET SALAD WITH ORANGE HONEY DRESSING

Makes 10 servings.

Nutrient Value Per Serving: 163 calories, 2 g protein, 15 g fat, 7 g carbohydrate, 121 mg sodium, 0 mg cholesterol.

1   *head leafy green lettuce*
1   *head romaine lettuce*
1   *long European-variety cucumber*
1   *fresh beet (about 8 ounces)*

Honey Orange Dressing:
3   *tablespoons orange juice*
1   *tablespoon lemon juice*
1   *tablespoon honey*
2   *teaspoons Dijon-style mustard*
2   *teaspoons grated orange zest*
     (orange part of rind only)
1/4 *to 1/2 teaspoon salt*
2/3 *cup vegetable oil*

1. Separate the leafy green lettuce head into individual leaves. Wash and blot them dry with paper toweling. Gather together half the leaves and cut them crosswise into 1-inch-wide strips. Repeat with the romaine lettuce.
2. Alternately place the whole lettuce leaves and the whole romaine leaves around the inside edge of a large salad bowl. Fill the center with the shredded lettuce and romaine strips. Cover the bowl with damp paper toweling and refrigerate until serving time.
3. Scrub the cucumber, cut it in half lengthwise and cut each half crosswise into thin half-moon slices. Place the slices in a plastic bag and refrigerate them.
4. Carefully peel the beet (beet juice will stain). Coarsely shred the beet, place it in a plastic bag and refrigerate it.
5. Prepare the Honey Orange Dressing: Combine the orange juice, lemon juice, honey, mustard, orange zest and salt in a small bowl. Whisk in the oil until it is well blended. Refrigerate the dressing until ready to use it.
6. To serve the salad, pour about half the dressing over the lettuce strips and toss to coat the strips. Arrange the cucumbers in a circle in the center of the bowl and arrange the shredded beet around the cucumber. Serve with the remaining dressing.

SAVORY BEETS WITH BACON

A hearty, flavorful vegetable dish that's a perfect foil for simply-cooked meats and poultry.

Makes 4 servings.

Nutrient Value Per Serving: 242 calories, 5 g protein, 17 g fat, 20 g carbohydrate, 579 mg sodium, 19 mg cholesterol.

2   *pounds fresh beets (about 2 bunches), scrubbed*
     and stems removed
1/4 *pound thickly sliced bacon, cut crosswise into*
     1/4-inch strips
1   *medium-size onion, halved and thinly sliced*
6   *tablespoons cider vinegar*
1 1/2 *teaspoons sugar*
1/2 *teaspoon salt*
1/4 *teaspoon freshly ground pepper*
1/4 *cup finely chopped parsley*

1. Place the beets in a 3-quart saucepan, cover them with water and bring to boiling. Cover and simmer until the beets are tender, for about 45 to 50 minutes. Drain the beets and cool them to room temperature. Peel the beets and slice them 1/4 inch thick.
2. Cook the bacon in the same saucepan until it is crisp. Remove it with a slotted spoon and set aside. Add the onion to the bacon fat and sauté for 3 minutes, stirring occasionally. Add the vinegar, sugar, salt and pepper. Bring to boiling, stirring constantly, and cook for 2 minutes, or until the dressing is slightly thickened. Remove the dressing from the heat.
3. Stir the beets into the dressing and heat briefly. Just before serving, sprinkle with the bacon and the parsley. Serve the beets warm.

Savory Beets with Bacon (recipe, page 222)

CORN AND SWEET PEPPER SAUTÉ

Makes 4 servings.

Nutrient Value Per Serving: 249 calories, 5 g protein, 14 g fat, 31 g carbohydrate, 663 mg sodium, 23 mg cholesterol.

3	tablespoons butter
1	tablespoon vegetable oil
4	cups fresh corn kernels (4 large or 6 medium-size ears)
2	tablespoons water
½	sweet green pepper, cut into ¼-inch cubes
½	sweet red pepper, cut into ¼-inch cubes
2	tablespoons finely chopped fresh cilantro OR: dillweed
1	teaspoon salt
¼	teaspoon freshly ground pepper

1. Heat the butter and the oil in a 12-inch skillet over medium-high heat. Add the corn and the water and sauté for 5 to 8 minutes, or until the corn is tender. Add the green and red peppers, and sauté for 2 more minutes.

2. Add the cilantro or dill, the salt and pepper. Toss well to combine all the ingredients, and serve.

SAVORY LENTIL STEW

Makes 4 servings.

Nutrient Value Per Serving: 177 calories, 15 g protein, 1 g fat, 30 g carbohydrate, 281 mg sodium, 0 mg cholesterol.

½	of 10½-ounce can condensed beef broth
1½	cups water
1	cup dried lentils, washed and picked over
¼	cup chopped celery
¼	cup chopped onion
¼	cup chopped sweet red or green pepper
1	large clove garlic, finely chopped
½	teaspoon leaf thyme, crumbled
⅛	teaspoon freshly ground pepper
1	small bay leaf

Combine all the ingredients in a medium-size saucepan. Cover the saucepan and bring to boiling. Lower the heat and simmer, stirring, for 30 minutes, or until the lentils are tender. Remove the bay leaf and serve at once.

CAULIFLOWER AND BEANS WITH CHEESE SAUCE

Cauliflower and beans are baked to perfection, then topped with a mustard-cheese sauce.

Bake at 350° for 50 minutes.
Makes 6 servings.

Nutrient Value Per Serving: 187 calories, 11 g protein, 10 g fat, 16 g carbohydrate, 725 mg sodium, 14 mg cholesterol.

1	small head cauliflower
½	pound green beans, tipped
½	pound wax beans, tipped
1	cup boiling water
1	teaspoon salt
1	teaspoon dillweed
¼	teaspoon lemon pepper
1	small can evaporated milk
4	slices processed American cheese, diced
1	tablespoon prepared mustard
	Chopped tomato, for garnish (optional)
	Sliced green onions, for garnish (optional)

1. Trim the cauliflower and soak it in salted hot water for 5 minutes.

2. Arrange the cauliflower and the beans in an 8-cup casserole dish. Add the boiling water, salt, dill and lemon pepper.

3. Bake in a moderate oven (350°) for 50 minutes, or until the vegetables are crisp-tender when pierced with a two-tined fork. Keep warm.

4. Heat the evaporated milk in a small saucepan over moderate heat until the milk is very warm. Stir in the cheese and the mustard until the cheese melts. Spoon the cheese sauce over the vegetables and garnish with the chopped tomato and sliced green onions.

Cauliflower is nothing but cabbage with a college education.
—Mark Twain

FRESH TOMATO CAKE

Bake at 350° for 40 to 45 minutes.
Makes 9 servings.

Nutrient Value Per Serving: 410 calories, 7 g protein, 19 g fat, 57 g carbohydrate, 332 mg sodium, 58 mg cholesterol.

10	ounces ripe tomatoes (2 medium-size tomatoes)
¼	cup white rum
1	cup raisins
1	cup slivered almonds
1¾	cups sifted all-purpose flour
1	teaspoon baking soda
½	teaspoon salt
2	teaspoons ground cinnamon
½	teaspoon ground cloves
½	cup (1 stick) butter or margarine, softened
1	cup granulated sugar
1	egg
	10X (confectioners' powdered) sugar, for garnish (optional)

1. Preheat the oven to moderate (350°). Grease and flour an 8-inch-square baking pan.
2. Core and coarsely chop the tomatoes. Place them in the container of an electric blender or a food processor. Cover and whirl until the tomatoes are puréed. Pour the purée into a 2-cup measure; you should have 1 cup of purée. Stir in the rum and set aside the mixture.
3. Combine the raisins with the almonds in a small bowl. Stir about 1 tablespoon of the flour into the almond mixture and set aside. Combine the remaining flour with the baking soda, salt, cinnamon and cloves in a second bowl. Mix well; set aside the flour mixture.
4. Beat the butter or margarine together with the granulated sugar until light and fluffy in a large bowl with an electric mixer. Beat in the egg until it is well mixed. Gradually beat in the puréed tomato mixture until smooth. Fold in the flour mixture and the almond mixture until they are blended. Pour the batter into the prepared pan.
5. Bake in the preheated moderate oven (350°) for 40 to 45 minutes, or until a cake tester inserted in the center of the cake comes out clean. Cool the cake in the pan on a wire rack for 10 minutes. Remove the cake from the pan to the wire rack and cool to room temperature. Slide the cake onto a serving plate. If you wish, sprinkle the top of the cake with 10X (confectioners' powdered) sugar, using a doily to create a pattern.

MINI CARROT CAKES WITH CREAM CHEESE SAUCE

A snack-size version of a familiar favorite.

Bake at 350° for 20 to 25 minutes.
Makes 24 mini-cakes.

Nutrient Value Per Cake: 251 calories, 2 g protein, 16 g fat, 26 g carbohydrate, 135 mg sodium, 32 mg cholesterol.

1½	cups unsifted all-purpose flour
2¼	teaspoons ground cinnamon
1	teaspoon baking soda
¾	teaspoon baking powder
¾	teaspoon ground nutmeg
½	teaspoon salt
1⅓	cups sugar
1	cup vegetable oil
2	eggs
3	cups grated carrots (about 1 pound)
1	cup coarsely chopped walnuts
	Cream Cheese Sauce (recipe follows)
	Shredded carrot, for garnish (optional)

1. Preheat the oven to moderate (350°). Line twenty-four 2½-inch muffin-pan cups with aluminum foil or paper baking cups.
2. Combine the flour, cinnamon, baking soda, baking powder, nutmeg and salt in a small bowl. Stir to mix the ingredients. Set aside the flour mixture.
3. Beat together the sugar, oil and eggs in a large bowl. Stir in the carrots. Add the flour mixture, stirring just until it is combined. Stir in the walnuts. Spoon the batter into the lined muffin-pan cups, dividing it equally among the cups.
4. Bake in the preheated moderate oven (350°) for 20 to 25 minutes, or until a wooden pick inserted in the centers of the cakes comes out clean. Remove the cakes from the pans to wire racks to cool.
5. Prepare the Cream Cheese Sauce.
6. Frost the cakes with the Cream Cheese Sauce. Garnish with shredded carrot, if you wish.

Cream Cheese Sauce: Beat ¼ cup (½ stick) of softened butter or margarine with 1 package (3 ounces) of softened cream cheese and 1 teaspoon of vanilla in a bowl until the ingredients are well blended. Gradually beat in 1½ cups of sifted 10X (confectioners' powdered) sugar until the sauce is smooth and creamy.

S·I·D·E D·I·S·H·E·S
A·N·D S·A·U·C·E·S

SWEET PEPPER APRICOT CHUTNEY

Serve this spicy condiment "as is" on crackers or toast. For a deliciously different treat, mix 2 tablespoons of the chutney into 3 ounces of cream cheese.

Makes 4 cups.

Nutrient Value Per 2 Tablespoons: 35 calories, 0 g protein, 0 g fat, 9 g carbohydrate, 53 mg sodium, 0 mg cholesterol.

1¼	pounds sweet red peppers, cored, seeded, and cut into ¼-inch dice (3 cups)
12	ounces dried apricots, cut into ¼-inch dice
1	cup raisins
1	large onion, finely chopped
5	cloves garlic, thinly slivered
1	3-inch piece fresh gingerroot, peeled and thinly slivered (3 tablespoons)
1½	teaspoons salt
1	to 1½ teaspoons crushed red pepper flakes, or to taste
1	teaspoon cumin seeds
¾	teaspoon mustard seeds
1	cup sugar
¾	cup red wine vinegar

1. Combine the red peppers, apricots, raisins, onion, garlic, ginger, salt, red pepper flakes, cumin seeds, mustard seeds and sugar in a large saucepan. Cook the mixture, uncovered, stirring occasionally, over medium heat until the sugar dissolves, for about 5 minutes.
2. Add the vinegar. Cook, stirring often, until the mixture is shiny and thick, for 30 to 35 minutes. Cool the chutney. Place the chutney in a bowl, cover the bowl and refrigerate the chutney.

GINGERED APPLE CHUTNEY

A tasty alternative to mango chutney.

Makes 6 cups.

Nutrient Value Per 2 Tablespoons: 49 calories, 0 g protein, 0 g fat, 12 g carbohydrate, 25 mg sodium, 0 mg cholesterol.

2	tablespoons yellow mustard seeds
½	teaspoon salt
1½	cups firmly packed dark brown sugar
2	cups cider vinegar
6	large, firm apples, such as Rome Beauty or Golden Delicious (2 pounds), peeled, cored and coarsely chopped
¼	cup finely chopped garlic
2	tablespoons finely chopped, peeled fresh gingerroot
1	cup dark seedless raisins
½	teaspoon ground hot red pepper

1. Heat the mustard seeds in a large saucepan over medium-high heat until they begin to color lightly and jump around the pan. Cover the saucepan and remove the mustard seeds from the heat until they settle down.
2. Add the salt, brown sugar and vinegar to the saucepan. Bring to boiling over medium-high heat. Lower the heat and simmer for 5 minutes. Add the apples, garlic, ginger, raisins and ground hot red pepper. Simmer gently for 20 minutes, or until the apples are transparent.
3. Ladle the hot chutney into hot, sterilized, 1-cup jars. Cover the jars tightly with sterilized lids. Refrigerate the chutney for at least 1 week for the flavors to mature. The chutney may be stored in the refrigerator for up to 1 month.

COUNTRY-STYLE CUCUMBER RELISH

This tangy relish takes one day to prepare and one day to finish.

Makes about 8 pints.

Nutrient Value Per ¼ Cup: 32 calories, 0 g protein, 0 g fat, 8 g carbohydrate, 225 mg sodium, 0 mg cholesterol.

5½   quarts medium-coarsely chopped, peeled
        small pickling cucumbers (about 5 pounds)
1   quart medium-coarsely chopped yellow onions
        (about 12 ounces)
1   quart medium-coarsely chopped, cored and
        seeded sweet green peppers (about 1 pound)
⅓   cup pickling salt OR: coarse (Kosher) salt
2   trays ice cubes
2   quarts cold water
7½   cups sugar
4½   cups cider vinegar
3   tablespoons celery seeds
2½   teaspoons ground turmeric

1. Layer the cucumbers, onion and green peppers in a very large, heavy, enamel or stainless steel kettle, sprinkling each layer with the salt. Place the ice cubes on top of the layered vegetables and pour in the cold water. Cover the kettle and let the vegetables stand for 24 hours.
2. Next day, drain the vegetables very well. Place them, in batches, in a clean dry cloth and twist the cloth hard to remove as much excess liquid as possible from the vegetables. Set aside the vegetables.
3. Combine the sugar, vinegar, celery seeds and turmeric in the large enamel or stainless steel kettle. Bring to boiling over medium heat and stir to dissolve the sugar. Lower the heat and simmer, uncovered, for 5 minutes.
4. Add the vegetables to the vinegar mixture, stirring well. Bring the mixture to a rolling boil. Remove the kettle from the heat. Ladle the relish immediately into hot, sterilized, 1-pint canning jars, filling to within ¼ inch of the tops. Run a thin-bladed nonmetallic spatula around the inside of each jar to release air bubbles. Wipe the jar rims with a damp cloth. Cover the jars with hot domed lids and metal rings.
5. Process the jars in a hot water bath for 10 minutes (the water should cover the jars by 1 to 2 inches). Remove the jars to a wire rack. Let them stand for twelve hours to cool thoroughly. Test the seals. Label, date and store the jars in a cool, dark place for at least 3 weeks before using the relish.

APPLE, ONION AND PEPPER RELISH

An old family recipe from the Blue Ridge Mountains of North Carolina.

Makes 10 to 11 pints.

Nutrient Value Per Tablespoon: 11 calories, 0 g protein, 0 g fat, 3 g carbohydrate, 26 mg sodium, 0 mg cholesterol.

12   large sweet red peppers (about 4½ pounds)
12   small yellow onions (about 2 pounds)
12   small Golden Delicious apples (about 4 pounds)
      About 3 quarts boiling water
2½   cups cider vinegar
2½   cups cold water
2½   cups sugar
4   teaspoons pickling salt OR: coarse (Kosher) salt

1. Core, seed and chop medium-coarsely the red peppers. Peel and medium-coarsely chop the onions. Peel, core and medium-coarsely chop the apples. Place the red peppers, onion and apples in a very large, heavy, enamel or stainless steel pot. Pour in just enough of the boiling water to cover. Let the vegetable-apple mixture stand for 10 minutes.
2. Meanwhile, combine the vinegar, cold water, sugar and salt in a medium-size, heavy, enamel or stainless steel pot. Bring to boiling over medium heat and stir to dissolve the sugar. Lower the heat and simmer, uncovered, for 5 minutes.
3. Drain the vegetable-apple mixture well and return it to the same pot. Pour in the vinegar mixture. Bring the combined mixture to a full rolling boil. Remove the pot from the heat. Immediately ladle the relish into hot, sterilized, 1-pint canning jars, filling to within ¼ inch of the tops. Run a thin-bladed nonmetallic spatula around the inside of each jar to release air bubbles. Wipe the jar rims with a damp cloth. Cover the jars with hot domed lids and metal rings.
4. Process the jars in a hot water bath for 10 minutes (the water should cover the jars by 1 to 2 inches). Remove the jars to a wire rack. Let them stand for twelve hours to cool thoroughly. Test the seals. Label, date and store the jars in a cool, dark place for at least 2 weeks before using the relish.

CUCUMBER STICK PICKLES

The best cucumbers to use for this recipe are small, unwaxed (so they needn't be peeled) pickling cucumbers; slim, foot-long "burpless" English or hot-house cucumbers can be substituted.

Makes about 6 pints.

Nutrient Value Per Stick: 32 calories, 0 g protein, 8 g fat, 32 g carbohydrate, 225 mg sodium, 0 mg cholesterol.

22	unwaxed pickling cucumbers, about 5 inches long (about 5 pounds)
3	quarts boiling water
1	quart cider vinegar
3	cups sugar
3	tablespoons pickling salt OR: coarse (Kosher) salt
2	teaspoons celery seeds
1	teaspoon ground turmeric
3/4	teaspoon mustard seeds

1. Scrub the cucumbers well in cool water. Trim and cut them into 4½-inch lengths to fit in 1-pint canning jars. Quarter the cucumbers lengthwise.
2. Place the cucumbers in a large, heavy kettle. Pour the boiling water over them. Cover the kettle and let the cucumbers stand 4 to 5 hours.
3. Drain the cucumbers well and set them aside.
4. Combine the vinegar, sugar, salt, celery seeds, turmeric and mustard seeds in a small, heavy, enamel or stainless steel pan. Bring the vinegar mixture to boiling over medium heat. Lower the heat and simmer, uncovered, for 5 minutes.
5. Meanwhile, stand the cucumber sticks upright in hot, sterilized, 1-pint canning jars, making a ring of the best-looking sticks around the outer edge and wedging less-than-perfect sticks in the middle. Pack the sticks snugly into each jar so that they stand straight; they should not wobble and should not start to float toward the tops of the jars when you add the vinegar mixture.
6. Return the vinegar mixture to boiling. Immediately ladle it into the jars, covering the sticks entirely and filling the jars to within ¼ inch of the tops. Run a thin-bladed nonmetallic spatula around the inside of each jar to release air bubbles. Wipe the jar rims with a damp cloth. Cover the jars with hot domed lids and metal rings.
7. Process the jars in a hot water bath for 10 minutes (the water should cover the jars by 1 to 2 inches).

Remove the jars to a wire rack. Let them stand for 12 hours to cool thoroughly. Test the seals. Label, date and store the jars in a cool, dark place for at least 2 weeks before using the pickles.

OLD-TIME YELLOW SQUASH PICKLES

Makes 4 pints.

Nutrient Value Per ¼ Cup: 93 calories, 1 g protein, 0 g fat, 23 g carbohydrate, 826 mg sodium, 0 mg cholesterol.

2	quarts thinly sliced small yellow squash (3 pounds)
1	quart thinly sliced white onions (about 1½ pounds)
1	large sweet green pepper, cored, seeded and coarsely chopped (½ pound)
¼	cup pickling salt OR: coarse (Kosher) salt
2	cups cider vinegar
3	cups sugar
2	teaspoons celery seeds
2	teaspoons mustard seeds
½	teaspoon ground turmeric

1. Layer the squash and the onions in a large bowl, sprinkling each layer with the green pepper and the salt. Cover the bowl and let stand for 1 hour.
2. Meanwhile, combine the vinegar, sugar, celery seeds, mustard seeds and turmeric in a large, heavy, enamel or stainless steel pot. Set aside.
3. Place the vegetables in a large colander and rinse them with cold water. Drain the vegetables well.
4. Bring the vinegar mixture to boiling. Add the vegetables and stir well. Bring the mixture to a full rolling boil. Remove the pot from the heat.
5. Immediately ladle the pickles into hot, sterilized, 1-pint canning jars, filling to within ¼ inch of the tops. Run a thin-bladed nonmetallic spatula around the inside of each jar to release air bubbles. Wipe the jar rims with a damp cloth. Cover the jars with hot domed lids and metal rings.
6. Process the jars in a hot water bath for 10 minutes (the water should cover the jars by 1 to 2 inches). Remove the jars to a wire rack. Let them stand for 12 hours. Test the seals. Label, date and store the jars in a cool, dark place for 2 weeks before using the relish.

CLASSIC PESTO

Toss this traditional Italian sauce with your favorite pasta or spoon a little on cooked vegetables or baked potatoes. You can even use pesto as a base for salad dressing.

Makes about 1 cup.

Nutrient Value Per ¼ Cup: 370 calories, 8 g protein, 36 g fat, 9 g carbohydrate, 326 mg sodium, 8 mg cholesterol.

¼	cup pine nuts (1½ ounces)
2	small cloves garlic, peeled
2	cups firmly packed fresh whole basil leaves
½	cup olive oil
½	cup grated Parmesan cheese
½	teaspoon freshly ground pepper
¼	teaspoon salt

Place the pine nuts and the garlic in the container of a food processor or an electric blender. Cover and whirl until they are finely chopped. Add the basil and whirl until it is coarsely chopped. With the motor running, pour the oil through the feed tube and whirl until the mixture is finely chopped but not puréed. Stir in the Parmesan cheese, pepper and salt. Refrigerate the pesto for up to 3 days, or freeze it for up to 3 months.

HERB-MARINATED MOZZARELLA

Makes 12 servings.

Nutrient Value Per Serving: 95 calories, 4 g protein, 9 g fat, 1 g carbohydrate, 62 mg sodium, 15 mg cholesterol.

1	cup extra-virgin olive oil
¼	cup chopped fresh oregano leaves
1	teaspoon crushed red pepper flakes
1	teaspoon chopped garlic
½	teaspoon salt
½	teaspoon freshly ground pepper
1	package (9 ounces) small mozzarella cheese balls, drained

Mix together the oil, oregano, red pepper flakes, garlic, salt and pepper in a small bowl. Arrange the mozzarella cheese balls in a nonmetal shallow pan just large enough to hold the balls in a single layer. Pour the oregano mixture over the mozzarella balls and roll the balls to coat them. Cover the pan and refrigerate the mozzarella balls overnight to allow the flavors to fully develop.

Note: *The marinade can be used as a base for salad dressing after the mozzarella balls have been eaten.*

SPINACH PESTO

This pesto, made with fresh spinach, is a delightful twist on the traditional basil pesto. Try it tossed with rotelle or ziti, or served over fresh steamed vegetables.

Makes 1½ cups.

Nutrient Value Per ¼ Cup: 342 calories, 9 g protein, 33 g fat, 7 g carbohydrate, 240 mg sodium, 5 mg cholesterol.

⅓	cup whole blanched almonds
2	small cloves garlic
2	cups firmly packed spinach leaves
1	cup firmly packed fresh flat-leaf Italian parsley leaves
½	cup olive oil
½	cup grated Parmesan cheese
½	teaspoon freshly ground pepper
¼	teaspoon salt

Combine the almonds and the garlic in the container of a food processor. Whirl until they are very finely ground. Add the spinach and the parsley. Whirl until they are coarsely chopped. With the motor running, pour the oil through the feed tube. Whirl until the mixture is finely chopped but not puréed. Stir in the Parmesan cheese, pepper and salt. Refrigerate the pesto for 2 or 3 days, or freeze it for up to 3 months.

C·R·A·F·T·S B·A·S·I·C·S & A·B·B·R·E·V·I·A·T·I·O·N·S

HOW TO KNIT

THE BASIC STITCHES

Get out your needles and yarn, and slowly read your way through this special section. Practice the basic stitches illustrated here as you go along. Once you know them, you're ready to start knitting.

CASTING ON: This puts the first row of stitches on the needle. Measure off about two yards of yarn (or about an inch for each stitch you are going to cast on). Make a slip knot at this point by making a medium-size loop of yarn; then pull another small loop through it. Place the slip knot on one needle and pull one end gently to tighten (FIG. 1).

FIG. 1

◆ Hold the needle in your right hand. Hold both strands of yarn in the palm of your left hand securely but not rigidly. Slide your left thumb and forefinger between the two strands and spread these two fingers out so that you have formed a triangle of yarn.

Your left thumb should hold the free end of yarn, your forefinger the yarn from the ball. The needle in your right hand holds the first stitch (FIG. 2).

FIG. 2

You are now in position to cast on.

◆ Bring the needle in your right hand toward you; slip the tip of the needle under the front strand of the loop on your left thumb (FIG. 3).

FIG. 3

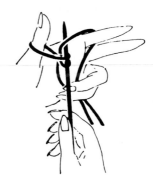

◆ Now, with the needle, catch the strand of yarn that is on your left forefinger (FIG. 4).

FIG. 4

◆ Draw it through the thumb loop to form a stitch on the needle (FIG. 5).

FIG. 5

♦ Holding the stitch on the needle with your right index finger, slip the loop off your left thumb (FIG. 6). Tighten up the stitch on the needle by pulling the freed strand back with your left thumb, bringing the yarn back into position for casting on more stitches (FIG. 2).

FIG. 6

♦ **Do not cast on too tightly.** Stitches should slide easily on the needle. Repeat from * until you have cast on the number of stitches specified in your instructions.

KNIT STITCH (k): Hold the needle with the cast-on stitches in your left hand (FIG. 7).

FIG. 7

♦ Pick up the other needle in your right hand. With yarn from the ball in **back** of the work, insert the tip of the right-hand needle from **left to right** through the front loop of the first stitch on the left-hand needle (FIG. 8).

FIG. 8

♦ Holding both needles in this position with your left hand, wrap the yarn over your little finger, under your two middle fingers and over the forefinger of your right hand. Hold the yarn firmly, but loosely enough so that it will slide through your fingers as you knit. Return the right-hand needle to your right hand.

♦ With your right forefinger, pass the yarn under (from right to left) and then over (from left to right) the tip of the right-hand needle, forming a loop on the needle (FIG. 9).

FIG. 9

♦ Now draw this loop through the stitch on the left-hand needle (FIG. 10).

FIG. 10

◆ Slip the original stitch off the left-hand needle, leaving the new stitch on right-hand needle (Fig. 11).

FIG. 11

Note: *Keep the stitches loose enough to slide along the needles, but tight enough to maintain their position on the needles until you want them to slide.* Continue until you have knitted all the stitches from the left-hand needle onto the right-hand needle.

◆ To start the next row, pass the needle with stitches on it to your left hand, reversing it, so that it is now the left-hand needle.

PURL STITCH (p): Purling is the reverse of knitting. Again, keep the stitches loose enough to slide, but firm enough to work with. To purl, hold the needle with the stitches in your left hand, with the yarn in ***front*** of your work. Insert the tip of the right-hand needle from ***right to left*** through the front loop of the first stitch on the left-hand needle (Fig. 12).

FIG. 12

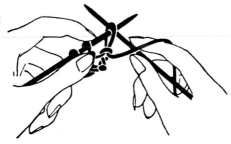

◆ With your right hand holding the yarn as you would to knit, but in ***front*** of the needles, pass the yarn over the tip of the right-hand needle, then under it, forming a loop on the needle. (Fig. 13).

FIG. 13

◆ Holding the yarn firmly so that it won't slip off, draw this loop through the stitch on the left-hand needle (Fig. 14).

FIG. 14

◆ Slip the original stitch off of the left-hand needle, leaving the new stitch on the right-hand needle (Fig. 15).

FIG. 15

SLIPSTITCH (sl st): Insert the tip of the right-hand needle into the next stitch on the left-hand needle, as if to purl, unless otherwise directed. Slip this stitch off the left-hand needle onto the right, but ***do not*** work the stitch (Fig. 16).

FIG. 16

BINDING OFF: This makes a finished edge and locks the stitches securely in place. Knit (or purl) two stitches. Then, with the tip of the left-hand needle, lift the first of these two stitches over the second stitch and drop it off the tip of the right-hand needle (FIG. 17).

FIG. 17

One stitch remains on the right-hand needle, and one stitch has been bound off.

♦ Knit (or purl) the next stitch; lift the first stitch over the last stitch and off the tip of the needle. Again, one stitch remains on the right-hand needle, and another stitch has been bound off. Repeat from * until the required number of stitches have been bound off.

♦ Remember that you work two stitches to bind off one stitch. If, for example, the directions read, "k 6, bind off the next 4 sts, k 6 . . . " you must knit six stitches, then knit **two more** stitches before starting to bind off. Bind off four times. After the four stitches have been bound off, count the last stitch remaining on the right-hand needle as the first stitch of the next six stitches. When binding off, always knit the knitted stitches and purl the purled stitches.

♦ Be careful not to bind off too tightly or too loosely. The tension should be the same as the rest of the knitting.

♦ To end off the last stitch on the bound-off edge, if you are ending this piece of work here, cut the yarn leaving a 6-inch end; pass the cut end through the remaining loop on the right-hand needle and pull snugly (FIG. 18).

FIG. 18

SHAPING TECHNIQUES

Now that you are familiar with the basic stitches, you are ready to learn the techniques for shaping your knitting projects.

INCREASING (inc): This means adding stitches in a given area to shape your work. There are several ways to increase.

1. To increase by knitting twice into the same stitch: Knit the stitch in the usual way through the front loop (FIG. 19), but **before** dropping the stitch from the left-hand needle, knit **another** stitch on the same loop by placing the needle into the back of the stitch. (FIG. 20). Slip the original stitch off your left-hand needle. You now have made two stitches from one stitch.

FIG. 19

FIG. 20

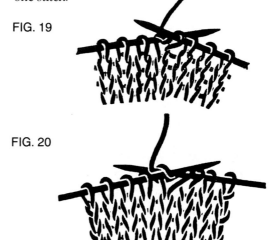

2. To increase by knitting between stitches: Insert the tip of the right-hand needle under the strand of yarn **between** the stitch you've just worked and the following stitch; slip it onto the tip of the left-hand needle (FIG. 21).

FIG. 21

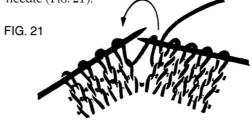

Now knit into the back of the loop (FIG. 22).

FIG. 22

3. To increase by "yarn-over" (yo): Pass the yarn **over** the right-hand needle after finishing one stitch and before starting the next stitch, making an extra stitch (see the arrow in Fig. 23). If you are knitting, bring the yarn **under** the needle to the back. If you are purling, wind the yarn **around** the needle once. On the next row, work all yarn-overs as stitches.

FIG. 23

DECREASING (dec): This means reducing the number of stitches in a given area to shape your work. Two methods for decreasing are:

1. To decrease by knitting (Fig. 24) **or purling** (Fig. 25) **two stitches together:**

FIG. 24

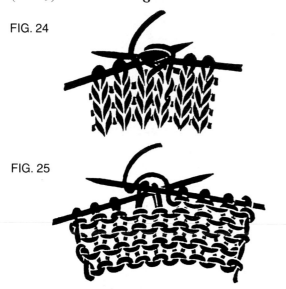

FIG. 25

Insert the right-hand needle through the loops of two stitches on the left-hand needle at the same time. Complete the stitch. This is written as "k 2 tog" or "p 2 tog."

♦ If you work through the **front** loops of the stitches, your decreasing stitch will slant to the right. If you work through the **back** loops of the stitches, your decreasing stitch will slant to the left.

2. Slip 1 stitch, knit 1 and psso: Insert the right-hand needle through the stitch on the left-hand needle, but instead of working it, just slip it off onto the right-hand needle (see Fig. 16). Work the next stitch in the usual way. With the tip of the left-hand needle, lift the slipped stitch over the last stitch worked and off the tip of the right-hand needle (Fig. 26). Your decreasing stitch will slant to the left. This is written as "sl 1, k 1, psso."

FIG. 26

Pass Slipped Stitch Over (psso): Slip one stitch from the left-hand needle to the right-hand needle and, being careful to keep it in position, work the next stitch. Then, with the tip of the left-hand needle, lift the slipped stitch over the last stitch and off the tip of the right-hand needle (Fig. 26).

ATTACHING YARN

When you finish one ball of yarn, or if you wish to change colors, attach the new ball of yarn at the start of a row. Tie the new yarn to an end of the previous yarn, making a secure knot to join the two yarns. Continue to work (Fig. 27).

FIG. 27

HOW TO CROCHET

THE BASIC STITCHES

Most crochet stitches are started from a base of chain stitches. However, our stitches are started from a row of single crochet stitches which gives body to the sample swatches and makes practice work easier to handle. When making a specific item, follow the stitch directions as given.

Holding the crochet hook properly (FIG. 1), start by practicing the slip knot (FIG. 2 through FIG. 2C) and base chain (FIG. 3 through FIG. 3B).

FIG. 1 HOLDING THE HOOK

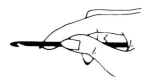

FIG. 2 THE SLIP KNOT (BASIS FOR CHAIN STITCH)

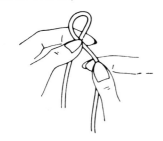

FIG. 2a

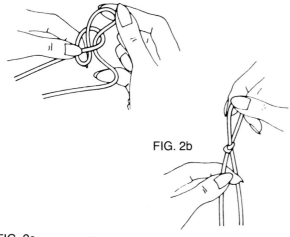

FIG. 2b

FIG. 2c

FIG. 3 CHAIN STITCH (CH)

YARN OVER (YO)

FIG. 3a

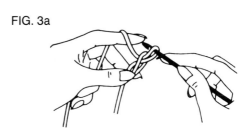

FIG. 3b

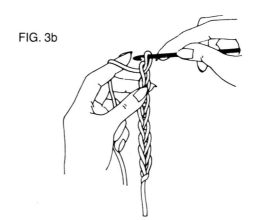

CHAIN STITCH (ch): Follow the steps in FIG. 3 through FIG. 3B. As you make the chain stitch loops, the yarn should slide easily between your index and middle fingers. Make about 15 loops. If they are all the same size, you have maintained even tension. If the stitches are uneven, rip them out by pulling on the long end of the yarn. Practice the chain stitch until you can crochet a perfect chain.

From here on, we won't be showing hands—just the hook and the stitches. **Note:** *Left-handed crocheters can use the illustrations for right-handed crocheting by turning the book upside down in front of a free-standing mirror. The reflected illustrations will provide left-handed instructions.*

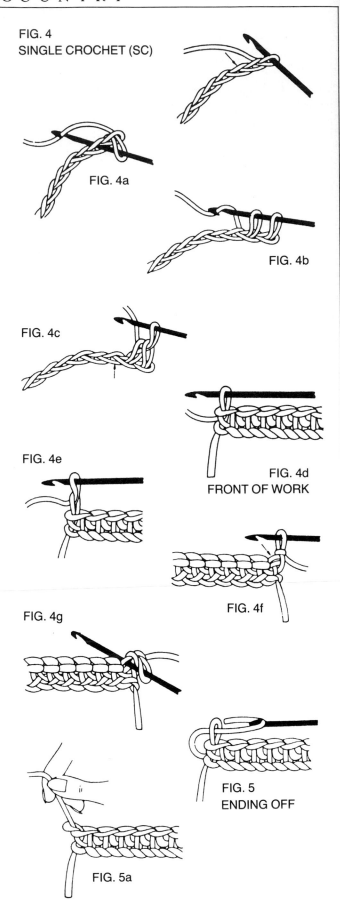

FIG. 4
SINGLE CROCHET (SC)

FIG. 4a

FIG. 4b

FIG. 4c

FIG. 4e

FIG. 4d
FRONT OF WORK

FIG. 4f

FIG. 4g

FIG. 5
ENDING OFF

FIG. 5a

SINGLE CROCHET (sc): Follow the steps in FIG. 4. To practice, make a 20-loop chain (this means 20 loops in addition to the slip knot). Turn the chain, as shown, and insert the hook in the second chain from the hook (see arrow) to make the first sc stitch. Yarn over (yo); for the second stitch, see the next arrow. Repeat to the end of the chain. Because you started in the second chain from the hook, you end up with only 19 sc. To add the 20th stitch, ch 1 (called a turning chain) and pull the yarn through. Now turn your work around (the "back" is now facing you) and start the second row of sc in the first stitch of the previous row (at the arrow). Make sure your hook goes under both of the strands at the top of the stitch. Don't forget to make a ch 1 turning chain at the end before turning your work. Keep practicing until your rows are perfect.

ENDING OFF: Follow the steps in FIG. 5. To finish off your crochet, cut off all but 6-inches of yarn and end off as shown. (To "break off and fasten," follow the same procedure.)

DOUBLE CROCHET (dc): Follow the steps in FIG. 6. To practice, ch 20, then make a row of 20 sc. Now, instead of a ch 1, you will make a ch 3. Turn your work, yo and insert the hook in the second stitch of the previous row (at the arrow), going under both strands at the top of the stitch. Pull the yarn through. You now have three loops on the hook. Yo and pull through the first two, then yo and pull through the remaining two—one double crochet (dc) made. Continue across the row, making a dc in each stitch (st) across. Dc in the top of the turning chain (see arrow in FIG. 7). Ch 3. Turn work. Dc in second stitch on the previous row and continue as before.

FIG. 7

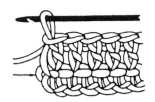

FIG. 8
STARTING
FROM A CHAIN

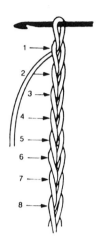

FIG. 6
DOUBLE CROCHET
(DC)

FIG. 6a

FIG. 6b

FIG. 6c

FIG. 6d

FIG. 6e

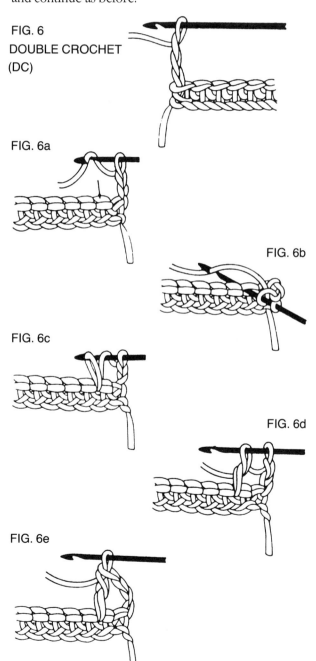

Note: You may also start a row of dc on a base chain (omitting the sc row). In this case, insert the hook in the fourth chain from the hook, instead of the second (FIG. 8).

SLIP STITCH (sl st): Follow the steps in FIG. 9. This is the stitch you will use for joining, shaping and ending off. After you chain and turn, **do not** yo. Just insert the hook into the **first** stitch of the previous row (see FIG. 9A), and pull the yarn through the stitch, then through the loop on the hook—the sl st is made.

FIG. 9
SLIP STITCH
(SL ST)

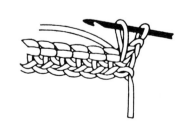

FIG. 9a

HALF DOUBLE CROCHET (hdc): Follow the steps in Fig. 10 and 10A.

To practice, make a chain and a row of sc. Ch 2 and turn; yo. Insert the hook in the second stitch, as shown; yo and pull through to make three loops on the hook. Yo and pull the yarn through *all* three loops at the same time — hdc made. This stitch primarily is used as a transitional stitch from an sc to a dc. Try it and see — starting with sc's, then an hdc and then dc's.

FIG. 10
HALF DOUBLE CROCHET (HDC)

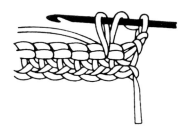

FIG. 10a

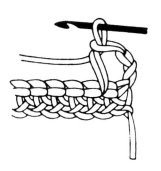

SHAPING TECHNIQUES FOR CROCHETING

Now that you have practiced and made sample squares of all the basic stitches, you are ready to learn the adding and subtracting stitches that will shape your project by changing the length of a row as per the instructions. This is done by increasing (inc) and decreasing (dec).

To increase (inc): Just make two stitches in the same stitch in the previous row (see arrow in Fig. 11). The technique is the same for any kind of stitch.

FIG. 11   INCREASING (INC)
FOR SINGLE CROCHET

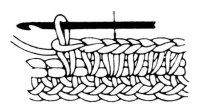

To decrease (dec) for single-crochet (sc): Yo and pull the yarn through two stitches to make three loops on the hook (see steps in Fig. 12). Pull the yarn through all the loops at once — dec made. Continue in the stitches called for in the instructions.

FIG. 12   DECREASING (DEC)

FOR SINGLE CROCHET   FIG. 12a

To decrease for double crochet (dc): In a dc row, make the next stitch and stop when you have two loops on the hook. Now yo and make a dc in the next stitch. At the point where you have three loops on the hook, pull yarn through all loops at the same time. Finish the row with regular dc.

HOW TO BLOCK LIKE A PRO

These step-by-step instructions for blocking will insure that your needlework has a professional finished look.

MATERIALS:

♦ *A Blocking Board* An absolute *must* for professional-looking blocking. You can usually buy a blocking board at craft and sewing centers.

♦ *Rustproof T-pins and Staples* Used to hold the needlework pieces in place.

♦ *Undyed Cotton Cloth* A dampened cloth covers the needlework while it is being pressed.

♦ *Iron* With a dry setting.

♦ *Yellow Soap* Dels Naptha or Kirkman. For blocking needlepoint. Restores natural sizing to canvas and helps prevent infestations of insects.

KNITTED OR CROCHETED WORK:

The purpose of blocking is to align the stitches, loft the yarn and straighten the knitted or crocheted pieces.

♦ Pin the work or the pieces, right side down, to the blocking board with the T-pins. Place the pins close together to avoid ripples in the work.

♦ Dampen a cotton cloth with water and wring it out; the cloth should be moist, not dripping wet. Place the cloth over the work on the board.

♦ Set the iron on "dry" and select a temperature setting suited to the fibers in the work.

♦ Gently iron over the cloth in the direction of the stitches. *Do not* apply pressure to the iron or iron against the grain. You may need to remoisten the cloth and iron the work several times, until it is moist and warm to the touch.

♦ Carefully remove the cloth. If the cloth clings, leaving the work damp and rippled, don't panic. This occurs when a synthetic fiber is pressed with steam that is too hot. No permanent damage can be done unless pressure is used and the stitches are flattened. To restore the work to the desired shape, pat the pieces gently with your hands.

♦ Allow the work to dry on the board in a flat position for at least 24 hours.

♦ When the work is completely dry, remove the pins; the pieces are ready to be assembled.

Note: You can ease or stretch pieces a bit to achieve the desired size, but you can't turn a size 10 sweater into a size 16, or shrink a size 40 vest into a size 34.

NEEDLEPOINT PROJECTS:

Blocking needlepoint realigns the threads of the canvas, lofts the yarn and naturally sets each stitch. *Note: Check for yarn color fastness before you begin to needlepoint. If you've competed a work, and are unsure of the color fastness, **do not block.** Press the work on the wrong side with a warm iron. This won't yield the same results, but avoids color streaking.*

♦ Place a bar of yellow soap *(see Materials)* in a bowl of warm water and let it stand until the water becomes slick to the touch.

♦ Place the needlepoint, right side down, on the blocking board.

♦ Dip a cotton cloth into the soapy water and wring it out. Place the damp cloth over the needlepoint.

♦ Set an iron on "dry" and select a temperature suited to the fibers in the work. Lightly pass the iron over the cloth; *do not* apply pressure.

♦ Repeat dampening the cloth and pressing until the canvas is very soft and flexible; moist, but not wet.

♦ Turn the needlepoint right side up on the board.

♦ Keeping the threads of the canvas parallel to the grid on the blocking board, staple the canvas to the board leaving 1 inch between the staples and the edge of the needlepoint. (Remove tape or selvages before stapling.) The staples should be fairly close together (staples are preferable to pins because they maintain a straight line and even tension across the work).

♦ Staple along the bottom edge of the canvas, again, maintaining an even tension across the work. Gently pull one side of the canvas to align the fabric grain with the grid lines on the board, and staple along this edge. Repeat on the other side of the canvas. (**Do not** stretch the canvas; just pull it gently into its original size.) As you are stretching the third and fourth sides, wrinkles may appear in the center of the work; as the fourth side is eased into alignment, these should disappear. If the canvas is pulled off the grain while being blocked, remove the staples and realign the sides. When the grain of the work is perfectly square, the stitching should be aligned; remember, you are not straightening the stitching, you are squaring the threads of the canvas.

♦ Allow the needlepoint to dry on the board for at least 24 hours.

♦ When the needlepoint is completely dry, gently pull it up from the board; the staples will pull out easily. Your needlepoint is now ready to be finished.

Note: If the design becomes distorted, reblock the piece. This can be avoided if you use enough soapy steam on the canvas and staple it carefully into a perfect square.

E·M·B·R·O·I·D·E·R·Y
S·T·I·T·C·H G·U·I·D·E

THE BLANKET STITCH

Work this stitch from left to right, with the point of the needle and the edge of the work toward you. The edge of the fabric can be folded under or left raw. Secure the thread and bring out the needle below the edge of the fabric. For each stitch, insert the needle through the fabric from the right side and bring it out at the edge. Keeping the thread from the previous stitch *under* the point of the needle, draw the needle and thread through, forming a stitch over the edge. The stitch size and spacing can be uniform or varied.

BLANKET STITCH

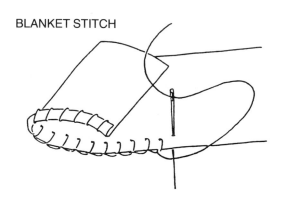

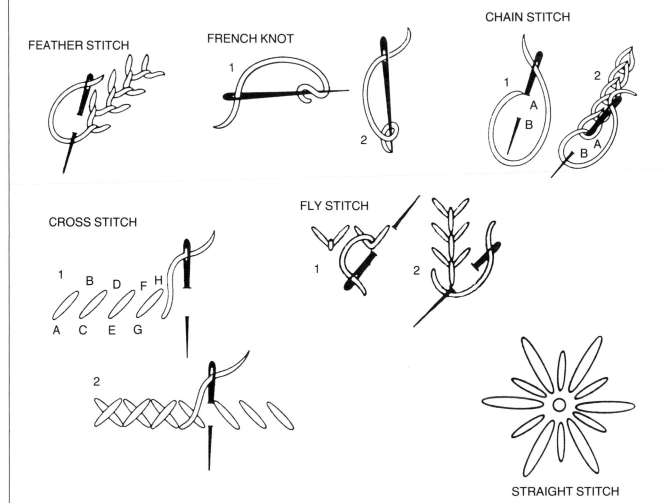

FEATHER STITCH

FRENCH KNOT

CHAIN STITCH

CROSS STITCH

FLY STITCH

STRAIGHT STITCH

TENT OR CONTINENTAL STITCH
OR PETIT POINT

BLIND STITCH

HOW TO ENLARGE PATTERNS AND DESIGNS

If the pattern or design is not already marked off in squares, make a tracing of it. Mark the tracing off in squares: For a small design, make the squares ¼-inch; for larger designs, use ½- or 2-inch squares, or use the size indicated in the directions. Check the instructions for desired size of the finished project. On a second piece of tracing paper, mark off an enlarged grid with the same number of squares as appears on the original pattern. For example, if you wish the finished project to be 6 times larger than the original pattern, each new square must be 6 times larger than on the original. Copy the design outline from the original pattern or tracing onto the second, enlarged grid, square by square. Using a dressmaker's carbon and a tracing wheel, transfer the enlarged design onto the material you are using for your project.

MOSAIC STITCH

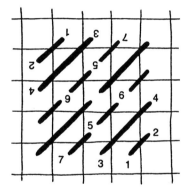

LONG AND SHORT STITCH

SCOTCH STITCH

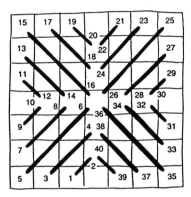

INTERLOCKING GOBELIN STITCH

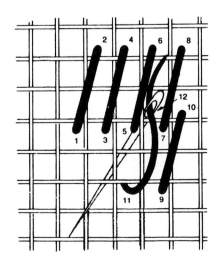

SLANTED GOBELIN STITCH
(worked vertically)

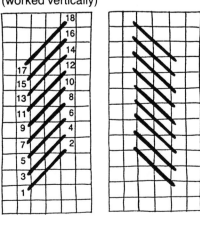

SCOTCH STITCH VARIATION

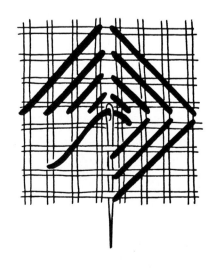

M·A·T·E·R·I·A·L·S
S·H·O·P·P·I·N·G G·U·I·D·E

MANUFACTURERS AND ADDRESSES

Vintage Wood Works
P.O. Box 980, Fredericksburg, TX 78624

Constantine & Son
2050 Eastchester Rd., Bronx, NY 10461

Plaid Enterprises
1649 International Blvd., Norcross, GA 30093

Rust-Oleum Corporation
11 Hawthorne Pkwy., Vernon Hills, IL 60061

Swedish Wood Dyes
T. Henningson & Assoc., P.O. Box 6004, Rockford IL 61125

Walnut Hollow Farm
Rt. 2, Dodgeville, WI 53533

Waverly Fabrics
(Division of S. Schumacher)
79 Madison Ave., New York NY 10016

PROJECTS AND PRODUCTS

Chapter II:
(page 50) Gingerbread-Style Bathroom Shelf: Fleur running trim and Shaker pegs from Vintage Wood Works.

(page 58) Six-Board Chest: Wood dye from Swedish Wood Dyes; water-based acrylic paint from Plaid Enterprises.

Chapter III:
(pages 88-89) A Little Love Pillows and Country Kitchen Towels: all fabric from Waverly Fabrics.

(page 101) Old Santa Fe Plates: wooden plates from Constantine & Son; latex paint from Plaid Enterprises. Animal Farm: Rustoleum® auto primer from Rust-Oleum Corporation.

(page 107) Home Sweet Home Wreath and "Our Town": acrylic paints from Plaid Enterprises; wooden houses from Walnut Hollow Farm.

(page 109) Portugese Pottery: Krylon® spray paint from Rust-Oleum Corporation.

I·N·D·E·X

Italicized Page Numbers Refer To Photographs

A

A Dried Flower Palette, 122-123
A Little Love Pillows, *88*
A Touch of Americana Samplers, *93-95*
acacia, *132*-133
afghan
  Country Charms, *81-83*
  Victorian Nosegay, *78-80*
African violets, *160-161*, 163
air-drying
  flowers, 122
  herbs, 172
Amaretto Cream Frosting, 195
Amish Folk Dolls, *102*-103
ammobium, *144-145*, 149
Anemones, *140*
Animal Farm, *101*
annual
  flowers, 149
  herbs, 170
antiques, 64-65
antiquing
  Jelly Cupboard, *61*
  Six-Board Chest, *56*, 58
apple, 211-213
  Applesauce Cake, 198
  Cheese, Cobbler, *210*, 213
  Cranberry and Sausage Stuffed, 212
  Gingered, Chutney, 226
  Glaze, 198
  Onion and Pepper Relish, 227
  Raisin Pie, 211
  Simmering, Spice, 117
  Spicy, Granola Muffins, 208
  Walnut Tart, *179*, 182
Applesauce Cake, 198
appliqué
  A Little Love Pillows, *88*
  Bed of Roses Comforter and Cover, 76-77
  Country Kitchen Towels, *88-89*
  Heart In Hand Potholder, *89*
  Rose Pillow, 76-77
Apricot, Sweet Pepper, Chutney, 226

arranging
  dried flowers, 126
  fresh flowers, *128-133*
artemesia, 148
asters, *133*, *146*, 149
avocado, 166

baby's
  Blossoms, *135*, 137
  breath, *162*
baking tips, 207
Banana Mocha Muffins, 208
basil, 170, 172-*173*
  Fresh, Dressing, 193
basket, *62*, 63
  Ruffle-and-Bow, *62*
  Twig, *18*, 20
bathing, 36
bathroom, *36, 37, 38, 39*
  Gingerbread-Style, Shelf, 50-*51*
  plants for, *162*
Bed of Roses Comforter and Cover, 76-77
bedroom, *2, 32, 33, 34*
beet, 219
  Cucumber, Salad with Orange Honey Dressing, 222
  Savory, with Bacon, 222-*223*
beverages
  Old-Fashioned Lemonade, 195
  Spicy Citrus Mulled Wine, 183
Birds 'n Blossoms Hooked Rug, *66*, 90-91
black-eyed Susan, 148
Blondies, Coconut Pecan, 197
Blossoming Braid, *127*
blueberry, 216
  Buttermilk Cake, 216
Boston fern, *162*-163
Boston Lettuce, Watercress and, with Cumin Vinaigrette, 180-181
bougainvillea, *151*
bouquet, *146*
  Simmering, 117

bow, 65
  Ruffle-and-, Basket, *62*
Braid, Blossoming, *127*
brass, 14
bread
  baking tips, 207
  Cranberry Nut, 218
  Cream Cheese Loaf, *202-203*
  Glazed Whole Wheat Raisin, *206*
  Mincemeat Braid, *202*, 205
  Moravian Lovefeast Buns, 199
  Old-Fashioned Wheat, 204
  Plums 'n Nuts Oatmeal, 214
  Spiraled Herb, 207
  Walnut Raisin Carrot Loaves, 204
Broccoli, Creamy Cheese and, Soup, 186
Brochettes, Marinated Chicken and Vegetable, 191
bromeliades, 163, *164-165*
Brownies, Fudge, with Amaretto Cream Frosting, 195
Buns, Moravian Lovefeast, 199
butter
  Corn with Lemon Lime, *189*, 191
  Fruit, 209
  Honey, 209
  Lemon, Cake, 183
  Spiced, 209
  Sweet, Glaze, 197
Buttercup Pillow, *84-85*
Buttermilk, Blueberry, Cake, 216

cacti, *162-163*
cake
  Applesauce, 198
  Blueberry Buttermilk, 216
  Fresh Tomato, 225
  Fudge Brownies with Amaretto Cream Frosting, 195
  Lemon Butter, 183
  Mini Carrot, with Cream Cheese Sauce, 225
  Moravian Sugar, 199
  Old Salem Gingerbread, 198
  Spicy Fruit and Nut, *196-197*

calendulas, *132*-133
candy, 200
Carolina Lily Quilt, *68-69, 72-75*
carrot
    Mini, Cakes with Cream Cheese
        Sauce, 225
    Walnut Raisin, Loaves, 204
casserole
    Creamy Corn, 182
    Shepherd's Pie, 181
cast iron, 217
Cauliflower and Beans with Cheese
    Sauce, 224
Cedar Balls, 117
chairs, 11
    Summer White Slipcovered, *26-27,
        28-30*
    Tie-On, Backs, *6, 9*
Chandelier, Green Glass, *18, 22-23*
cheese
    Apple Cobbler, *210, 213*
    Cauliflower and Beans with, Sauce,
        224
    Creamy, and Broccoli Soup, 186
    Herb-Marinated Mozzarella, 229
    Sautéed Tomatoes with Blue, Sauce,
        220
Chest, Six-Board, *56, 58*
chicken
    grilling tips, 191
    Marinated, and Vegetable
        Brochettes, 191
    Stock, 185
Chinese
    evergreen 163, *164-165*
    star apple, 166
chives, 171-*173*
Chocolate Chip Oatmeal Cookies, 201
chutney
    Gingered Apple, 226
    Sweet Pepper Apricot, 226
cilantro, 170, 172-*173*
Citrus Pomanders, *114-115*
clarkia, *144-145, 149*
Classic Pesto, 229
climbing plants, 150-151, 156-157
cobbler
    Cheese Apple, *210, 213*
    Strawberry Rhubarb, 194
cockscomb, *146, 149*
Coconut Pecan Blondies, 197
coffee tree, 167
collectibles, 64-65
Comforter, Bed of Roses, and Cover,
    76-77

condiments
    Apple, Onion and Pepper Relish, 227
    Country-Style Cucumber Relish, 227
    Cucumber Stick Pickles, 228
    Gingered Apple Chutney, 226
    Old-Time Yellow Squash Pickles,
        228
    Sweet Pepper Apricot Chutney, 226
Confetti Salad with Fresh Basil
    Dressing, 193
cookies
    Chocolate Chip Oatmeal, 201
    Coconut Pecan Blondies, 197
    Fudge Brownies with Amaretto
        Cream Frosting, 195
    Old-Fashioned Sugar, 201
corn, 219
    Creamy, Casserole, 182
    Hush Puppies, 194
    Husk Dolls, *104-106*
    with Lemon Lime Butter, *189,* 191
    Marinated, Salad, 221
    Strawberry, Muffins, 209
    and Sweet Pepper Sauté, 224
Cornucopia
    Old English, *96-97*
    Sachet, *113,* 118
country
    Charms Afghan, *81-83*
    Garden Potpourri, *112,* 116
    Ham with Honey Mustard, *189,* 192
    Kitchen Towels, *88-89*
    Style Cucumber Relish, 227
Cover, Bed of Roses Comforter and,
    76-77
cranberry
    Nut Bread, 218
    and Sausage Stuffed Apples, 212
Crazy Quilt Pillows, 86-87
cream
    Cheese Loaf, *202*-203
    Cheese Sauce, 225
    Peaches and, Tart, 218
    Raspberries, In, 216
creamy
    Cheese and Broccoli Soup, 186
    Corn Casserole, 182
crochet
    Country Charms Afghan, *81-83*
    Victorian Nosegay Afghan, 78-80
Crocuses, 138-*139*
cross stitch, 96-97
    A Touch of Americana Samplers,
        93-95
    Country Charms Afghan, *81-83*
    Victorian Nosegay Afghan, 78-80
croton, 163, *164-165*

cucumber
    Beet Salad with Orange Honey
        Dressing, 222
    Country-Style Relish, 227
    Stick Pickles, 228
Cumin Vinaigrette, 180
Cupboard, Jelly, *61*
curtain
    Floral, Pole, *18, 20*
    Pinch-Pleated Drapes, 35
    Shirred, 35

Daffodils, *134,* 136
Dainty Wreath, *124-125,* 127
dill, 170, 172-*173*
dining rooms, *10, 11, 12-13, 16*
Dollar-Wise Decorating tips,
    9, 11, 13, 15, 17, 31, 35, 39, 43
dolls
    Amish Folk, *102-103*
    Corn Husk, *104-106*
dracaena, 163, *164-165*
Drapes, Pinch-Pleated, 35
dressing
    Cumin Vinaigrette, 180
    Fresh Basil, 193
    Orange Honey, 222
    Oriental, 219
dried flower, 17, *120-121*
    air-drying, 122
    arranging, 126
    Blossoming Braid, *127*
    Dainty Wreath, *124-125, 127*
    drying in medium, 123
    Making A, Wreath, *124-125, 127*
    palette, 122-123
    preparing for display, 126
    preserving greens, 123
    Wreath, *110*
drop cloths
    decorating tips, 29
    Summer White Slipcovered Chairs,
        26-27, 28-30

eggplant, 219
    Stir-Fried, with Oriental Dressing,
        219
entryway, *42, 43*
eucalyptus, *133*
    Rose and, Potpourri, 114
    Rose and, Wreath, *114-115*

F

fabric
  face-lift, 24
  Floral, Screen, 18-19
  Flowers That Last Forever, *134-141*
Fan, Floral, *113*, 118
feverfew, *146*, 148
ficus, *164-165*
firethorn, *155*
floral
  Curtain Pole, *18, 22*
  Fabric Screen, *18-19*
  Fan, *113, 118*
flower, 126, 131, 148-149
  African violets, 160-*161*, 163
  air drying, 122
  annuals, 149
  arranging, dried, 126
  arranging, fresh, *128-133*
  Blossoming Braid, *127*
  bougainvillea, *151*
  bouquet, *146*
  Dainty Wreath, *124-125*, 127
  dried, 17, *120-121*
  dried, palette, 122-123
  Dried, Wreath, *110*
  drying in medium 123
  fabric, *134-141*
  forsythia, 158-*159*
  garden, *144-145*, 147
  geraniums, *160*
  ideas, 17, 120
  Making A Dried, Wreath, *124-125*, 127
  perennials, 148
  planting a, garden, 147
  primroses, 160-*161*
  Rose and Eucalyptus Wreath, *114-115*
  roses, 152
  Wax, 128-*129*
flowering vines, 150-*151*
Flowers That Last Forever, *134-141*
forsythia, 158-*159*
fresh
  Basil Dressing, 193
  Tomato Cake, 225
Frosting, Amaretto Cream, 195
fruit
  Apple, Onion and Pepper Relish, 227
  Apple Raisin Pie, 211
  Apple Walnut Tart, *179*, 182
  Butter, 209
  Cheese Apple Cobbler, *210*, 213
  Cranberry Nut Bread, 218
  Cranberry and Sausage Stuffed Apples, 212
  Mixed, with Lemon Juice and Port, 193
  Oranges with Raspberries and Ruby Port, 213
  Peaches and Cream Tart, 218
  Plum Chiffon Pie, *215*
  Plums 'n Nuts Oatmeal Bread, 214
  Spicy, and Nut Cake, *196*-197
  Strawberry Kropsua, 217
  Strawberry Rhubarb Cobbler, 194
Fudge Brownies with Amaretto Cream Frosting, 195
furniture, *54, 55*
  Jelly Cupboard, *61*
  Rhapsody In Blue Table, *57, 59*
  Rustic Hutch, *60*
  Six-Board Chest, *56, 58*
  Victorian Sideboard, *18, 24-25*

G

garden, *144-145*, 147
  annual flowers, 149
  annual herbs, 170
  herb, *168-169*, 170
  perennial flowers, 148
  perennial herbs, 171
  plants for walls, fences & arbors, 156-157
  plants from produce, 166-167
  roses, growing, 152
  tender perennial herbs, 171
  window boxes, *160*
gardening
  advice referrals, 147
  terms, 158
  tools, 148, 171
Garlic, Mint and, Marinated Zucchini, 221
geraniums, *160*
gingerbread
  Old Salem, 198
  Style Bathroom Shelf, 50-*51*
Gingered Apple Chutney, 226
glaze
  Apple, 198
  Sugar, 205
  Sweet Butter, 197
Glazed Whole Wheat Raisin Bread, *206*
glue gun, 18-20
gloxinias, 163, *164-165*
glycerin, preserving greens in, 123
granola
  Homemade, Crunch, *200*
  Spicy Apple, Muffins, 208
grape hyacinths, *130-131*
grapevine, *146, 150*

Green Glass Chandelier, *18, 22-23*
green beans, 219
  Cauliflower and, with Cheese Sauce, 224
greens, preserving, 123

H

Ham, Country, with Honey Mustard, *189, 192*
Hangers, Pretty Padded, *108*
heart
  In Hand Potholder, *89*
  Sweet, *113*, 119
Hearty Tomato and Rice Soup, *184, 186*
herb, *173*, 192
  annual, 170
  cooking with, 172
  drying, 172
  Fresh Basil Dressing, 193
  gardens, *168-169*, 170
  Marinated Mozzarella, 229
  perennial, 171
  in pots, *168-169*
  Sautéed Summer Squash, 221
  and Spice Potpourri, *113*, 116
  Spiraled, Bread, 207
  tender perennial, 171
Home Sweet Home Wreath, *107*
Homemade Granola Crunch, *200*
honey
  Butter, 209
  Glazed Peas, 181
  Mustard, *189*, 192
  Orange, Dressing, 222
hot glue, 18-20
houseplants, 162, 164
  chart, 163
  from produce, 166-167
Hush Puppies, 194
hutch, *54, 65*
  Rustic, *60*
hyacinths, *130-131*

I, J

ivy, 151, *160*
Jelly Cupboard, *61*

K

kitchen, *4-5, 7, 46, 48, 49, 50, 52*
  Country, Towels, *88-89*
  ideas, 8, 9
kumquat, 166

Lace, Ruffles and, Pillows, *26-27*, 31
lamp
  Green Glass Chandelier, *18, 22-23*
  decorating, 31
  Rhapsody In Blue, Shades, *57, 59*
larkspur, 149
lavender
  Dainty Wreath, *124-125*, 127
  Lovely In, Tree, Wreath and Ball, *113*, 118
  Potpourri, *113,* 116
  Teddy Bear, *113*, 118
Leek, Savory, Soup, 185
lemon, 166
  Butter Cake, 183
  Corn with, Lime Butter, *189*, 191
  Mixed Fruit with, Juice and Port, 193
  Old-Fashioned Lemonade, 195
  Spritzer, 195
Lemonade, Old-Fashioned, 195
lights, 31
  Green Glass Chandelier, *18, 22-23*
  decorating, 31
  Rhapsody In Blue Lamp Shades, *57, 59*
Lilies, 141
Lime, Corn with Lemon, Butter, *189*, 191
living rooms, *14, 16, 18, 26-27, 47*
Lentil, Savory, Stew, 224
Lovely In Lavender: Tree, Wreath and Ball, *113*, 118

Making A Dried Flower Wreath, *124-125*, 127
mango, 167
marigold, *144-145*, 149
marinated
  Chicken and Vegetable Brochettes, 191
  Corn Salad, 221
  Herb, Mozzarella, 229
  Mint and Garlic, Zucchini, 221
marjoram, 171-*173*
Mincemeat Braid, *202*, 205
Mini Carrot Cakes with Cream Cheese Sauce, 225
mint, 171-*173*
  and Garlic Marinated Zucchini, 221
mirror
  decorating with, 13
  Pier Glass, *18, 21*

Mixed Fruit with Lemon Juice and Port, 193
Moravian
  Lovefeast Buns, 199
  Sugar Cake, 199
mosquitos, 149
Mozzarella, Herb-Marinated, 229
muffins
  Banana Mocha, 208
  Pineapple Oatmeal, 209
  Spicy Apple Granola, 208
  Strawberry Corn, 209
mushroom, 187
  Wild, Soup, 187
Mustard, Honey, *189*, 192

Napkins, Springtime Tablecloth and, 6, 8
needlepoint, 96-97
  Old English Cornucopia, *96-97*
New England Spice Potpourri, *113*, 116
nut
  Apple Walnut Tart, *172*, 182
  Coconut Pecan Blondies, 197
  Cranberry, Bread, 218
  Plums 'n, Oatmeal Bread, 214
  Spicy Fruit and, Cake, *196-197*
  Walnut Raisin Carrot Loaves, 204

oatmeal
  Chocolate Chip, Cookies, 201
  Pineapple, Muffins, 209
  Plums 'n Nuts, Bread, 214
Old English Cornucopia, *96-97*
Old-Fashioned
  Lemonade, 195
  Rose Potpourri, 116
  Sugar Cookies, 201
  Wheat Bread, 204
Old Salem Gingerbread, 198
Old Santa Fe Plates, *100*-101
Old-Time Yellow Squash Pickles, 228
Onion, Apple, and Pepper Relish, 227
orange, 166
  Honey Dressing, 222
  with Raspberries and Ruby Port, 213
orchid, *131, 162*
oregano, 171-*173*
Oriental
  Dressing, 219
  Rugs, 15
"Our Town", *107*

painting
  decorating, 9, 11
  Old Santa Fe Plates, *100*-101
  "Our Town", *107*
  Portuguese Pottery, *109*
  sponge technique, *57, 59*
  stencil, *56, 58*
pancake, Strawberry Kropsua, 217
parsley, 170-*173*
passion flower, 167
patchwork
  Buttercup Pillow, *84-85*
  Carolina Lily Quilt, *68-69, 72-75*
  Crazy Quilt Pillows, *86-87*
  Pretty Puzzle Pillow, *84*, 86
  Springtime Table Setting, *6, 8*
  Sunshine and Shadow Quilt, *70-71*
  Table Runner, *98-99*
Peaches and Cream Tart, 218
peanut, 167
Peas, Honey-Glazed, 181
Pecan, Coconut, Blondies, 197
Pennsylvania Dutch
  stencil, *56, 58*
  Tin Punch, *92*
pepper
  Apple, Onion and, Relish, 227
  Sautéed, Salad, 220
  Sweet, Tomato Soup, 180
perennial
  flowers, 148
  herbs, 171
pesto
  Classic, 229
  Spinach, 229
pickles
  Cucumber Stick, 228
  Old-Time Yellow Squash, 228
pie
  Apple Raisin, 211
  Apple Walnut Tart, *179*, 182
  Peaches and Cream Tart, 218
  Plum Chiffon, *215*
  Shepherd's, 181
Pier Glass Mirror, *18, 21*
pillow, *17*
  A Little Love, *88*
  Buttercup, *84-85*
  Crazy Quilt Pillows, *86-87*
  Pretty Puzzle, *84*, 86
  Rose, 76-77
  Ruffles and Lace, *26-27*, 31
  Shining Star, *84*
  Springtime, Seats, *6, 9*
Pinch-Pleated Drapes, 35

Pineapple Oatmeal Muffins, 209
planting, 147
plants
    climbing, 150-151, 156-157
    from produce, 166-167
    house, 162-164
Plates, Old Santa Fe, *100*-101
plum 214
    Chiffon Pie, *215*
    'n Nuts Oatmeal Bread, 214
Pomanders, Citrus, *114-115*
pomegranate, 167
porch, 40-*41*
Portuguese Pottery, *109*
pot racks, 8
Potholder, Heart In Hand, *89*
potpourri, 117
    Country Garden, *112*, 116
    Herbs and Spice, *113*, 116
    Lavender, *113*, 116
    New England Spice, *113*, 116
    Old-Fashioned Rose, 116
    Rose and Eucalyptus, 114
    Simmering Apple Spice, 117
    Simmering Bouquet, 117
    Simmering Scents, 117
    Summer Breeze Simmering Scent, 117
Pottery, Portuguese, *109*
preserving greens, 123
pretty
    Padded Hangers, *108*
    Puzzle Pillow, *84*, 86
primroses, 160-*161*

Queen Anne's lace, 148
quilt, 74
    Bed of Roses Comforter and Cover, 76-77
    Carolina Lily, *68-69*, 72-75
    Crazy, Pillows, 86-87
    Sunshine and Shadow, *70-71*

raisin
    Apple Pie, 211
    Glazed Whole Wheat, Bread, *206*
    Walnut, Carrot Loaves, 204
raspberries, 216
    In Cream, 216
    Oranges with, and Ruby Port, 213
relish
    Apple, Onion and Pepper, 227
    Country-Style Cucumber, 227

Rhapsody In Blue Table and Lamp
    Shades, *57*, 59
Rhubarb, Strawberry, Cobbler, 194
Rice, Hearty Tomato and, Soup, *184*, 186
rose, *128, 152-153*
    Bed of, Comforter and Cover, 76-77
    and Eucalyptus Potpourri, 114
    and Eucalyptus Wreath, *114-115*
    fabric, *135*, 138
    growing tips, 152
    Old-Fashioned, Potpourri, 116
    Pillow, 76-77
    "The Fairy", *146*, 148
rosemary, 171-*173*
ruffle
    and-Bow Basket, *62*
    and Lace Pillows, *26-27*, 31
rug
    Birds 'n Blossoms Hooked, *66*, 90-91
    Oriental, 15
    Stenciled Scatter, 15
Rustic Hutch, *60*

sachet
    Cornucopia, *113*, 118
    Floral Fan, *113*, 118
    Lavender Teddy Bear, *113*, 118
    Lovely In Lavender: Tree, Wreath
        and Ball, *113*, 118
    Stocking, *113*, 119
    Sweet Heart, *113*, 119
sage, 171-*173*
salad
    Confetti, with Fresh Basil Dressing, 193
    Cucumber Beet, with Orange Honey
        Dressing, 222
    Marinated Corn, 221
    Mixed Fruit with Lemon Juice and
        Port, 193
    Sautéed Pepper, 220
    Tangy Vegetable, 192
    Watercress and Boston Lettuce with
        Cumin Vinaigrette, 180-181
salvia, 149
Samplers, A Touch of Americana, *93-95*
sand, drying flowers in, 123
sauce
    Blue Cheese, 220
    Cauliflower and Beans with Cheese, 224
    Classic Pesto, 229
    Cream Cheese, 225
    Spinach Pesto, 229

Sausage, Cranberry and, Stuffed
    Apples, 212
sautéed
    Corn and Sweet Pepper, 224
    Herb, Summer Squash, 221
    Pepper Salad, 220
    Tomatoes with Blue Cheese Sauce, 220
savory
    Beets with Bacon, 222-*223*
    Leek Soup, 185
    Lentil Stew, 224
scents
    bathing, 36
    Simmering, 117
    Summer Breeze Simmering, 117
schefflera, 163, *164-165*
Screen, Floral Fabric, *18*-19
Seat Covers, Summer White, *26-27*, 30
Seats, Springtime Pillow, *6*, 9
Sensational Spinach Soup, 190
sewing
    Amish Folk Dolls, *102*-103
    Bed of Roses Comforter and Cover, 76-77
    Pinch-Pleated Drapes, 35
    Shirred Curtains, 35
    Springtime Pillow Seats, *6*, 9
    Springtime Tablecloth and Napkins, *6*, 8-9
    Summer White Seat Covers, *26-27*, 30
    Summer White Slipcovered Chairs, *26-27*, 28-30
    Tie-On Chair Backs, *6*, 9
shelf, *47*, 50
    Gingerbread-Style Bathroom, 50-*51*
    Jelly Cupboard, *61*
    Rustic Hutch, *60*
    Victorian Sideboard, *18*, 24-25
Shepherd's Pie, 181
Shining Star Pillow, *84*
Shirred Curtains, 35
Shrimp, Spicy Pickled, 190
silica gel, drying flowers in, 123
simmering
    Apple Spice, 117
    Bouquet, 117
    Scents, 117
    Summer Breeze, Scent, 117
Six-Board Chest, *56*, 58
Skirted Table, *18*, 20
Slipcovers, Summer White, *26-27*, 28-30
snapdragons, 128-*129*
soup
    Chicken Stock, 185
    Creamy Cheese and Broccoli, 186

Hearty Tomato and Rice, *184*, 186
Savory Leek, 185
Sensational Spinach, 190
Sweet Pepper Tomato, 180
Wild Mushroom, 187
spice
  Herbs and, Potpourri, *113*, 116
  jars, as vases, *133*
  New England, Potpourri, *113*, 116
  Simmering Apple, 117
Spiced Butter, 209
spicy
  Apple Granola Muffins, 208
  Citrus Mulled Wine, 183
  Fruit and Nut Cake, *196*-197
  Pickled Shrimp, 190
spinach, 219
  Pesto, 229
  Sensational, Soup, 190
Spiraled Herb Bread, 207
springtime
  Pillow Seats, *6*, 9
  Table Setting, *6*, 8-9
squash, 219
  Herb Sautéed Summer, 221
  Old-Time Yellow, Pickles, 228
staircase, *42*
statice, 149
stencil
  Jelly Cupboard, *61*
  Rhapsody In Blue Table, *57*, 59
  scatter rugs, 15
  Six-Board Chest, *56*, 58
Stew, Savory Lentil, 224
Stir-Fried Eggplant with Oriental
  Dressing, 219
Stock, Chicken, 185
Stocking Sachet, *113*, 119
Strawberry, 216
  Corn Muffins, 209
  Kropsua, 217
  Rhubarb Cobbler, 194
strawflowers, 149
succulents, *162*-163
sugar
  Glaze, 205
  Moravian, Cake, 199
  Old-Fashioned, Cookies, 201
summer
  Breeze Simmering Scent, 117
  White Seat Covers, *26-27*, 30
  White Slipcovered Chairs, *26-27*,
  28-30
Sunshine and Shadow Quilt, 70-71
sweet
  Butter Glaze, 197
  Heart, *113*, 119
  marjoram, 171

sweet pepper, 219
  Apricot Chutney, 226
  Corn and, Sauté, 224
  Tomato Soup, 180
sweet potato, 167

table
  Patchwork, Runner, 98-99
  Rhapsody In Blue, *57*, 59
  Skirted, *18*, 20
Tablecloth, Springtime, and Napkins,
  6, 8
tangerine centerpiece, *132*-133
Tangy Vegetable Salad, 192
tarragon, 171-*173*
tart
  Apple Walnut, *179*, 182
  Peaches and Cream, 218
Teddy Bear, Lavender, *113*, 118
thyme, 171-*173*
Tie-On Chair Backs, *6*, 9
tin, Animal Farm, *101*
tin punch
  Pennsylvania Dutch, *92*
  "Welcome Friends", *92*
tomato, 219-220
  Fresh, Cake, 225
  Hearty, and Rice Soup, *184*, 186
  Sautéed, with Blue Cheese Sauce,
  220
  Sweet Pepper, Soup, 180
towels, 39
  Country Kitchen, *88-89*
Tree, Lovely In Lavender, *113*, 118
trunk, 39
  Six-Board Chest, *56*, 58
tulips, *132*
Twig Basket, *18*, 20

vases, ideas for, 131
vegetables, 219
  Cauliflower and Beans with Cheese
  Sauce, 224
  Corn with Lemon Lime Butter,
  189, 191
  Corn and Sweet Pepper Sauté, 224
  Herb Sautéed Summer Squash, 221
  Honey-Glazed Peas, 181
  Marinated Chicken and, Brochettes,
  191
  Marinated Corn Salad, 221
  Mint and Garlic Marinated Zucchini,
  221

Sautéed Pepper Salad, 220
Sautéed Tomatoes with Blue Cheese
  Sauce, 220
Savory Beets with Bacon, 222-*223*
Stir Fried Eggplant with Oriental
  Dressing, 219
Tangy Salad, 192
Victorian
  Nosegay Afghan, 78-80
  Sideboard, *18*, 24-25
Vinaigrette, Cumin, 180
violet
  African, 160-*161*, 163
  trumpet vine, *154*-155

wagon, for gardening, 158
walnut
  Apple Tart, *179*, 182
  Raisin Carrot Loaves, 204
Watercress and Boston Lettuce with
  Cumin Vinaigrette, 180-181
wax flowers, 128-*129*
"Welcome Friends" Tin Punch, *92*
wheat
  Glazed Whole, Raisin Bread, *206*
Wild Mushroom Soup, 187
willow, corkscrew, *132*-133
window, 35
  boxes, *160*
wine
  Mixed Fruit with Lemon Juice and
  Port, 193
  Oranges with Raspberries and Ruby
  Port, 213
  Spicy Citrus Mulled, 183
wisteria, *142*
wreath
  Dainty, *124-125*, 127
  Dried Flower, *110*
  Home Sweet Home, *107*
  Lovely In Lavender, *113*, 118
  Making A Dried Flower, *124-125*,
  127
  Rose and Eucalyptus, *114-115*

yarrow, *121*
zinnia, *144-145, 146*, 149
zucchini, 219
  Mint and Garlic Marinated, 221

PHOTOGRAPHY CREDITS

Laurie Black & Roslyn Banish/ARX: Page 53. **Ralph Bogertman:** Pages 12-13, 14, 18, 21, 22, 23, 24, 36, 40, 42 (bottom left), 50, 54, 102, 104, 109, 160, 161, 162, 164-165, 168. **Chuck Crandall:** Pages 142, 150, 151, 152-153, 154, 155. **David Frazier:** Pages 17, 57, 78. **David Glomb:** Pages 7, 44, 52. **Kari Haavisto:** Pages 11, 33, 34, 41, 43, 120, 121, 124-125, 223. **Ronald G. Harris:** Pages 189, 210. **Lizzie Himmel:** Page 46. **Lynn Karlin:** Page 81. **James Kozyra:** Pages 112, 113, 114-115. **Michael Luppino:** Page 39. **Tom McCavera:** Page 6. **Bill McGinn:** Pages 70, 84, 93, 94, 95, 127, 144-145, 146, 202. **Chris Mead:** Pages 2, 64, 169, 173. **Rudy Muller:** Pages 56, 66, 88, 100, 101, 107, 181, 196. **Leonard Nones:** Pages 62, 68-69, 87, 96, 99, 134, 135, 139, 140. **Dean Powell:** Pages 89, 108. **Lilo Raymond:** Pages 26-27. **Carin Riley:** Pages 51, 77, 179. **Carin & David Riley:** Pages 60, 61. **Jerry Simpson:** Page 215. **Joe Standart:** Page 110 (From *The Scented Room* by Barbara Milo Ohrbach. Published by Clarkson N. Potter, Inc., New York, New York. Copyright ©1986 by Barbara Milo Ohrbach). **William P. Steele:** Pages 38, 47, 55, 174, 176-177. **William Stites:** Cover Photo, Pages 4-5, 10, 16, 32, 37, 42 (top right), 48, 49. **Bob Stoller:** Pages 128, 129, 130, 131, 132, 133. **George Taloumis:** Page 159. **René Velez:** Pages 92, 200, 206.

SPECIAL THANKS

We would like to extend our heartfelt appreciation to Margit Echols, designer of the Shining Star, Buttercup and Pretty Puzzle Pillows *(pages 84-86)* and to Doris Chaconas, designer of the Country Charms Afghan *(page 81)*.